Shockwave 3D

201 West 103rd Street, Indianapolis, Indiana 46290

By Jason Wolf

Shockwave 3D

Copyright © 2002 by New Riders Publishing

All rights reserved. No part of this book shall be reproduced, stored in a retrieval system, or transmitted by any means—electronic, mechanical, photocopying, recording, or otherwise—without written permission from the publisher. No patent liability is assumed with respect to the use of the information contained herein. Although every precaution has been taken in the preparation of this book, the publisher and author(s) assume no responsibility for errors or omissions. Neither is any liability assumed for damages resulting from the use of the information contained herein.

International Standard Book Number: 0-7357-1197-6

Library of Congress Catalog Card Number: 2001097084

Printed in the United States of America

First Printing: April 2002

06 05 04 03 02   7 6 5 4 3 2 1

Interpretation of the printing code: The rightmost double-digit number is the year of the book's printing; the rightmost single-digit number is the number of the book's printing. For example, the printing code 02-1 shows that the first printing of the book occurred in 2002.

Trademarks

All terms mentioned in this book that are known to be trademarks or service marks have been appropriately capitalized. New Riders Publishing cannot attest to the accuracy of this information. Use of a term in this book should not be regarded as affecting the validity of any trademark or service mark. The name havok.com is copyrighted to Havok.com, Inc. Maya® is a registered trademark of Alias|Wavefront. Maya Real-Time Author™ is a registered trademark of Alias|Wavefront.

Warning and Disclaimer

Every effort has been made to make this book as complete and as accurate as possible, but no warranty of fitness is implied. The information provided is on an "as is" basis. The authors and the publisher shall have neither liability nor responsibility to any person or entity with respect to any loss or damages arising from the information contained in this book or from the use of the CD or programs accompanying it.

Permissions

Havok Xtra Lingo Reference

© Copyright 2000/2001 Havok.com, Inc.

www.havok.com

Publisher
David Dwyer

Associate Publisher
Stephanie Wall

Executive Editor
Steve Weiss

Production Manager
Gina Kanouse

Managing Editor
Sarah Kearns

Acquisitions Editor
Theresa Gheen

Development Editor
Ginny Bess

Project Editor
Sarah Kearns

Copy Editor
Ginny Bess

Product Marketing Manager
Kathy Malmloff

Publicity Manager
Susan Nixon

Manufacturing Coordinator
Jim Conway

Cover Designer
Aren Howell

Interior Designer
Kim Scott, www.bumpy.com

Compositor
Kim Scott

Proofreader
Linda Seifert

Senior Indexer
Cheryl Lenser

Media Developer
Jay Payne

Contents at a Glance

	Foreword	ix
	Introduction	1
Chapter 1	What's New?	5
Chapter 2	Oh Behave!	17
Chapter 3	Architecture Fly-Through	45
Chapter 4	Wreaking Havok	79
Chapter 5	Havok Lingo Reference	113
Chapter 6	Building a Virtual City Tour	143
Chapter 7	Places to Go, People to See!	165
Chapter 8	Sneak Peek at the Maya® RTA™	189
Appendix A	What's on the CD-ROM	197
	Index	199

Table of Contents

Foreword — ix

Introduction — 1

1 What's New? — 5
The Extra Dimension — 6
    Coding Considerations — 7
Why Size Doesn't Matter — 8
Streaming — 8
Behaviors: Programming without Code — 10
3D Applications — 11
    The Shockwave 3D Plug-In — 11
    Delivering to the Web or a Projector — 13

2 Oh Behave! — 17
What Are Behaviors? — 18
Lingo Compared to Behaviors: A Closer Look — 19
Actions and Triggers: Reference Tables — 20
Adding Behaviors to 3D Sprites — 41
    Changing Behavior Settings — 41
Making Your Text Stand Out — 41

3 Architecture Fly-Through — 45
Storyboarding — 46
Building the Model — 46
Naming Models — 52
Lighting — 53
Texture Mapping — 55
Setting Up the Camera — 57
Exporting Options — 57
    A Piece of the Pie — 63
Working in Director — 64
    File Size Considerations — 65
    Score Setup — 65
    Color and Visibility — 66
    Redrawing Issues — 66
    Adding Lingo — 67
Testing—"Test Early, Test Often" — 73
    Projector Testing — 74
    Web Testing — 75
    Xtra Embedding — 76
    Graphic Dithering — 77
    Completing the Movie — 78

4 Wreaking Havok — 79
Storyboarding the Car Simulation — 80
Constructing the 3D Environment — 81
    Textures — 85
    Lighting the Scene — 86
Physics Time — 87
    Rigid Body Collection — 88
    Setting the Model's Physical Properties — 89
    Friction — 91
Speeding Up Simulations — 92
Testing and Exporting Your Scene — 93
    Exporting in Shockwave — 94

Texture Warning	96	
The Pie Chart	96	
In Director	97	
The Havok Behaviors	97	
Importing the .W3D File and the .HKE File	107	
Playing God	110	
Exporting the Movie	111	
Creating a Cross-Platform File	111	
What About Lingo?	112	

5 Havok Lingo Reference   113

Havok Cast Member Lingo Property Reference	114
Havok Cast Member Lingo Function Reference	117
Rigid Body Lingo Property Reference	126
Rigid Body Lingo Function Reference	132
Spring Lingo Property Reference	135
Spring Lingo Function Reference	136
Linear Dashpot Lingo Property Reference	137
Linear Dashpot Lingo Function Reference	138
Angular Dashpot Lingo Property Reference	139
Angular Dashpot Lingo Function Reference	140

6 Building a Virtual City Tour   143

Picking a Part of the City	144
Modeling the Buildings	147
Editing Photos to Create Textures	150
Texture Mapping	152
Exporting the Virtual City Tour Movie	153
Working with the .W3D File in Director	153
Navigation Using Lingo	155
Lingo Camera Angles	156
Buttons and Sliders	158
Sliders and Rotation	159
The Hot Spots	161

7 Places to Go, People to See!   165

Shockwave 3D Software and Application Developers	167
3D Model Makers and Suppliers	174
Inspiration Sites	176
Xtras and Plug-Ins	180
Shockwave 3D Content Developers	183

8 Sneak Peek at the Maya® RTA™   189

What Is the RTA?	191
What Comes with RTA?	192
RTA Features	192
Why RTA?	194
Concluding Remarks	196

A What's on the CD-ROM?   197

Index   199

About the Author

Jason Wolf has been working with Macromedia Director since version 1.42 and with 3D applications since the days of Swivel 3D. Jason's first jobs were for Lucas Film's Games and Koei Corporation. Jason also spent five years at Macromedia where he authored the first book on Shockwave, *Macromedia Shockwave for Director, the Complete Guide*, and where he developed the award-winning **Macromedia.com**. He also authored several interactive CD-ROMs, videos, and demos for Fortune 500 clients. At Macromedia, Jason had the pleasure of working with Natalie Zee and Hillman Curtis in the creative services department.

Jason also worked for CKS Partners, the agency of record for companies such as Apple, Pixar, Lexis, Nike, and GM. CKS Partners eventually merged into what is known as marchFIRST. Jason served as Director of Multimedia and Research and Development for marchFIRST. Currently, Jason works from his home as an independent contractor doing freelance multimedia engineering work and CTO work. In his spare time, Jason writes books, such as this one and *The Last Mile, Broadband and the Next Internet Revolution*, a *New York Times* bestseller. In his free time, Jason likes to ride his CBR F4 or build electronic devices.

About the Technical Editors

Perry Board is the Art Director for Gabriel Interactive, Inc., a multimedia and game development company in Indianapolis, Indiana. He studied art at Taylor University. Perry developed a proficiency in programming through his work with Macromedia Director over the past six years. He has been responsible for a wide variety of interactive media projects ranging from business applications to retail computer games. Involved with Shockwave from its beginning, Perry also wrote *Creating Shockwave Web Pages* in 1996.

Jerome Givens is an interactive designer from Indianapolis, Indiana. He studied multimedia at Indiana University and developed a proficiency in programming through his work with Macromedia Director over the past five years. He has been involved with several interactive media projects ranging from business applications to 3D gaming applications and DVD-ROM titles.

Dedication

This book is dedicated to all of the people I ignored or avoided during the time that I wrote this book, especially to Marthe and my mom. And this book is dedicated to my grandparents for teaching me so much about the world and for teaching me to never stop asking questions. I promise I'll come and visit soon!

Acknowledgments

I would like to acknowledge a lot of people who made this book possible. First, I'd like to thank Natalie Zee for putting me in touch with Steve Weiss. When I wrote my first book, I gave Natalie my contact information so that she could write her first book, and now I'm thankful she returned the favor! Next, I'd like to thank Steve Weiss for talking me into writing this book. Next up are Theresa Gheen and Ginny Bess. These are the people who actually do the work that make a book real.

And of course, I cannot forget the following people: Andrea Kavanagh at Havok; Peter Ryce, Jake Sapirstein, and Thomas Higgins at Macromedia; Dan Prochazka and Kevin Clark at Discreet; and last, but not least, Mike Wilson at Alias|Wavefront. These people work on the technology that makes interactive dreams come true.

And lastly, I'm thankful for the wonderful distracting episodes of *SpongeBob* and *The Simpsons*!

New Riders Acknowledgments

New Riders wishes to thank Havok.com, Inc. for their generous permission to reproduce some materials for this book.

A Message from New Riders

As the reader of this book, you are our most important critic and commentator. We value your opinion and want to know what we're doing right, what we could do better, in what areas you'd like to see us publish, and any other words of wisdom you're willing to pass our way.

As Executive Editor at New Riders, I welcome your comments. You can fax, email, or write me directly to let me know what you did or didn't like about this book—as well as what we can do to make our books better. When you write, please be sure to include this book's title, ISBN, and author, as well as your name and phone or fax number. I will carefully review your comments and share them with the authors and editors who worked on the book.

Please note that I cannot help you with technical problems related to the topic of this book, and that due to the high volume of email I receive, I might not be able to reply to every message. Thanks.

Fax: 317-581-4663

Email: steve.weiss@newriders.com

Mail: Steve Weiss
Executive Editor
New Riders Publishing
201 West 103rd Street
Indianapolis, IN 46290 USA

Visit Our Web Site: www.newriders.com

On our web site, you'll find information about our other books, the authors we partner with, book updates and file downloads, promotions, discussion boards for online interaction with other users and with technology experts, and a calendar of trade shows and other professional events with which we'll be involved. We hope to see you around.

Email Us from Our Web Site

Go to www.newriders.com and click on the Contact Us link if you

> Have comments or questions about this book.

> Want to report errors that you have found in this book.

> Have a book proposal or are interested in writing for New Riders.

> Would like us to send you one of our author kits.

> Are an expert in a computer topic or technology and are interested in being a reviewer or technical editor.

> Want to find a distributor for our titles in your area.

> Are an educator/instructor who wants to preview New Riders books for classroom use. In the body/comments area, include your name, school, department, address, phone number, office days/hours, text currently in use, and enrollment in your department, along with your request for either desk/examination copies or additional information.

Foreword

Think back a few years and recall what 3D on the web was like for web developers and designers. VRML promised to make our greatest 3D dreams come to life. We could live in virtual space as avatars while navigating the nebulous ether of this new space. Of course, this never happened for most of us. Unfortunately, bandwidth and technology first needed to catch up to the idealistic dreams we were conjuring up for the Internet.

Today, there is a promising future for interactive 3D on the web—with the arrival of Shockwave 3D. I was lucky enough to be a part of the original Shockwave team at Macromedia in 1995, along with the author of this book, Jason Wolf. Jason was my former co-worker at Macromedia and then at marchFIRST. Back then, Shockwave was just a pioneer technology for interactivity on the web. I was curious to see how it had evolved five years later.

At a special preview of Shockwave 3D at the Macromedia office, I was amazed at what was displayed on the screen—pure 3D quality merged with the interactive power of Director. "Finally!" I thought to myself. I was excited that 3D on the web was no longer going to get a bad reputation. Shockwave 3D is making that inspiring first step that will lead us into the broadband future, one that ensures we can have richer experiences online through interactive video games, shopping, home buying, 3D chat rooms, and perhaps, ultimately, 3D movies.

There's no better expert for Director or 3D than Jason Wolf. Having taught me Director while working together at Macromedia, I know firsthand that Jason has the technical expertise in Director as well as the artistic passion for 3D. This book reflects both his expertise and his passion, a combination of stellar qualities that will benefit you.

As web designers and developers, we hold the vision of the Internet future. With this book in hand, we now have the know-how to take what the web has to offer to new heights with Shockwave 3D.

Natalie Zee
Creative Director of Rich Media, SBI & Company
Co-author, *HTML & Web Artistry 2* and *The Last Mile*

Introduction

What Is Shockwave 3D?

I am sure that you have, at the very least, heard of the term Shockwave. But what is Shockwave? Hopefully, I can answer your question with a digression on Macromedia Director, Lingo, and the third dimension.

Macromedia's Director allows the creation of interactive multimedia content. Director content can include text, sounds, graphics, and video. With Director, you can choreograph this content into an interactive show that users can navigate through, or a path you define for them can automatically take them through it. You can create compelling content and integrated user experiences with Director. Thousands upon thousands of interactive CD-ROMs are created with Director. There are even cases where larger corporations purchased the runtime engine from Macromedia. This engine allows interactive content to play on a Macintosh or Windows PC for use with custom content. This book assumes that you already have some understanding of Director.

Director is an enormous application. It is written in the programming language C and C++ with over a million lines of code. Director is at the heart of Shockwave. That is, Director is the *authoring environment* for Shockwave content. This is where you, the developer, spend your time creating and linking the navigation that your users will use. Think of it this way: The name of the application is Director because you are the director of a *movie*. The application uses metaphors such as the *Score window*, where you can score the animation of your movie, and the *Cast window*, where you can import assets from your hard drive and treat them just like the cast members of a movie. Fortunately, you won't have to deal with union and SAG (Screen Actors Guild) issues with digital actors!

In Director, your completed work or interactive pieces are called *movies*. You have a few delivery choices with your movies. You can compile your completed movie into a standalone application that can be played by your audience on a Macintosh or Windows machine. This application needs nothing else to run. The Director application doesn't have to run on a computer or in a browser.

The second delivery option is a Play in the browser option. This option, called either a Shockwave movie or Java applet, requires a copy of a browser such as Internet Explorer or Netscape Navigator. In this book, I focus on Shockwave movies, as Java applets are too limited as a delivery option. The Shockwave .DCR file (named after its Windows dot-three extension) is a format that is perfectly suited for streaming your interactive Director movie over the Internet. Once you have completed your Director movie, you can save the movie as a .DCR (Director-compressed resource) file. This file format arranges the content in your movies in a fashion that is perfectly suited for streaming. Thus, your users can start interacting with your movie before downloading it to their computer.

Once you get to the point where you have a .DCR file, you have created a Shockwave movie. That is all there is to it. However, if you're not using the latest version of Director that supports the Shockwave 3D format (version 8.5), then you can't take advantage of the 3D aspects of Shockwave and Director. If you are using a non-3D version, upgrade it and download the latest plug-in, which is also provided on the CD that accompanies this book.

The older version of the Shockwave plug-in for your browser is not as useful for working with this book, as you will not be able to take advantage of the new 3D features.

Lingo

What about Lingo? Yes, it's true that you might have to get your hands dirty with some Lingo code. You need to have some familiarity with Lingo to understand the concepts and examples in this book, and like I said earlier, I do recommend that you at least understand what Lingo is, what it can do, and where you can type code into Director. For this book, it's not as important that you know what Lingo does as it is that you know where code should be typed into Director. For example, you should know how to open the Movie Script window and understand the difference between typing the following script, as opposed to putting it into one frame in the score:

```
on exitframe
    beep
end
```

This simple script behaves very differently depending on where you put it in Director.

Who You Are

This book is for you. If you picked up this book, you have already heard of Shockwave. If you are a computer user (who isn't these days?) who needs to (or wants to) create a compelling experience using some of the latest 3D technology for the web, then this book can help. As a reader of this book, you should be familiar with either the Macintosh or Windows operating system, and you should have some familiarity with Director and 3D applications. To follow the examples in this book, you should have access to Director version 8.5 and a 3D application that supports the export of the .W3D file format. Application designers, interactive designers, multimedia programmers or engineers, motion graphics designers, and 3D animators will gain the most meaning from this book. In addition, if you are aspiring to learn about Director, Shockwave, or 3D applications, this book is the perfect solution, as it discusses all of these and funnels the combination of these into complete Shockwave 3D movies.

What's in This Book

This book contains both tutorial-style chapters and reference chapters. My intention is to couple these styles to provide you the optimal learning experience. I find that many people learn by example, while others simply want to find the quick solution or they want to use information as a reference. This book's design is set up to accommodate both learning styles.

I will "catch you up" by teaching you what you might have missed with the introduction of Shockwave 3D. I also offer you practical, real-world examples that you can apply to your projects. These examples are intended to give you hands-on experience with Shockwave. Finally, the book concludes with a discussion of where you might look for more information and inspiration.

The CD-ROM

This book comes with a CD-ROM that contains real-world examples from third-party developers, links to several HTML developers, installers for Shockwave 3D, and sample files that are referenced in the chapters. See Appendix A, "What's on the CD-ROM," at the end of this book for more information regarding the CD-ROM.

Assumptions of This Book

I hate making assumptions, but as an author I have to start somewhere. That somewhere is based on the assumption of knowledge you already have about Director, Lingo, and Shockwave 3D. When writing this book, here is what I assume you already know:

> You already know what Director is, and you have worked with Lingo. Even if you aren't very skilled with Lingo, you know what it is, where you can find it, and where Lingo code gets typed into Director when programming.

> I'm assuming that you have heard of Shockwave 3D, and you are interested in learning more about it. I also assume that you have a limited knowledge of Shockwave 3D.

> You have seen 3D applications, and you likely have one on your hard drive. Or, you are aspiring to get into 3D and want to learn more about it.

> I'm assuming you want to learn more about the software technologies that make up Shockwave 3D. Shockwave 3D is the combination of two software technologies—3D technology and Macromedia's Director technology. When you use a 3D application, such as 3ds max, you can make 3D models. When you use Director, you can make interactive content. When you put the two together, you get interactive 3D content that is delivered via Shockwave 3D technology.

Conventions Used in This Book

Every computer book has its own style of presenting information. As you flip through this book, you'll notice an interesting layout. The team of people working on this book customized the layout for each chapter so that you grasp the concepts based on the concepts, and not based on rules about how a book should look.

Because I know most of you are really into graphics, the chapters contain way-cool eye candy. Along with the graphics, you'll find screen captions, illustrating the steps for producing an effect or explaining a reference.

You'll also find notes and tips, which will provide you with additional contextual information or customization techniques. I provide as many tips and examples of what you can do with the techniques you learn in each chapter so that you can apply them to your work. I also provide extensive reference sections, such as the behaviors reference in Chapter 2, so that you can quickly find information as you do your own projects.

CHAPTER 1

- **In This Chapter**
  - The Extra Dimension, 6
    - Coding Considerations, 7
  - Why Size Doesn't Matter, 8
  - Streaming, 8
  - Behaviors: Programming without Code, 10
  - 3D Applications, 11
    - The Shockwave 3D Plug-In, 11
    - Delivering to the Web or a Projector, 13

What's New?

Welcome to the revolution. I have been a user of Macromedia Director since before it was called Director, and I have never seen an upgrade that has incorporated such amazing technology as Shockwave 3D. The closest thing I can relate it to is the release of version 2.0 of Director. When version 2.0 came out, Macromedia (called Macromind at the time) introduced a scripting language, Lingo. This hyper-card language allowed people to interact with animation while it was occurring onscreen. It took a few years for people to understand the potential of this technology, but they must have "gotten it," because Director has been the number-one multimedia-authoring tool for almost 10 years now.

Other multimedia companies tout their application as the "Director killer" only to see it fail in a couple of years. Director is here to stay. It is a good investment regardless of whether you are an engineer or analyst. As of October 22, 2001, Macromedia and Intel announced that the Shockwave 3D player would be distributed with all Intel motherboards. This certainly secures the future of Shockwave 3D.

So let's get started. This chapter provides an overview of Shockwave 3D technology. I discuss what Shockwave 3D is and how it came about. I also discuss the languages you need to know to use Shockwave, and how to work around these languages (if you don't know how to code in them) by using 3D behaviors. This chapter also discusses how to stream your movies efficiently, what 3D applications consist of, discussion of the Shockwave 3D exporter, and tips on developing and delivering content via the web or a stand-alone projector.

The Extra Dimension

The hype about Shockwave 3D is centered on the simple fact that it now supports an extra axis, the Z-axis. It's really Director, the authoring environment that sets the tone for the capabilities of Shockwave. In fact, the new version of Director is what allows Shockwave (and you) to use 3D files. Originally, the application only allowed you to move objects around the screen using an X- and/or Y-coordinate system. This resulted in Lingo code statements that looked like this:

```
-- point(523, 262)
```

In this code, you can see that when I asked Director for the location of sprite 1, it returned a two-value answer. These numbers correspond to the X and Y points on the computer screen. If you have a monitor that is set at 1024×768 resolution, the middle point of the screen would be at the following location:

```
put the loc of sprite 1
      -- point(512, 384)
```

This is how Director has worked since Lingo was first added to version 2.0 of the program. Now, with the release of Director 8.5, the application has a third coordinate number added to it that allows objects (or sprites) to not only move left to right and up and down, but also in and out; that is, closer and further away from the viewer. In Director 8.5, you see and control a three-axis number when dealing with Shockwave 3D castmembers. That three-axis number could look like this:

```
put member("3d").camera[1].transform
-- transform(1.0,0.0,0.0,0.0, 0.0,0.0,1.0,0.0, 0.0,
➥-1.0,0.0,0.0, 37.24396,-668.81323,82.07935,1.0)
```

This third number is what is part of something called the Cartesian coordinate system, and it is the standard way that almost every 3D application on the market allows you to move and manipulate 3D objects inside the computer. Director has adopted this same convention, making it easy to learn the Lingo code necessary for 3D object movement inside the application.

With the introduction of a 3D-dimensional axis into Director and the vast capabilities that come with lighting, rendering, texturing, and moving of 3D objects, you can bet there is a considerable amount of new Lingo code to accommodate these features. The following section tells you what you need to know about this new code.

Coding Considerations

If you already have Director 8.5, I imagine you have seen the new 597-page "what's new" manual, most of which is comprised of the new Lingo code that Shockwave 3D uses. I'll bet that manual is so big that it has led you to purchase this book!

To truly master Director's Shockwave 3D, you should become good at using Lingo (at least you should have a good understanding of it); however, you definitely don't have to be an expert. In fact, with some of your movies you don't have to worry about Lingo ever, thanks to *behaviors*. Macromedia knows that non-programmers want to create compelling applications or web content. Thus, they created a library of previously written code (behaviors) that you can drag and drop into your movie, giving your movie the functionality that originally only programmers could do by writing code. Behaviors are discussed later in this chapter and in more detail in Chapter 2, "Oh Behave!."

Lingo is similar to English, and it's a syntax programming language that is easy to understand once you understand two concepts. First, you need to know the different places you can type Lingo code, and you need to understand your code's behavior when it is typed into those places. In other words, you need to recognize that the exact same Lingo command(s) typed into two different places in Director can give you completely different results. If you don't already understand this concept, you should consider taking the Lingo tutorials. In addition, I would recommend that you deconstruct Director or Shockwave 3D movies from CDs, friends, or the web. In order to open a Shockwave 3D movie, however, you must have the master Director (DIR) file. Some web sites will let you download the source DIR files to help you learn more. A great web resource is the DOUG web site, which can be found at **http://www.director-online.com**, or go to the Director Dev site, which can be found at **http://www.directordev.com**. Regardless of whether you know Lingo or not, this book should help you excel at Shockwave 3D.

In order to start writing Lingo code to control your Shockwave 3D movie, you first need a 3D object that you can import into Director. There are specific ways to create simple, generic shapes in Director, such as spheres and cubes, that you can map textures onto and your users can interact with. However, a generic, primitive shape, such as a cube, is not as compelling as a 3D model of a more complex object, such as a table. To create 3D models, you have many options. You can type specific Lingo commands, you can use behaviors, you can import 3D models from the .Obj file format, or you can import pre-made Shockwave 3D scenes from the W3D (Web 3D) file format. The W3D file format is the recommended method. With it, you gain much more control over the look and feel of your scene and animations, and interactions can be included inside the W3D file.

Why Size Doesn't Matter

One of the great reasons for working with 3D is that just like vector file formats, images can be scaled to any size without affecting the quality of their appearance. For those familiar with 3D applications, this isn't anything new. However, this is new to Director, a formerly bitmapped-only application.

The best way to explain this is to compare it to other applications, such as Illustrator or Freehand. In these applications, the graphics you create are resolution-independent. That is, you can zoom in to the letter T by 2600%, for example, and the image still looks perfect. This isn't the case with a bitmapped image from Photoshop, for example. A photograph has a specific resolution associated with it that prevents you from zooming in any more than 150%–200% before it starts to look bad.

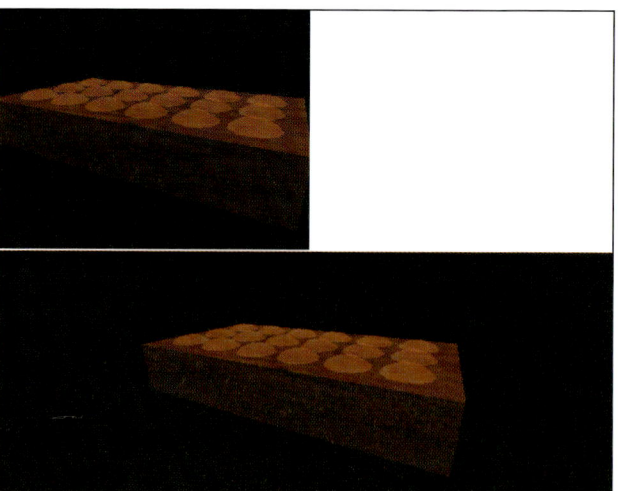

[1.1] Shockwave 3D movies can be any aspect ratio inside Director.

The 3D castmember that gets imported into Director can be scaled and positioned in a similar way to a Flash asset castmember. That is, you can scale it to any size or shape, as long as that shape has right-angle corners.

This means that you can create a 3D scene of a room with a table in it, import it into Director, and then decide on the size you want that 3D window to be on your stage [1.1]. For example, if your stage is 800×600 and you imported your 3D scene in as 320×240, you can stretch it to look like a letterbox movie.

Another option you have with scaling your movies is the ability to easily make a full-screen or mini-screen version. If you have an interface that has a Shockwave 3D movie in it at a fixed size of 320×240, for example, and you want to give the user the ability to play a full-screen mode version, then all you have to do is jump to another frame in the score that has your new UI layout and a re-scaled version of the same castmember. You do not have to import another copy of your Shockwave castmember. You can treat it just like any other Director object that can be scaled and moved via the Score window [1.2].

Streaming

Once your movie is set up and ready for delivery, you have a few options for delivery, one of which is *progressive streaming*. There are two widely used streaming technologies for the Internet—RTSP (real-time streaming protocol) and progressive. Both of these technologies make the delivery of large, streaming content files possible, such as digital video and Shockwave movies.

Built into Director is the capability for movies to work with progressive streaming technology. For example, in Director, under the Modify menu, choose Movie, then choose Playback. A dialog box appears [1.3] that allows you to control how your movie delivers its content to your users. Enable the Play While Downloading Movie option. This starts your movie as soon as the first piece of content arrives.

If you enable this option, you will want to test your movie with different bandwidths. When this option is checked, your movie will start up as quickly as possible, even if the content (graphics, Shockwave 3D, text, or sounds) has not loaded yet. This is both good and bad. If you design your movie to start with very small amounts of content (by small, I mean from about 50–100KB in size), then you can have a welcome page that allows the user to read the instructions of your game while it is loading. At the very least, turn on the Show Placeholders option if you don't have the ability or time to conduct a bandwidth test. This allows an empty box to show up where your content will be placed. This gives the user the impression that something is about to load into the box.

In addition to the Movie Playback Properties dialog box, there are a host of Lingo commands that allow you to better design the users' experience of your movie based on user bandwidth. For example, the Frame Ready command is used to test whether a streaming movie is ready for display, and it should be used in conjunction with the Play While Downloading Movie option. If you enable the option for streaming, then you should use Lingo to test your frames to see if they are

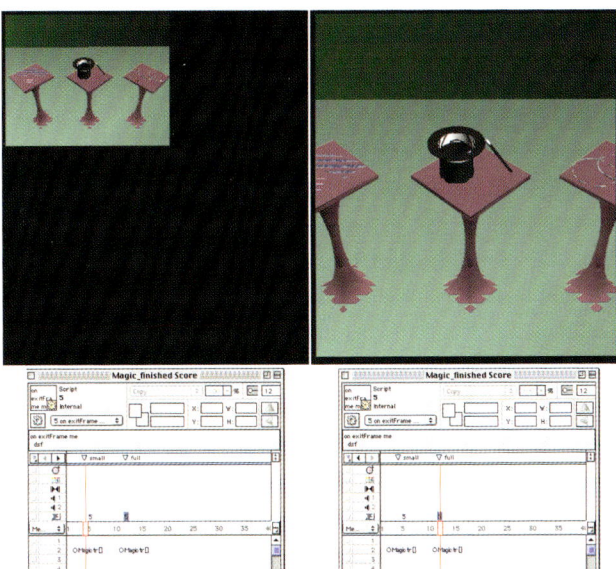

[1.2] Use the Score window to show different size versions of the same Shockwave 3D castmember.

[1.3] Enable the Play While Downloading Movie option to allow your movies to start streaming.

> **Note**
> I would highly recommend that if you do not know what the Lingo command Frame Ready is used for, then leave the Play While Downloading Movie option unchecked.

ready before letting the score go to those frames. For example, use the following Lingo code:

```
on exitFrame
    if frameReady(10) then
        go to frame 10
    else
        go to the frame
    end if
end
```

This simple exit frame handler tests to see if the sprites that compose frame 10 have been downloaded from the Internet. If they have been downloaded, then the handler instructs the score to go to frame number 10; however, if frame number 10's sprites have not finished downloading, the user will continue to wait for the current frame to download.

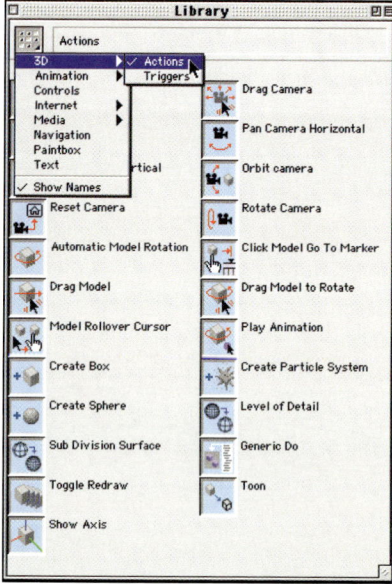

[1.4] Find prewritten Lingo in the Library window.

Behaviors: Programming without Code

Regardless of your knowledge of Lingo, you can still achieve amazing creations with Shockwave 3D, thanks to little prewritten libraries of Lingo code called behaviors. These are located in the Library window [1.4].

Behaviors will become your savior if you need to make a movie fast and don't have time to learn Lingo, not to mention the new Shockwave 3D Lingo. Just some of the things that you are able to do without code are navigation controlling (such as pausing), jumping to frames, and looping or jumping to another movie. There are several kinds of controls for text, such as allowing the user to automatically enter text while allowing a typewriter sound to be heard. You can also create a paint box effect where your users can automatically draw on pictures that you have imported. If you are compelled to, you can even create your own behaviors. This book concentrates specifically on Shockwave 3D behaviors.

The behaviors that were specifically written for Shockwave 3D allow you to program your own 3D scenes and perform neat actions that typically would require very complex Lingo programming. Some of the behaviors include functionalities that allow you to "dolly a virtual camera," automatically rotate 3D models in your scene, adjust the subdivision of your 3D model surfaces to accommodate different bandwidths, and draw or render your 3D scenes in the style of cartoons. You get these capabilities and more without having to code them! See Chapter 2, "Oh Behave," for more on behaviors.

3D Applications

So, you want to learn Shockwave 3D? You have a 3D application, right? If you are considering learning Shockwave 3D, then you should have a fairly good 3D application with regular access to it. Preferably, you should have 3ds max version 3 or 4, because this application is one of the only 3D applications that can support the direct export of the Shockwave 3D file format known as the W3D. Other applications will soon support the W3D exporter.

With the W3D exporter and 3ds max 4, you not only have control over the models you create, but you also have control over the light placement, texture mapping, and animation key frames, and you can even use the real-time physics engine known as Havok® [1.5]. The Havok system is a soft- and rigid-body physics interaction plug-in that both 3ds max and Director understand. This means that you can animate collisions between models to simulate how they would interact in the real world.

This is great if you are a 3D artist or animator that wants to get into Shockwave 3D, because again, you don't have to learn much to create your own Shockwave movies and animations. You are going to need the exporter plug-in. The plug-in can be found on the CD-ROM or you can find it on the Macromedia web site at **https://www.macromedia.com**. I would recommend using the one on the web site to ensure that you have the most recent release.

[1.5] You can use the Havok real-time physics engine in conjunction with Director 8.5 to create cool-looking animated collisions like this one.

Once you have an application that supports W3D, you need an application that will allow you to save a W3D file. You can then deliver your movie to the web or to a projector. The following section discusses the type of application you need to save a W3D file, the Shockwave 3D plug-in.

The Shockwave 3D Plug-In

The Shockwave 3D plug-in is the software that you add to your 3D application to allow it to save a W3D file. The W3D file is the type of file that Director 8.5 imports as a Shockwave 3D castmember. If you have 3ds max, the plug-in can simply be added to the plug-in folder. Then, you just restart the application, and the plug-in will work.

The 3ds max plug-in is easy to deal with, and it provides valuable information about the scene you are trying to export. For example, it shows you a percentage breakdown of your movie's components [1.6]. Apart from appearances, the Maya exporter is similar in feature set [1.7].

The Shockwave 3D plug-in can be obtained from Alias|Wavefront at **http://www.aliaswavefront.com/sw3d** or from the companion CD-ROM. In addition, there is a Shockwave 3D plug-in for Caligari's trueSpace. Note that customers are required to pay $250.00 for the trueSpace version, which includes the Shockwave 3D exporter. The other two software developers that have a plug-in are Discreet, located at **http://www.discreet.com/products/3dsmax/exporter/register**, and MAXON. At the time of this writing, Softimage was close to releasing their plug-in.

Following is a list of developers who are either working on Shockwave 3D plug-ins or already have one:

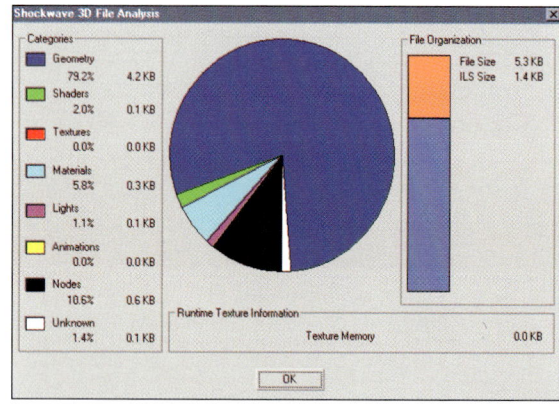

[1.6] The 3ds max Shockwave 3D export pie chart is a great way to see a percentage breakdown of your Shockwave movie.

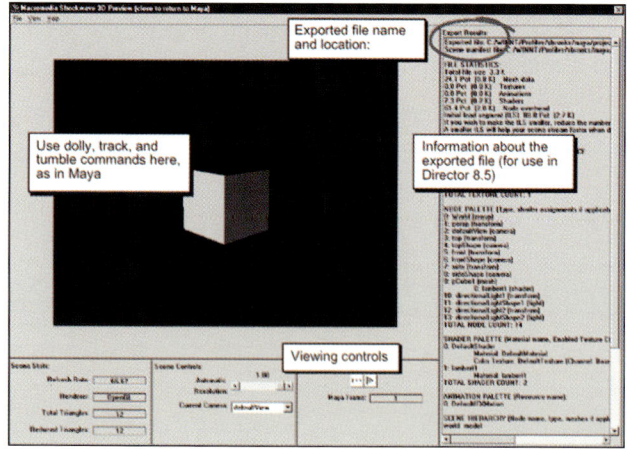

[1.7] The Shockwave 3D export window for Maya.

Company	Application
Alias|Wavefront	Maya
Ashlar-Vellum	Argon version 4
Caligari	trueSpace 5
Curious Labs	Poser Pro
D Vision Works	D Sculptor
Discreet	3ds max
EON Reality	EON Studio
MAXON	Cinema 4D
NewTek	LightWave
REALVIZ	ImageModeler and Stitcher
Softimage/Avid	Softimage XSI
Tabuleiro	ShapeShifter 3D
TGS	AMAPI 3D

If you do not see the 3D application that you use listed here, then there might not be a direct plug-in to support your application. However, you should check the current partner list at the Macromedia web site to see if it has been added. Check for it at **http://www.macromedia.com/software/director/3d/partners**. If you still don't see your application listed, then you can export from your 3D application into the .Obj file format or into another file format that Director supports with an Xtra. Check the Macromedia web site for the latest details on Xtras.

Delivering to the Web or a Projector

The final technology discussed is the delivery of your movie application. If you are a Director user, you already know that you have two delivery options. You can export a Shockwave DCR file and upload it to a web server where people can view your movie over the web, or you can compile your movie into a stand-alone application that can play on either a Macintosh or Windows PC without the use of another supporting application. With Shockwave 3D, both export options apply.

Project Stand-Alone Applications

When you compile your Director movie into a stand-alone application, called a *projector*, your Shockwave 3D castmember is embedded into your application and there is no way that someone can reverse-engineer it for her own use. This is a great way to distribute your work if you are planning on sending a CD-ROM, DVD, or email file to someone. There are a few options that are often overlooked when compiling a projector [1.8].

If you plan to publish your movie to the web as a Shockwave DCR file, it is recommended that you save and compact your file. This is the equivalent of telling Director that you are done working on your file and you are ready to have it compressed. The compression is done in a run-length-encoding fashion where the file is arranged in an order that allows for extremely efficient decompression. If you open and edit something in the file after choosing the save and compress method, you should save and compress it again when you are done.

If you decide to create a projector, you have a few options to choose that will determine how your movie is played back. Your Shockwave 3D castmember normally takes more time to open and render than any other type of castmember. Because of the loading lag time already associated with the Shockwave 3D castmembers, I would recommend that you set your projector options the way I did [1.8]. Turning off Compress (Shockwave Format) for the media option keeps your content in a noncompressed state and allows faster startup for your projector. The same goes for the compression options of the playback engine. I recommend the Standard player option to save time during loading. Enabling the Use System Temporary Memory is also a good idea. With a Shockwave 3D movie, your projector could require more memory than is currently allocated to it. Enabling this option will use the memory that is allocated for the system. Turning this option off could potentially cause an out of memory error message for the user. The

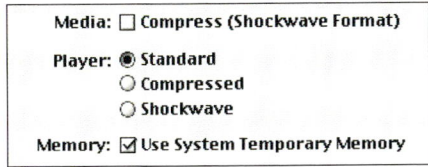

[1.8] The options for creating a stand-alone application.

Shockwave 3D

System Temp Memory option is only available to Macintosh users; Windows manages memory using a virtual swap file method that ensures your application has plenty of memory, which comes at a slight performance expense.

DXR Format Stand-Alone Applications

Director movies that are converted to the DXR format allow you to develop a quicker stand-alone application [1.9].

[1.9] The elusive DXR file is the recommended method of projector delivery!

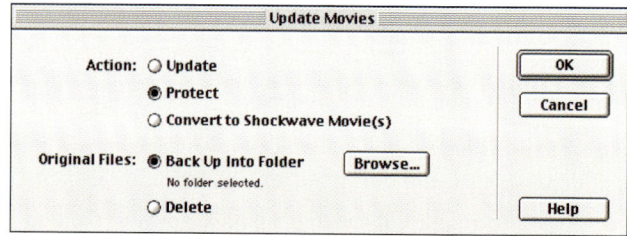

[1.10] Use the Protect option to create DXR files for your projectors.

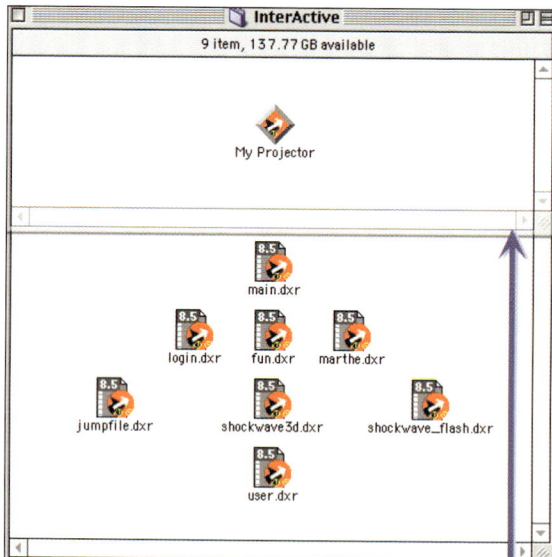

[1.11] DXRs are faster to use, but they create more clutter. Just hide the files under the window.

The DXR format is an uncompressed, secure version of your Director movie, and therefore no decompression is necessary to play back your movie. This is the preferred method of file delivery if disk space isn't an issue. However, the DXR option can cause problems. Someone cannot attempt to open your DXR movie to edit it or reverse-engineer the code. However, DXRs can only be played back by a projector, so don't ever delete your original source file. There is no recovering it!

To create a DXR, you need to be in Director. Then, go to the Xtras menu and choose Update Movies. The Update Movies dialog box appears [1.10]. Next, you simply choose the files you want to protect, and Director automatically creates DXRs out of them.

Another reason DXRs are troublesome is because they are not files that get included inside your projector; thus, when you create a directory or CD-ROM with your projector, you also need to externally include your DXR files. Although you will have to deal with several more files, the speed increase is worth it. To eliminate the distraction of so many files, just hide your files in the window [1.11]. Do this if you are making a CD-ROM, for example.

In order to use the DXR format, you first need a calling movie that is embedded into your projector. DXR files cannot be added to a projector, so you will need to make a simple Director movie that uses Lingo's Open Movie command to "jump" to your DXR. Then, add this Director movie to your projector only. Once your movie starts playing, you can navigate from DXR to DXR using the same Open Movie command.

Web Publishing: DCR Format

If you're planning on delivering Director movies via the web, then you will need to publish your movies to the DCR (Director compressed resource) format. A DCR file is what you need to upload your application to a web server in order to embed it into a web page [1.12]. Director can automatically create DCR files for you and will automatically write the HTML file with all the necessary code for playing your movies.

From the File menu, choose Publish Setting. Here, you can select the format that you want your movie to be written in; plus, you have many other options, such as naming conventions, progress bars, and compression settings. Once you pick and choose how you want your DCR movie to be formatted, simply choose Publish from the File menu. Director automatically creates a web DCR file and its corresponding HTML file in the same directory as the source DIR file.

There are no secrets or special tips about the DCR file format, except that you should make your file as small as possible. This decreases download times for your users. Generally, the DCR file size can be reduced by deleting unused castmembers, reducing the bit depth of castmembers, reducing the sample rate of sound files, or by using quickdraw shapes whenever possible instead of bitmapped shapes. This is covered in more detail in Chapter 3, "Architecture Fly-Through," and Chapter 4, "Wreaking Havok."

Another thing to remember is that there is a difference between the size of the DCR file on your hard drive versus the one on the Internet. On a web page, people like a file size description next to the Shockwave DCR movie that they are about to click on. The file size should come from the size of the file, not the size of space the file is taking up on disk [1.13].

Here [1.13], 15,650 is the exact size of the file, while the computer reports the file to be 16KB. This is not a rounding-up feature; it has to do with the block sizes the hard drive is partitioned into. My drive, for example, has 4KB block sizes, so anything that uses four blocks uses 16KB of hard drive space whether the file is 13, 14, 15, or 16KB in size. Some hard drives are formatted differently, especially Windows drives. On Windows NT, for example, the files can actually take less space on the drive because some hard drive drivers perform disk compression. So make sure to read the size in parentheses when referencing the size for downloading.

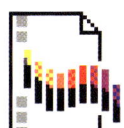

[1.12] Use the DCR file format to embed your movies into web pages.

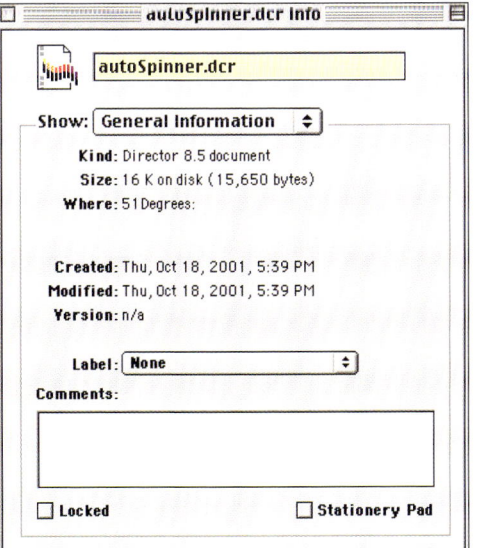

[1.13] Be sure to read the actual file size in parentheses, not the size on the disk.

CHAPTER 2

In This Chapter

What Are Behaviors?, 18

Lingo Compared to Behaviors: A Closer Look, 19

Actions and Triggers: Reference Tables, 20

Adding Behaviors to 3D Sprites, 41

    Changing Behavior Settings, 41

Making Your Text Stand Out, 41

Oh Behave!

In this chapter, I discuss what behaviors are and how to use them. If you are not a Lingo programmer and you don't have time to learn Lingo, you'll want to use behaviors to produce your Director movies. They will allow you to create interactive Shockwave 3D movies very quickly without compromising the quality of user interactions. When you understand what behaviors are and how to apply them, you can use this chapter as a reference.

If you consider yourself to be more of an artistic person than a programmer, you are likely going to use behaviors. This is especially true if you are a 3D animator trying to learn how to create Shockwave games or animation. Also, if you are new to Director, using behaviors is an effective way to achieve interactive results that can make you look like you know a lot more about Lingo than you actually do!

What Are Behaviors?

Director includes a library of pre-written Lingo scripts that are named behaviors. With this library of scripts, you have access to literally hundreds of pre-written pieces of code that you can simply drag-and-drop into your movie. Behaviors add functionality to your 3D scenes, ranging from simple user navigation to particle systems. The only complexity is in filling in the attributes for the behavior you select. In most cases, the attributes are selected as either value sliders or pull-down menus.

To access the Behavior palette, go to the Window menu and choose Library palette [2.1]. (Are you wondering why they didn't just call it the Behavior palette?) It's here that you'll find the behaviors that shipped with Director.

The list of behaviors in the Library palette is broken down into the following categories:

> 3D
> Animation
> Controls
> Internet
> Media
> Navigation
> Paintbox
> Text

Because we are focusing on Shockwave 3D, I explain only the specifics of the first category, 3D. I do, however, recommend that you go through each list of behaviors and discover for yourself what they can do. Even if you are an experienced Lingo programmer, the time you save using some of the new behaviors is worth the exploration time. For example, the Media list now contains the behaviors for working with Director's RealMedia file format.

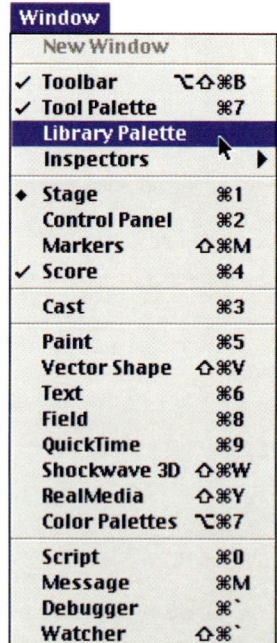

[2.1] Access the Library palette through the Window menu.

The 3D list of behaviors contains two sublists—actions and triggers. The actions are a collection of behaviors that perform functions on your Shockwave 3D castmember(s), such as playing 3D animations or dragging around 3D models. The triggers are used to activate or trigger actions. Actions and triggers work in conjunction with one another; in most cases you have to use a trigger with every action. First, the action you want to perform is applied to your castmember. You fill in the options that are presented to you, and then you apply a trigger that allows your action to run. Manual coding in Lingo is not necessary.

Now that you understand what a behavior is, it's time to learn about the various functionalities of the behaviors in the 3D category.

Lingo Compared to Behaviors: A Closer Look

I'm the first to admit that there are a lot of programmers who love to code in Lingo (I'm one of them), but there are ten times as many people who don't know how to program. If you are not interested in Lingo or if you just don't have natural programming ability (as some proclaim), you should definitely learn how every 3D behavior functions. Learning what each behavior can do now will help you plan for functionality needs later and prevent you from agreeing to do something that you don't know how to do.

Take a look at these two images [2.2–2.3]. Note the substantial difference between using a behavior versus Lingo code to create a simple 3D box in Shockwave 3D. For the behavior, you only need to identify parameters that define the box, whereas, in Lingo, you have to manually write a lot of code to achieve the same result.

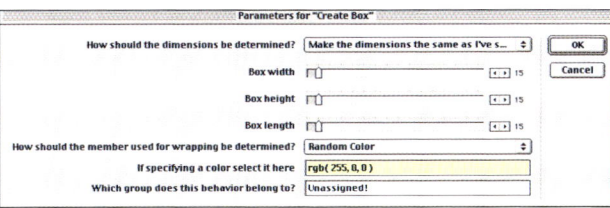

[2.2] If this looks like something you can work with, then behaviors will be a snap for you.

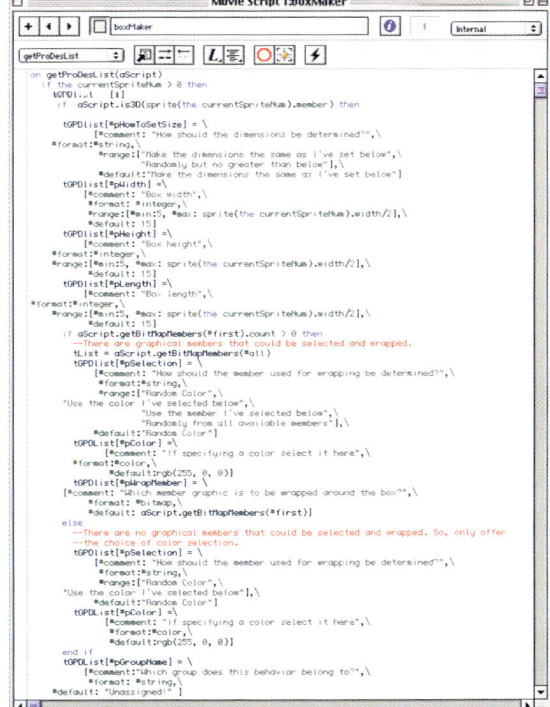

[2.3] This is about 10 percent of the Lingo code needed to create a 3D box.

> **Note**
>
> **Director Coupled with Lingo** Remember that Director can do just about anything you want it to, especially when it's coupled with Lingo. If you are in a job role that competes for work, and you aren't comfortable programming in Lingo, you can always outsource your Lingo programming work for more complex projects, such as games or multi-user movies.

Actions and Triggers: Reference Tables

In this section, I explain in detail each of the behaviors and their respective attributes. The first table provides a reference for behavior actions. The second table shows you the triggers for each action.

Use these tables to reference the Shockwave 3D behavior actions. First, choose an action, and then choose a trigger that will allow your action to run.

ACTIONS

Create Box

The Create Box [2.4] behavior adds a 3D box to your Shockwave 3D castmember. This can be tied to a trigger or frame so that when the user performs an action, the result is a 3D box. Add a Grab and Rotate action to give the user the ability to grab and rotate the box.

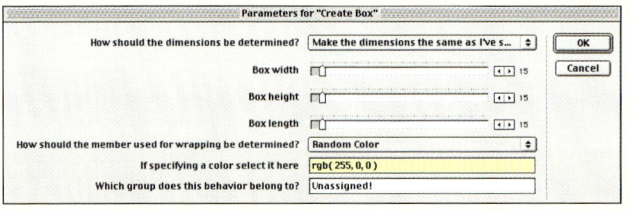

[2.4] Create a 3D box using this behavior.

Create Box Options

Size   You can choose the length, width, and height, or you can just specify the size to be random. When choosing a random size, you can specify the maximum size.

Color of wrapping   You can choose random for the color of wrapping, which allows Director to pick the color, or you can type in an RGB value.

Behavior belongs to   Potentially, you can have a lot of actions and triggers. To organize them, this option allows you to group multiple actions to one trigger by naming the group of actions the behavior belongs to with the same name. You simply make up the group name. For example, BoxMakerGroup would work for this action.

ACTIONS *(continued)*

Create Particle System

This is the coolest and most complex behavior [2.5] in that it defines how your particle system works. Particle systems are complex. How you define them will determine a great deal about how they look when starting and ending. With this behavior, you can create particles that look like fireworks are going off or water is flowing. The best way to learn how to use this is to play with the different settings and discover for yourself the potential of this behavior.

[2.5] The elaborate particle dialog behavior.

Create Particle System Options

Number of particles This determines how many particle dots appear in an image. The more dots, the more realistic an image will appear, but it also means that the CPU activity is more intensive. Values of 5,000 to 10,000 can give spectacular firework-like results.

Particle life Each particle that is emitted can show up for a specific duration of time. A setting of 1 second is comparable to sparks from a welder, whereas 5–10 seconds of time is comparable to fireworks.

Starting size The particle system will emit pixels as a representation of the particle. The starting size determines how big that pixel is at creation time. You can also adjust the size to give the illusion that the particle emission is closer or farther away.

Final size The final size determines how big the particle emission is before vanishing. If the starting and ending size are the same, the particle does not change in size during its life.

continues…

ACTIONS (continued)

Create Particle System (continued)

Angle of emission This setting [2.6–2.8] determines the angle at which the particles propagate away from the center point. Lower numbers produce tighter cones of emissions, and higher numbers (up to 180) produce wider emissions.

Max and min speed These two settings are used together to set a fixed range of speed. The particles cannot go faster or slower than this range of speed. In a fireworks explosion, for example, while all the particles should propagate out at the same rate, this is never the case. Factors, such as wind, temperature, manufacturing process, chemical composition, moisture, and so on will independently affect each particle separately. This setting attempts to vary each particle to achieve more realistic, real-world, chaotic movement.

Distribution method This setting determines how particles move over time. Linear causes the particles to have an equal velocity; Gaussian causes a more natural effect, allowing each particle to gradually slow down.

Gravity along X, Y, Z This allows you to add the pull of gravity to your particle emission. A setting of –1 in the Y will pull down your particles just as natural gravity would. Positive numbers in the X move particles right; negative numbers move them left. Positive numbers in the Y move particles up; negative Y values move them down. Positive values in the Z move toward the viewer, and negative values push particles away from the screen. Thus, X values equate to left and right, Y values equate to up and down, and Z values equate to in and out.

[2.6] An angle emission setting of 180 degrees.

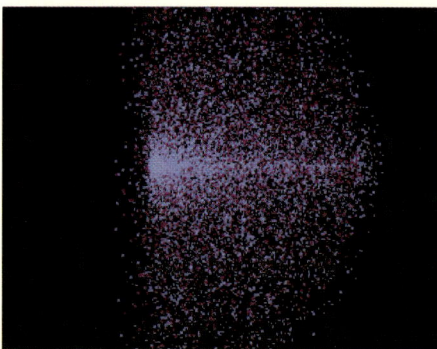

[2.7] An angle emission setting of 90 degrees.

[2.8] An angle emission setting of 15 degrees.

ACTIONS (continued)

Create Particle System (continued)

Wind X, Y, Z   These settings are similar to the gravity settings, except that they are more subtle in their result. For example, they can make a water fountain look like wind is blowing through it. The X, Y, and Z settings follow the same directions as the gravity X, Y, and Z settings, respectively.

Color selection   The particles can be randomly picked colors or you can specify the starting and ending colors. When you specify the starting and ending colors, Shockwave will blend the particle through those colors as the particle's lifetime comes to an end.

Starting and ending blend   These settings determine when the color cycling of particle colors starts and stops. The values are in percentages and represent 0–100 percent of the lifetime of the particle. If, for example, you set your particle lifetime to 2.0, a starting blend setting of 50 (think of it as 50 percent of the life of the particle emission) would start the color blending at 1.0 second into the particle emission.

Repeat emissions   This check box is for starting your particle emission continually. This would be used for a flowing fluid emission, but not for something such as fireworks, because fireworks aren't fluid or liquid-like.

Emission released   The all at once setting lets the particles you specified in the how many particles option out in one burst. The streaming setting calculates the number of particles divided by the particle life and releases a continuous stream (like water).

Group belong to   This text field allows you to name the trigger group that will activate the particle emission. This way you can group multiple actions to one trigger.

Create Sphere

The Create Sphere behavior [2.9] adds a 3D sphere to your Shockwave 3D castmember. This is the same as the Create Box, which allows you to trigger a sphere to be created by different types of user inputs.

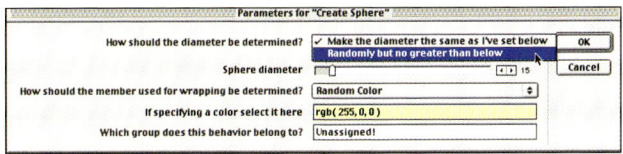

[2.9] The options for creating a generic sphere using a behavior.

Create Sphere Options

The diameter   This option determines the size of the sphere. You can use the slider to pick an exact size or have Director pick a "random but not greater then" size.

continues...

ACTIONS (continued)

Create Sphere (continued)

Color of wrapping   For this setting, you can choose random, and Director will pick the color of wrapping, or you can type your own RGB value for the sphere.

Group name   With this setting, you specify the name of the trigger group. The name can be anything you want it to be.

Drag Camera

This behavior [2.10] allows you to move freely in the X- and Y-axis. You can also enable the zoom check box to zoom in and out of the Z-axis. This is a good behavior for moving your entire view in a fluid motion. The controls are similar to what you might feel if you were flying an airplane. When pulling the mouse down the scene goes up, and rotations bank left or right. This behavior needs three triggers to work correctly. One trigger is used for each direction. You can also click on the Left button of the mouse and trigger it three times; then assign the horizontal and vertical pan to a mouse click. Assign zoom and rotate to the Shift-mouse-click and Control-mouse-click, respectively.

[2.10] Use this behavior to move around your Shockwave scene.

Drag Camera Options

Horizontal pan   This allows you to move left and right without constraint. The action is a dragging motion, where you click and drag the mouse to move around.

Vertical pan   This option is the same as the Horizontal pan, except that you are panning up and down instead of side-to-side.

Include zoom   When this is checked, you can move forward and backward through your Shockwave 3D world.

Sensitivity   This slider determines how quickly your 3D world responds to your mouse's movements.

Group name   With this option, you specify the name of the trigger group; the name can be whatever you want it to be.

ACTIONS   *(continued)*

Drag Model

The Drag Model behavior [2.11] is a simple behavior that allows you to pick any of your 3D model or models and give the user control to move it around. The movement is constrained to the X- and Y-axis. This behavior needs a mouse trigger to simulate mouse clicks and other mouse actions, such as grabbing and dragging.

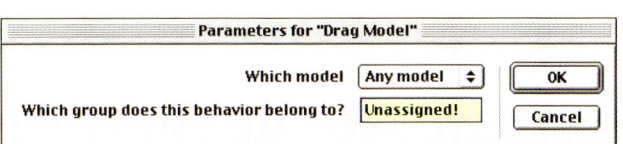

[2.11] You can pick any 3D model that you want the user to move around.

Drag Model Options

Which model   This is a pull-down list that contains every model in your Shockwave 3D castmember. Scroll through it and pick the model you want to drag.

Group name   This specifies the name of the trigger group that activates the Drag Model behavior.

Drag Model to Rotate

The Drag Model to Rotate behavior [2.12] is similar to Drag Model, except that with this behavior, your model spins around a 3D axis when dragged. Clicking and dragging from left to right spins the 3D model around its Y-axis, for example.

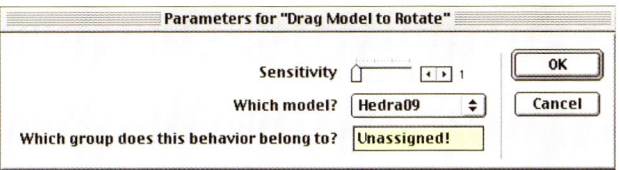

[2.12] The Drag Model to Rotate behavior.

Drag Model to Rotate Options

Sensitivity   This setting determines how far the mouse has to travel before the model starts to rotate. Smaller settings result in less rotation per mouse movement, and higher settings result in a greater rotation.

Which model   This allows you to pick a specific model to control.

Group name   This option specifies the name of the trigger group that can activate the Drag Model to Rotate behavior.

continues...

ACTIONS *(continued)*

Fly Through

Fly Through is a great behavior for traveling through 3D space [2.13]. Attach a mouse trigger, and this behavior will act as the flight joystick that controls your flight path. It can automatically move you forward and backward, and roll you left or right, which is similar to the banking of a plane. Pushing the cursor up moves you forward and pulling it back slows you down gradually.

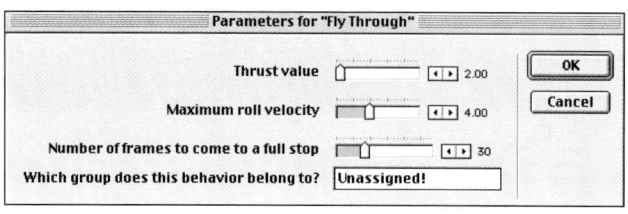

[2.13] Simulate flying with this simple behavior.

Fly Through Options

Thrust value For this setting, start with the default value of 2.0 and increase it if your 3D world is large and you need to get around faster. Decrease the default value if you want to travel more slowly. Also realize that a faster setting is more CPU-intensive depending on your 3D model's complexity.

Roll velocity This determines the maximum speed the user can turn to the left or right depending on the cursor's position. Smaller numbers result in slower speeds or more gradual turns.

Group name Group name specifies the name of the trigger group that can activate this behavior.

Click Model Go to Marker

The Click Model Go to Marker behavior [2.14] allows you to pick a specific 3D model that when clicked jumps to a marker that you have created in the Score window. Or, it can jump to the next or previous marker. You can use this as a simple method to change the area surrounding your Shockwave 3D sprite. If, for example, a user clicks a 3D model of a TV, the user might be sent to a marker that contains text that says, "TV." This text would be located next to your Shockwave 3D sprite.

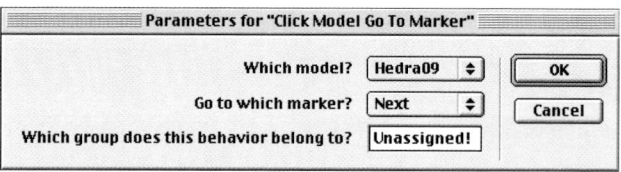

[2.14] Your 3D models can be used to navigate from marker to marker in your score.

Click Model Go to Marker Options

Which model This pull-down list allows you to scroll through your models and choose the one that will respond to the click.

ACTIONS   (continued)

Click Model Go to Marker   (continued)

Which marker   This scrolling list contains the markers you have already created.

Group name   Here, you specify the name of the trigger group that can activate this behavior.

Orbit Camera

The Orbit Camera behavior [2.15] allows you to place a camera orbit around the 3D model you've selected. This behavior simulates a QuickTime VR object movie.

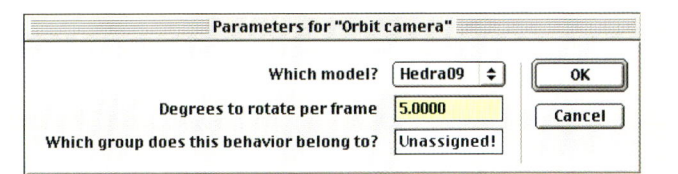

[2.15] You can orbit around a 3D object with the Orbit Camera behavior.

Orbit Camera Options

Which model   This pull-down list allows you to scroll through your models and choose the one to orbit around.

Degree per frame   This setting, coupled with the frames per second, determines how fast and how smooth your camera movements will be. The slower and smoothest movements are smaller values.

Group name   This option specifies the name of the trigger group that can activate this behavior.

Play Animation

The Play Animation behavior [2.16] controls the animation that is key-framed in your Shockwave 3D castmember. You must use a Shockwave 3D castmember that already contains animation. This behavior doesn't create new animation. It can, however, move your animation from model to model, a new concept that is a bit tricky to grasp. If, for example, you have two spheres (sphere A and sphere B) and you animate sphere A to bounce in your 3D program, then you export your 3D movie as a Shockwave 3D .W3D file and bring it into Director. This behavior will view sphere A, sphere B, and the sphere A-key (or keyframes) as three separate things. You can easily tell sphere A to animate, but you can also tell sphere B to animate using sphere A's animation keyframes. This way you can share different animations with different models.

Play Animation Options

Which model is to be clicked on   This pull-down list allows you to scroll through your models and choose the one that when clicked will activate the animation playback. This doesn't have to be the same model that you animated in your 3D application.

continues...

ACTIONS *(continued)*

Play Animation *(continued)*

Model going into motion   This option is a pull-down list of your models. You pick the model that is going to be animated from this list.

Start which animation   This is a pull-down list of the possible animation key frames that you can choose to animate the model that is "going into motion." In other words, you will choose which animation to start first (if you animated more than one model).

Initial state of animation   This is a pull-down list that lets you choose whether the animation should start playing automatically or if it should initially wait for a trigger to start it.

How should the animation playback   This list allows you to choose if the animation plays once and stops at the end, plays once then resets to start, or loops continuously.

Restrict the model to its origin   This pull-down list lets you determine if you want the model to change the X, Y, and Z position, and the X, Y, and Z rotation. If you set the option to yes, the model will animate in one place; it will not move from its current location.

Initial state of all other animations   If you have animated more than one object, you can choose from this pull-down menu whether or not the objects are activated or if they are stopped when this behavior is activated.

Group name   This specifies the name of the trigger group that can activate this behavior.

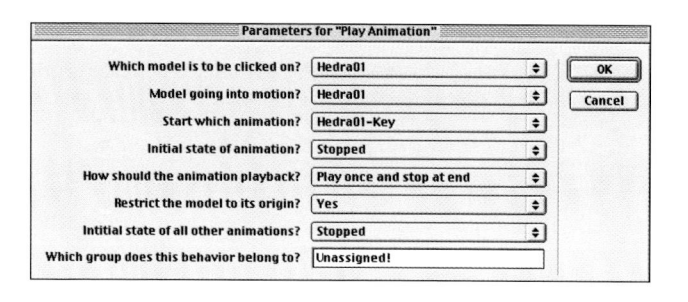

[2.16] Play animations that you created in your 3D application.

Dolly Camera

Dolly Camera [2.17] is a simple behavior that allows you to move the point of view in and out. The Hollywood term for this is a dolly.

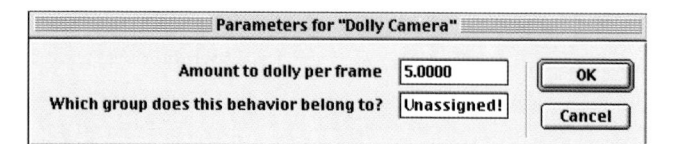

[2.17] Move in and out of your 3D scene with this behavior.

ACTIONS *(continued)*

Dolly Camera *(continued)*

Dolly Camera Options

Amount to dolly per frame This setting, coupled with the frames per second, determines the speed and smoothness of the camera movements. The slowest, smoothest movements have smaller values, such as 1.0 or even .75.

Group name This option specifies the name of the trigger group that can activate this behavior.

Generic Do

The Generic Do behavior [2.18] is for Lingo programmers. It allows you to attach a Lingo command to a Shockwave 3D castmember.

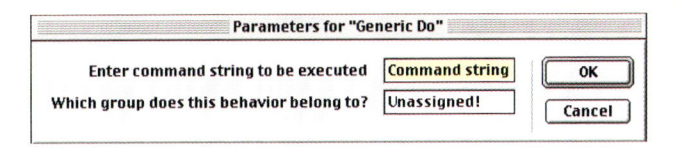

[2.18] You can assign 3D models to call custom Lingo handlers with this behavior.

Gonoric Do Options

Command string to be executed This is where the custom Lingo command, such as a handler name, is typed.

Group name This specifies the name of the trigger group that can activate this behavior.

Following is a very simple example of the passing of a Lingo command string:

1. In Director, open the movie script (Command-Shift-U) and type the following code:

   ```
   On beepTest
        Beep 2
   End
   ```

2. Attach the Generic Do behavior to your Shockwave 3D castmember and type **beepTest** as the command string to be executed.

3. Name the group to which the behavior belongs to mousebeep.

4. Attach a Mouse Left trigger to the Shockwave 3D castmember, choose the mousebeep group, and then execute this command option from the group pull-down menu. Click OK.

5. Make sure your movie has a go to the frame loop or the loop command, and then play your movie. Note that clicking the Shockwave 3D castmember should activate the system beep twice.

continues…

ACTIONS *(continued)*

Pan Camera Horizontal

Pan Camera Horizontal [2.19] is a simple behavior that allows you to move the point of view to the left and to the right. Attach a Mouse Left trigger, and you can use the mouse to drag elements around on the screen.

[2.19] Move your 3D camera smoothly with this behavior.

Pan Camera Horizontal Options

Degrees to pan per frame This setting, coupled with the frames per second, determines how fast and how smooth your camera movements become. The slowest and smoothest movement has smaller values, such as 1.0 or even .75.

Group name This specifies the name of the trigger group that can activate this behavior.

Pan Camera Vertical

The Pan Camera Vertical behavior [2.20] is identical to the pan camera horizontal except that this behavior is for vertical movement. It allows you to move the point of view to up and down. Attach a Mouse Left trigger, and you can use the mouse to drag elements around on the screen.

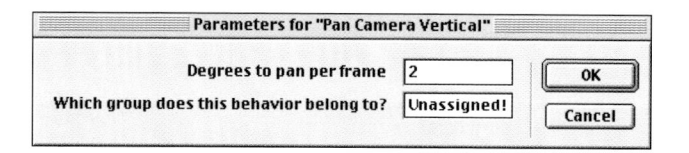

[2.20] Move the camera in one axis with this behavior.

Pan Camera Vertical Options

Degrees to pan per frame This setting, coupled with the frames per second setting, determines both how fast and how smooth your camera movements will be.

Group name This option specifies the name of the trigger group that can activate this behavior.

ACTIONS *(continued)*

Reset Camera

The Reset Camera behavior [2.21] is an important behavior to use. I recommend you use the Reset Camera behavior whenever you give navigation control to your users. If you are using a Pan or Fly Through behavior, you can easily become lost in your 3D world. When this behavior is triggered, it will reset the camera view to the same view your movie first started at.

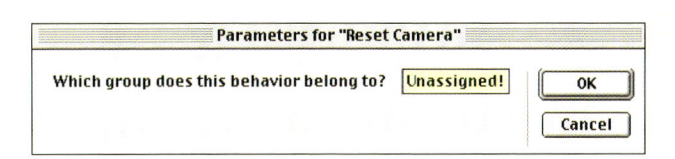

[2.21] If you get lost in your scene, you can use the Reset Camera behavior to take you back to your starting place.

Reset Camera Options

Group name This options specifies the name of the trigger group that can activate this behavior. It is a good idea to attach a Keyboard input trigger and use the spacebar as the trigger for the Reset Camera action. Then, if you are lost in your 3D world, you can reset your view by simply clicking the spacebar.

Rotate Camera

The Rotate Camera behavior [2.22] allows the camera to bank or rotate in place. There is no translation of position with this behavior. An example of this type of movement is viewing the world from the cockpit of a plane and spinning left or right.

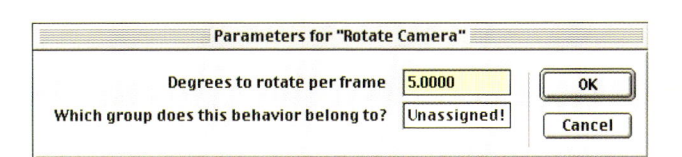

[2.22] Spin about an axis with this behavior.

Rotate Camera Options

Degrees to rotate per frame This setting, coupled with the frames per second setting, determines how fast and how smooth your camera rotations will be.

Group name This option specifies the name of the trigger group that can activate this behavior.

Toggle Redraw

This behavior [2.23] is similar to a 3D special effect. This behavior is like the Trails ink effect in Director. When turned off, you will see visible trails of your 3D models and elements as they move.

continues...

ACTIONS *(continued)*

Toggle Redraw *(continued)*

Toggle Redraw Options

Initial redraw state   This pull-down list lets you enable or disable the redrawing of your 3D models. By default, it is enabled.

Group name   This specifies the name of the trigger group that can activate this behavior.

[2.23] If you get delayed when redrawing, use this behavior.

Automatic Model Rotation

The Automatic Model Rotation behavior [2.24] lets you pick your 3D models or a specific one, which you rotate around a selected axis. You can control the speed of the spin, and you can attach multiple copies of this behavior to the same model in order for it to spin on two or three axes. The spinning starts automatically when the movie starts playing. You cannot control this behavior after it is applied.

Automatic Model Rotation Options

Rotation speed   This value slider determines the speed of the spin.

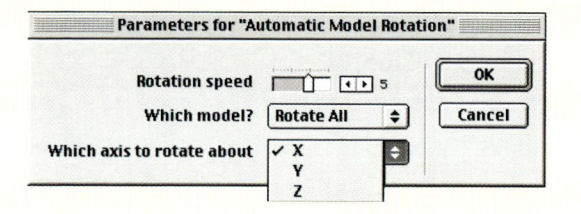

[2.24] Permanent spin can be added to any model.

Which model   Use this pull-down menu to select a specific model or choose all of your models.

Which axis to rotate about   A pull-down menu that lets you choose the X, Y, or Z axis to spin around.

Level of Detail

This behavior [2.25] controls a few things. It was designed to adjust the quality (or detail) of your 3D models relative to the distance the model is from the viewer. As the models (or a specific model) move closer to the viewer, their quality increases. Adding or subtracting polygons from the 3D model

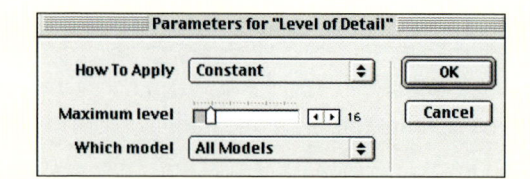

[2.25] Models can adjust quality in real time with this behavior.

ACTIONS   (continued)

Level of Detail   (continued)

adjusts the quality. This behavior can produce bad-looking models. Because this behavior pulls polygons out of your models, objects, such as spheres, can end up looking like pyramids or another unintentional object. This behavior is useful for large movies that are going to be streamed over the Internet. Be careful to test this setting with different types of connections so that you know what your audience is seeing.

Level of Detail Options

How to apply   This pull-down menu gives you the three choices—constant, randomly, and cyclic. Constant keeps your model or models at a fixed level of detail. This is the most useful setting. Randomly picks your models at random and picks random times to remove the detail. The random setting typically results in strange-looking models, though at times, the models will look as intended. The final choice is cyclic. This setting cycles the quality of your models from the maximum setting to zero and back again in a loop.

Maximum level   This slider determines the maximum quality setting of your models. A setting of 100 is the same as not using the behavior, whereas a setting of 0 removes so many polygons from your models that they are almost unrecognizable.

Which model   This pull-down menu lets you choose whether this behavior affects all your models or just one.

[2.26] This shows a Shockwave 3D model with the Level of Detail set to 100.

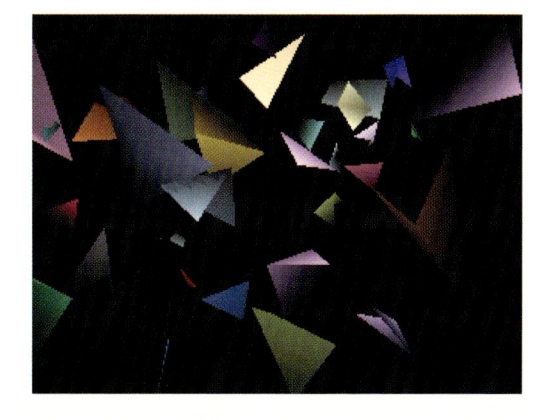

[2.27] This figure shows the same Shockwave 3D member with a Level of Detail setting of 10.

continues…

ACTIONS *(continued)*

Model Rollover Cursor

This behavior [2.28] changes your cursor when you rollover a model. This is useful if you have a model that goes to another marker when it's clicked.

Model Rollover Cursor Options

Which model   This pull-down menu lets you select a model that when rolled over with the mouse changes the cursor.

Which cursor   Use this pull-down menu to pick the cursor you want to use. Your choices are: Arrow, I-Beam, Crosshair, Crossbar, Watch, Blank, Help, Finger, Hand, Closed hand, No drop hand, Copy closed hand, Pencil, Eraser, Select, Bucket, Lasso, Dropper, Air Brush, Zoom in, Zoom out, Vertical size, Horizontal size, and Diagonal size.

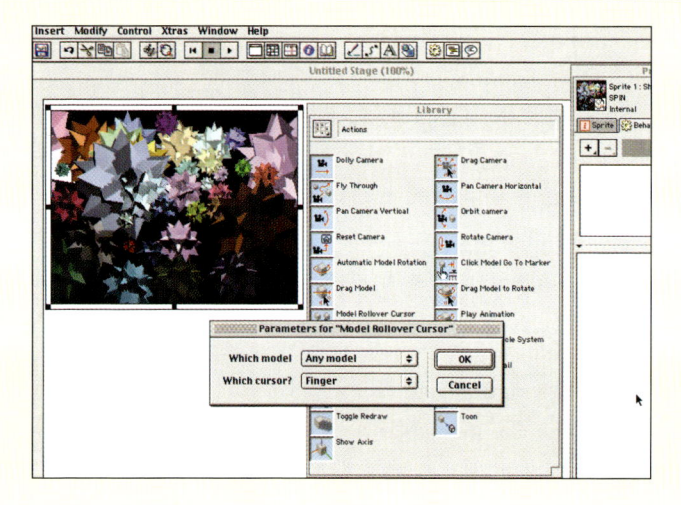

[2.28] Assign custom cursors to your models.

Show Axis

This behavior [2.29] shows the axis (X, Y, and Z) of a specific model that you choose or all of your models. The behavior draws a wireframe around your model and draws a line to each of the three axes options. This is a visual effect that works well for rotating models.

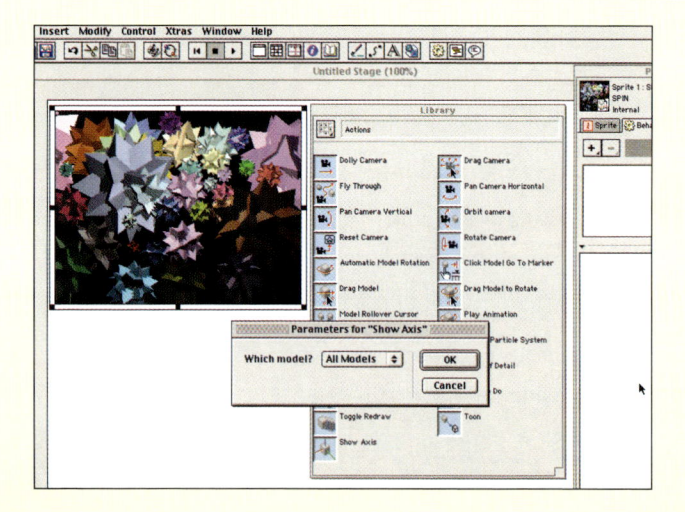

[2.29] Shockwave 3D can show you the axis of any model.

ACTIONS *(continued)*

Show Axis *(continued)*

Show Axis Options

Which model The pull-down lets you choose a specific model or you can choose all of your models [2.30].

[2.30] In this image, Show Axis is turned on for all models.

Sub Division Surface

This behavior [2.31] is almost the opposite of the Level of Detail behavior. With it, you can add detail to your models. To add detail, you have to increase the polygon count; thus, the smoothness of the model comes at the expense of more CPU time.

[2.31] Add more detail to your models with the SDS behavior. Here, the behavior is turned on for all models.

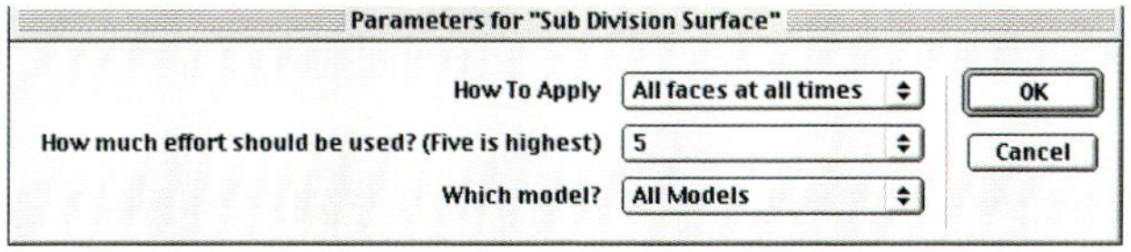

Sub Division Surface Options

How to apply Your choices from this pull-down menu are the all faces at all times option or the only when visible option. Using only when visible will give you great results with less CPU requirements. Using all faces increases the quality of the backside of your models as well.

Effort used This pull-down menu lets you choose the quality and CPU effort that the SDS behavior will use to make your model(s) look good.

Which model This pull-down lets you choose if the behavior is applied to all your models or to a specific model.

continues...

ACTIONS *(continued)*

Toon

The Toon behavior [2.32] attempts to color your Shockwave 3D castmember as you would a cartoon. The number of colors is reduced and models can be outlined with a solid color of your choice. The result is a model or animation that looks like it was drawn with markers. This behavior requires a lot of tweaking to get ideal results.

Toon Options

Toon style   This pull-down lets you pick the toon shader style. The Sharp choice gives your models sharp edges that require a lot of light. Smooth gives a gradual (or more airbrushed) look to your models. The Black and White option strips the color from your models [2.33].

Number of colors for lighting   This pull-down lets you choose the number of colors for the Toon Shaders palette. Choices range from 2–16 colors [2.34].

Percentage of lighting colors used for shadows   This slider lets you set a percentage from 0–100. The setting lets you select how many colors to extract from the original models(s) to use for shadows.

How dark should the shadowed areas be   This slider allows you to select when the darker areas will turn to black.

Percentage of lighting colors used for highlighting   This slider lets you select the percentage for how much color will be extracted from the original models and used to shade the areas where light strikes your models.

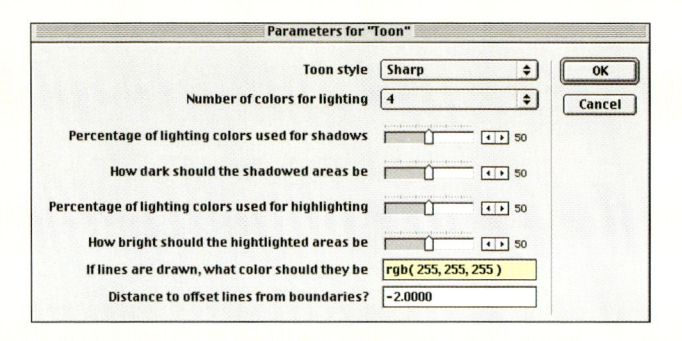

[2.32] There are several options with the toon behavior that allow you to make your 3D models look hand-sketched.

[2.33] A sample of the sharp toon shader with all the lights adjusted to remove the color.

[2.34] An example of the smooth shader with the light adjusted to show four colors.

ACTIONS (continued)

Toon (continued)

How bright should the highlighted areas be   This slider is used as a way to adjust how bright hot spots will be.

If lines are drawn, what color should they be   These RGB values allow you to choose the outline color that will surround your models.

Distance to offset lines from boundaries   This text field allows you to type in the value that determines where the outline surrounding your model is drawn.

[2.35] The original image with all its colors.

TRIGGERS

Mouse Left

The Mouse Left trigger [2.36] is used to trigger an applied action with the mouse. On the Macintosh, the Mouse Left is the behavior to use, as opposed to the Mouse Right, which only works on the PC.

Mouse Left Options

When does action occur   This pull-down lets you choose when the trigger becomes active. Your choices are anytime the left mouse button is being pressed, only when the mouse button is released, and only when the mouse button is first pressed. If you choose anytime the button is being pressed, some actions will occur continually. To simulate a normal mouse click, the button released option is the best choice.

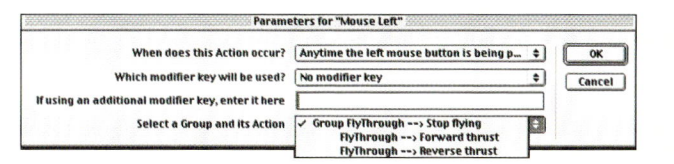

[2.36] The Mouse Left trigger will activate your action behavior when the left mouse button is pressed.

Which modifier key will be used   This option lets you choose an additional key to be pressed before the trigger will activate your action. Your choices are no modifier key, shift, control, and shift and control. Picking one of these means that you must also press that modifier key and mouse click to activate the action. This adds an additional key to your trigger, giving you a practically unlimited number of possible key choices to choose from.

continues...

TRIGGERS *(continued)*

Mouse Left *(continued)*

Custom modifier key The custom key text field lets you enter your own keyboard character. For this to work, you must first set the modifier key option to shift, control, or shift and control. Then, you can add an additional key. This function simply allows you to pick a key combination to activate your trigger.

Select a group and its action This pull-down menu lets you choose which action the trigger effects and which attribute of that action. For example, if you attach the Fly Through behavior, you will need to attach three triggers to handle the fact that the Fly Through can perform three actions—move forward, stop, and move backward. You can attach the Mouse Left trigger three times and assign a different modifier key for each action.

Mouse Enter

The Mouse Enter trigger [2.37] will activate your action anytime the mouse is rolled into the Shockwave 3D sprite.

The only option for this trigger is Select group and its action. This pull-down menu will let you choose which action this trigger will be effecting. There are no settings for this trigger.

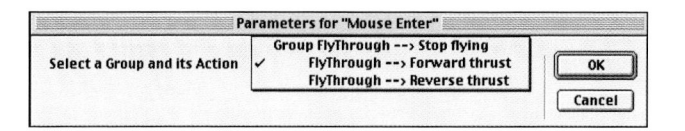

[2.37] The Mouse Enter trigger activates a behavior when your mouse rolls over a 3D sprite.

Mouse Leave

The Mouse Leave trigger [2.38] activates an action when the mouse is rolled off the Shockwave 3D sprite. You could potentially use a Mouse Enter and a Mouse Leave trigger together to start an action when the cursor is rolled over the Shockwave 3D sprite. Then, make the action stop when the mouse is rolled off it.

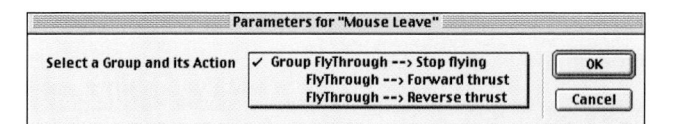

[2.38] The Mouse Leave trigger activates a behavior when your mouse rolls off your 3D sprite.

TRIGGERS *(continued)*

Mouse Leave *(continued)*

The only option to set for this trigger is the Select group and its action option. This pull-down menu lets you choose which action this trigger effects. There are no other settings for this trigger.

Mouse Right

The Mouse Right trigger [2.39] is used to trigger an applied action with the mouse. This trigger does not function on a Macintosh, unless you have a non-Apple mouse with more than one button.

[2.39] Use the Mouse Right trigger to activate a behavior with a mouse that has two or more buttons.

Mouse Right Options

When does this action occur This pull-down lets you choose when the trigger becomes active. Your choices are anytime the right mouse button is being pressed, only when the mouse button is released, and only when the mouse button is first pressed.

Which modifier key will be used This lets you choose an additional key to be pressed before the trigger activates an action. Your choices are no modifier key, shift, control, and shift and control.

Custom modifier key The custom key text field lets you enter your own keyboard character. For this to work, you must first set the modifier key option to shift, control, or shift and control, and then you can add an additional key.

Select a group and its action This pull-down menu lets you choose which action the trigger effects and which attribute of that action. For example, if you attach the Fly Through behavior, you will need to attach three triggers to handle the fact that the Fly Through can perform three actions—move forward, stop, and move backward. You can attach the Mouse Right trigger three times and assign a different modifier key for each action.

continues...

TRIGGERS *(continued)*

Mouse Within

The Mouse Within trigger [2.40] is almost identical to the Mouse Enter trigger, except that the trigger continuously sends the event message to the behavior that the mouse is in the Shockwave 3D sprite.

The only option for this trigger is the Select group and its action option. This pull-down menu lets you choose which action this trigger effects.

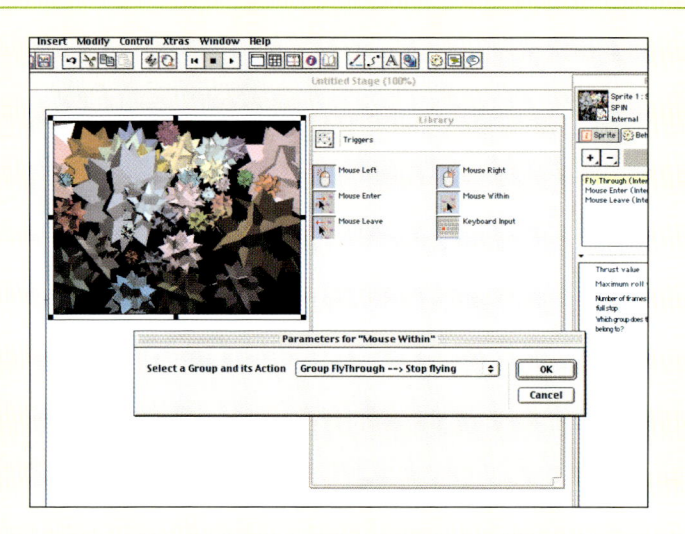

[2.40] Mouse Within triggers a behavior by rolling over your 3D sprite with the mouse in the action.

Keyboard Input

This trigger [2.41] allows you to specify a custom keyboard key that will trigger your action.

Keyboard Input Options

Which key will be used This pull-down menu allows you to enter your own custom key or choose from a list of arrow keys.

Enter custom key This empty text field is where you type in the key.

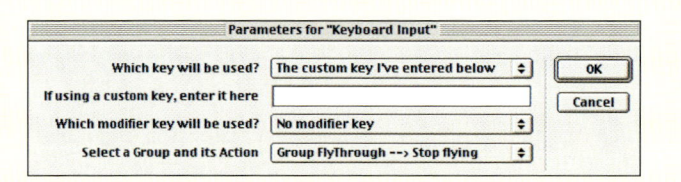

[2.41] Activate a behavior by simply pressing a key with this action.

Which modifier key will be used You can choose an additional modifier key to be pressed from this menu.

Select a group and its action This pull-down menu lets you choose which action this trigger effects.

Adding Behaviors to 3D Sprites

To attach a behavior to a castmember, you simply drag the behavior on to it. To do this, open the Behaviors library, choose the behavior you want, and drag it on top of the sprite, either on the stage or in the score window [2.42]. Do the same thing to attach triggers.

There are some cases when a behavior won't attach itself to a sprite. This is not unusual. If, for example, there is no animation in your Shockwave 3D castmember, you cannot attach the Play Animation behavior. Don't attach behaviors when it isn't logical to attach them.

Changing Behavior Settings

After you attach a behavior or trigger to your Shockwave 3D sprite, simply delete the behavior and reattach it with a new setting, or you can adjust the existing setting in the Property Inspector [2.43]. To open the Inspector window, go to the Windows menu and choose Inspectors; then, choose Property.

Whenever you change setting values, you are required to start and stop the movie to see the effects of the changes.

Making Your Text Stand Out

This section describes a new feature in Director 8.5 that allows you to create 3D text. The Shockwave 3D engine now supports 3D functions; thus, the normal text generation engine has been enhanced to allow you to turn your normal fonts into extruded 3D text.

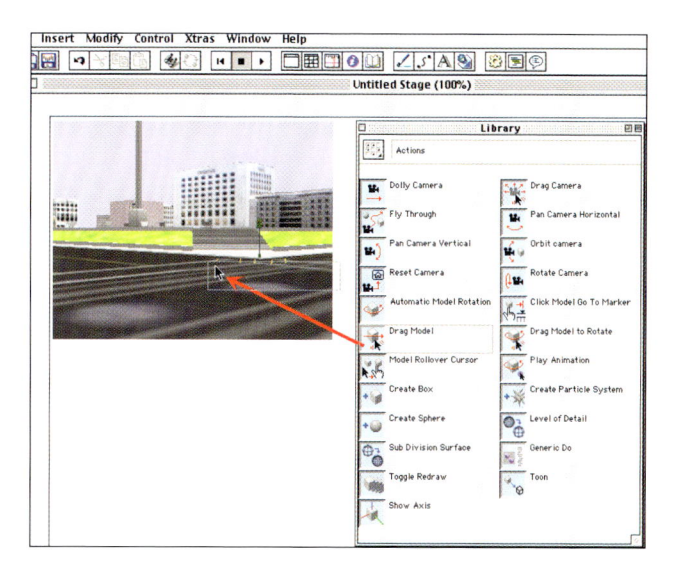

[2.42] To add a behavior, drag it onto your Shockwave 3D sprite.

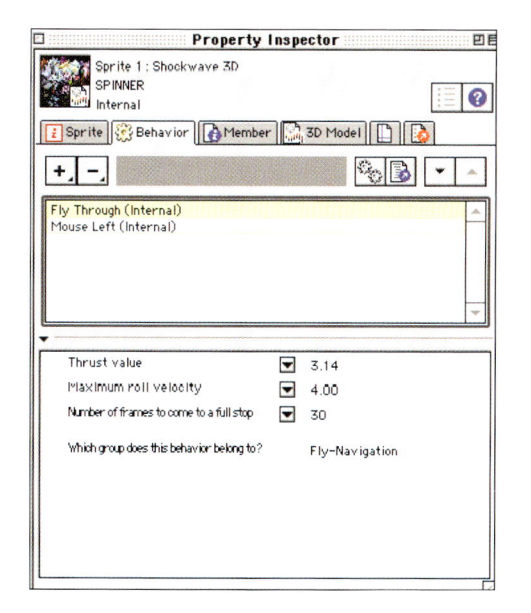

[2.43] The Property Inspector is where you modify the values of behaviors that have already been attached to sprites.

[2.44] Type some text on the stage.

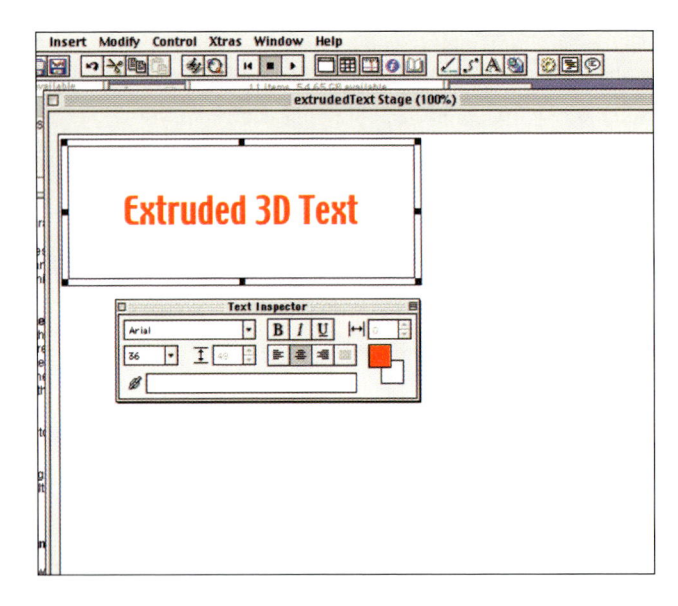

[2.45] With the Property Inspector, you can change your text to 3D text.

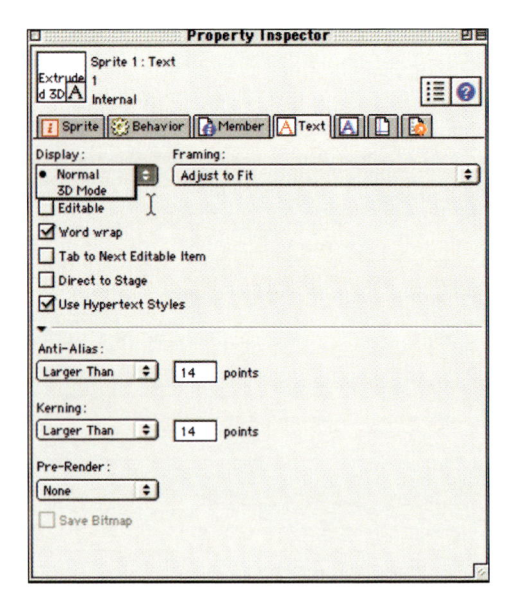

You can open the sample movie in this section from the CD-ROM accompanying this book. It is titled textextrude.dir. Or, you can recreate it following these steps:

1. In Director, create a new text window on the stage. You can use the text tool to create the text on the Macintosh. You open it with by selecting Command-7 on the Macintosh or Ctrl-7 on Windows. Then, go to the Window menu and choose the Tool Palette. Type some sample text on the stage **[2.44]**.

2. Next, extrude the text. Open the Property Inspector window. Make sure your text is selected. Switch to the Text tab and change the display setting to 3D Mode. Your text should have changed to 3D text **[2.45]**.

3. Switch to the 3D Extruder tab and adjust the settings. With the Extruder tab checkboxes—front face, tunnel, and back face—you can turn on or off the front, middle, or back of the 3D text. The result is text that looks like a container. There is no right or wrong option for the settings you pick. They are used for visual effects. The tunnel option connects the front face and the back face together to make the 3D text look real. However, if you turn off this option, less CPU is needed to draw your 3D text. This is good, for example, if your 3D text is spinning around an axis. It can spin much faster if the tunnel option is turned off.

4. Experiment with the other settings to adjust the length of the 3D extrusion, the surrounding bevel, and the lighting positions. Use these settings to customize the 3D text. They do not require you to change them in order for the effect to work. Optionally, you can add an automatic rotation behavior to the 3D text sprite, because it is now contains a 3D model—the text.

5. Drag the behavior over the 3D text castmember and select the Y rotation axis. You can choose any axis of rotation or add multiple copies of this behavior. You can also have your 3D text rotate in the X- and Y-axis.

6. When you are done experimenting with the settings, click OK, and play your movie.

As you can see, creating 3D text in Director is a simpler process than creating it in an external 3D program, which requires you to export it as a .W3D file. In addition, you can't make changes to Shockwave 3D text that comes from another application, such as 3ds max.

Now that you understand behaviors, their associated actions and triggers, and how to create 3D text, you are ready to take on more Shockwave 3D examples. The following chapters promise to supply plenty of these.

CHAPTER 3

■ **In This Chapter**

Storyboarding, 46

Building the Model, 46

Naming Models, 52

Lighting, 53

Texture Mapping, 55

Setting Up the Camera, 57

Exporting Options, 57

    A Piece of the Pie, 63

Working in Director, 64

    File Size Considerations, 65

    Score Setup, 65

    Color and Visibility, 66

    Redrawing Issues, 66

    Adding Lingo, 67

Testing—"Test Early, Test Often", 73

    Projector Testing, 74

    Web Testing, 75

    Xtra Embedding, 76

    Graphic Dithering, 77

    Completing the Movie, 78

Architecture Fly-Through

This chapter is the first hands-on example in this book. It walks you through the process of creating a Shockwave 3D file. For this chapter, we will use the example of a fly-through house. Imagine that your house is for sale and that you want to put more than a photo of it on the Internet. In Shockwave 3D, you can easily create an interactive, fly-through version that allows viewers to literally see the inside of your house.

When building a 3D model, you should first storyboard it, then 3D model it, and then move your model into Director via the Shockwave exporter. After your model is in Director, you can apply behaviors or Lingo to it to make it interactive, or to give the interface a design. Finally, once you've finished it, you'll export it to the Internet for delivery.

Note, in the previous chapter, I showed you how behaviors can accomplish complicated tasks. In this chapter, I show you how to build the fly-through house model without behaviors. Leave it to me to task you with the hard stuff before you get half way through the book! Don't worry. I walk you through the details step by step.

[3.1] A sketch of the initial floor plan of the fly-through house.

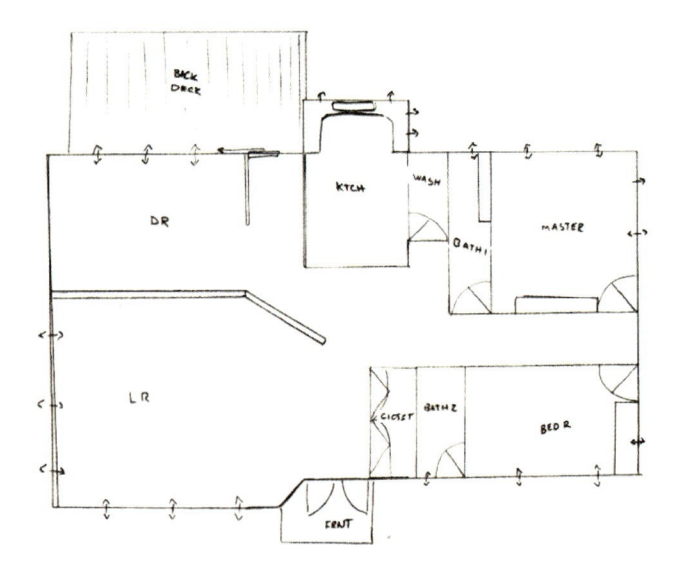

Storyboarding

The first step in building a 3D model is to storyboard the model. Depending on your 3D modeling program, storyboarding (or drawing a model) can be precise or it can just be a rough sketch, such as those you might draw on a napkin or scrap piece of paper [3.1]. If you have a 3D modeling application that allows you to trace or extrude scanned in images, then you might want to draw your model with ruler accuracy. This creates perfectly straight lines, which makes extruding them easy. In the fly-through house example, the sketch is just a reference for the model and was not traced.

When drawing your 3D models, try to sketch out as much detail as possible, so that when you begin working in the modeling application, you can create the objects the first time through the process of creating the model. In this example, you should sketch where you want the windows, doors (and how they open), and the places you want lighting.

Building the Model

Before you start modeling a final product, you should conduct experiments to determine how much detail you should include in your models. Keep in mind this simple formula—the more detail you include, the slower the animation. Making this formula even more fun to work with is the fact that the speed of your animations will vary from PC to PC, due to CPU differences. Generally, Shockwave 3D can handle as much detail as you want, because it can adaptively adjust the model quality (the number of polygons) on-the-fly. However, note that performing these on-the-fly adjustments causes a reduction in frames per second, rendering slower animation speeds.

There is no best-practice policy when modeling for Shockwave 3D because there are many options to work with to get the desired quality or animation effect. I generally favor modeling very high-quality and detail-oriented models. I then output my model to Shockwave 3D to see what type of performance I'm going to get. As might be predicted, the model is usually too slow. Thus, I go back to 3ds max and make changes to reduce the number of details I'm going to use.

3ds max 4 has a great Polygon Counter tool [3.2] that allows you to see the total polygon count for an entire scene and for specific models. This tool is located in the Utilities tab. The counter will also let you set a color range if your models start to get close to 10,000 polygons, for example.

Because one of the biggest performance factors is the video card that is in your target machine, you should either find out as much as possible about your target audience or tell your target audience that you recommend specific hardware for the best performance, such as an OpenGL or DirectX capable video card.

The Polygon Counter tool is useful when you build parts that are in the range of 10,000 polygons. With the tool, you can also see different parts of a model that are complex or that have too many polygons. The more sections included in a geometrical piece, the more polygons needed. Again, the more polygons needed for a model, the slower the animation.

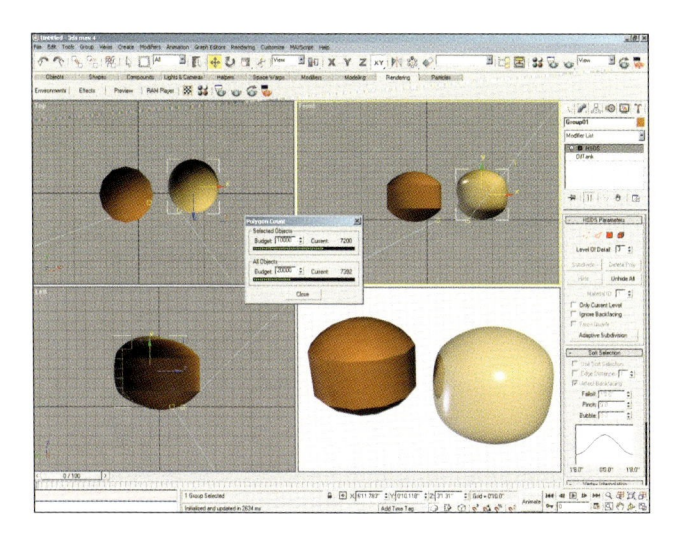

[3.2] Use the polygon counter to help create models with the smallest polygon count possible while still maintaining quality.

The other option that you have is to use Shockwave's Polygon Reduction and Addition tools. These are great tools. Included in these is the Lingo LOD modifier that adjusts the level of detail of a model as it moves closer or further away from the camera. You can hard-set the detail with a slider value from 0 to 100. Values of 0 turn your models off, whereas values of 100 perform no polygon reduction. The LOD command is not only used for polygon reduction, but also to make models disappear and reappear by setting the option to 0 to represent an invisible state. Another way to use this is to adjust the setting based on the animation. If your model is not moving, then the LOD setting can be high, such as 70. When, however, the model is about to transition into an animation state or it is about to be moved by the user, you can quickly reduce the LOD setting to 20. Then, you can reset it to 70 when the model comes to a standstill.

You should experiment with the LOD setting for each model independently, because each model is going to require customized adjustments. Be careful with this setting! The LOD command can turn perfect spheres into pyramids or other unintended shapes if you set its values too low. Experimentation is the only way to learn how to use this setting. Okay, now it's time to get back to our house model.

Recall that we decided on a rough look for the sketch. With a drawing in hand, we can start the modeling process. Because I want to focus on the Shockwave 3D aspects more than the modeling aspects, I'm only going to give brief descriptions of the creation process for this house.

The modeling application I use here is 3ds max, version 4.2 (3ds max 4). If you don't have 3ds max and you are using another modeling application that can perform simple extrusions and Booleans, then this should work for you. Do ensure that you have the Shockwave 3D exporter for your application. If it isn't included on the CD-ROM that came with this book, then check the manufacturer's web site. If you don't have a 3D application that can support Boolean subtractions, I highly recommend you obtain one. Booleans are at the heart of the best photo-realistic models, and they are the fastest way to create geometry.

The 3D cube is drawn to closely resemble the rectangular shape of the house, and is extruded in proportion to the length. If you have a scanner, and your 3D application supports the viewing of bitmapped images, you can trace a polyline to the exact shape of your house perimeter, then extrude it with both ends capped for the same result.

Next, the base cube you extruded is going to be duplicated and positioned above the original cube in the z-axis [3.3]. We are going to use a copy of the original cube to create a Boolean subtraction that will become the empty volume of the house's interior.

Perform a uniform scale on the copy of the house. The result is a scaled piece that is going to be used for the subtraction. The scaled piece needs to be approximately 96% of the size of the original [3.4]. You can use a more non-uniform scaling to match the sides as closely as possible if you are trying to make the Boolean interior perfect. Additionally, you could scale a copy of the polyline *before* extruding it into a 3D shape.

You want the scaled copy of the house's sides to be almost exactly the same size of the original house. This is easy to do on a square shape, but it's not easy to do on a rectangular shape, unless you scale the length of the sides to a different percentage.

After you get the copied shape scaled, move it in the z-axis back to the original shape. Try to watch the left wireframe view as you are positioning the copied cube; position it so that the distance from the bottom is equal (as accurately as possible) to the distance from the sides [3.5].

Perform the Boolean subtraction to eliminate the overlap of the images. After the two shapes are lined up, subtract the copy from the original using the Compound tool in 3ds max. This will form the box shape of your house [3.6]. This is the fastest way to construct this type of room or house shape.

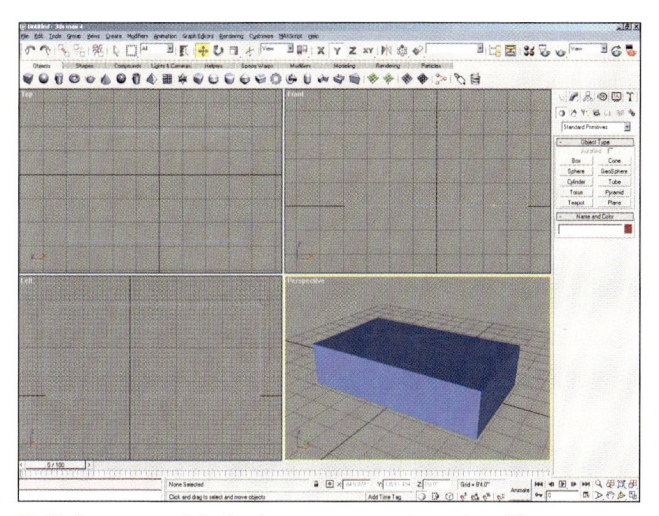

Chapter 3 Architecture Fly-Through | 49

[3.3] Copy your original cube to use as a subtraction object.

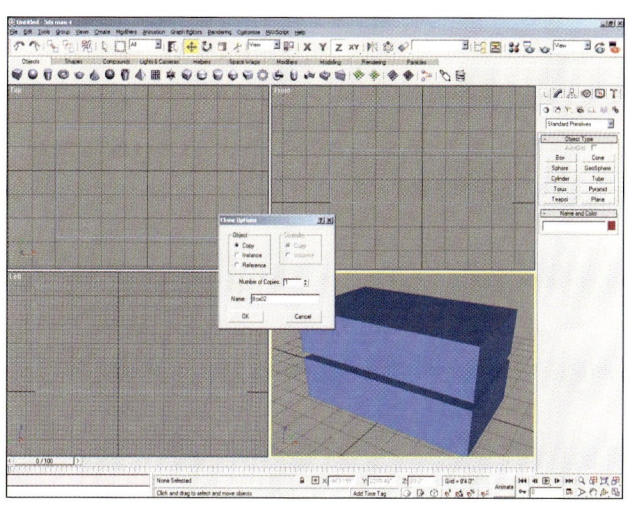

[3.4] Using the Scale tool, scale the copied box 96%.

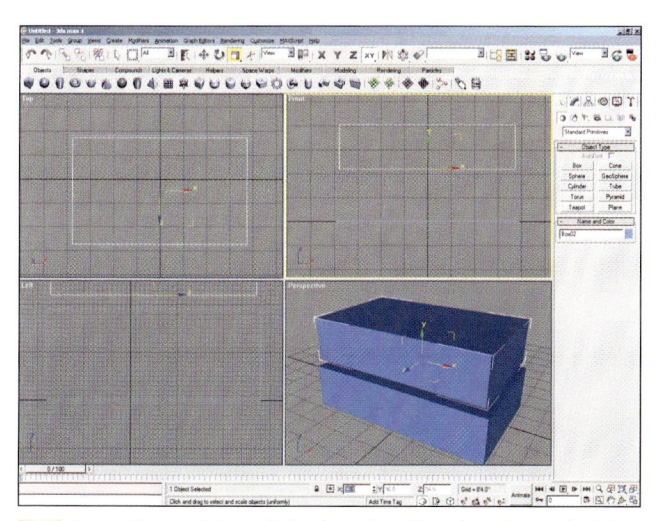

[3.5] Lower the copied, scaled subtraction block into the original, but leave a part of it sticking out at the top.

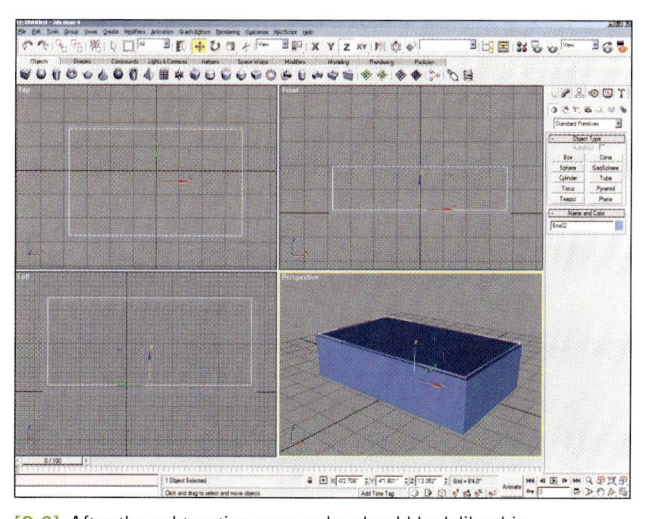

[3.6] After the subtraction, your cube should look like this.

Shockwave 3D

[3.7] Draw and extrude your walls.

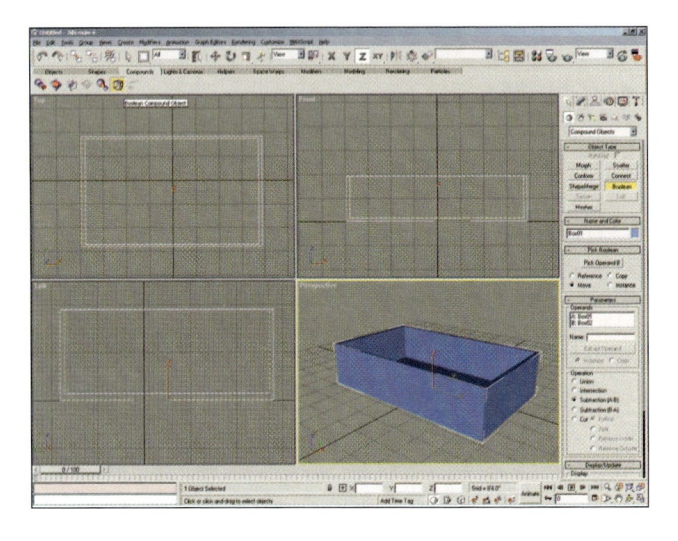

[3.8] After the walls are done, you are ready to add the doors and windows.

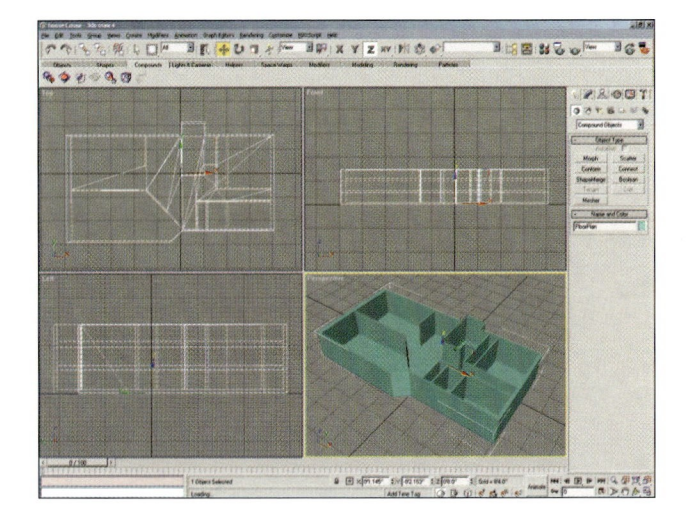

> **Note**
>
> **Empty Cubes** Empty cubes are used so often, it is a puzzle why they are not just added as generic primitives to the toolbar!

Next, you need to insert the walls and extrude them. This is easy to do. First, draw where the walls are going to exist, then extrude them to the same height as the original surrounding cube walls. The simplest way to do this is to switch to the top view and use either the Polyline tool or the 3D box tool and draw where your walls should go, then extrude them up **[3.7]**.

Mark the doors and windows for a Boolean subtraction by switching to the side or front view and drawing a cube wherever you want a new window or door **[3.8]**. Just like the huge subtraction you did on the house foundation, do the same for the doors and windows. The easiest way to do this is to draw your windows and door shapes from the front, left, and right views **[3.9]**. The depth of the cube(s) is not important as long as it doesn't run through another object causing you to inadvertently create a hole in another wall during the Boolean operation.

After the subtraction pieces are lined up and you have performed the Boolean, your shape should look like a house **[3.10–3.12]**.

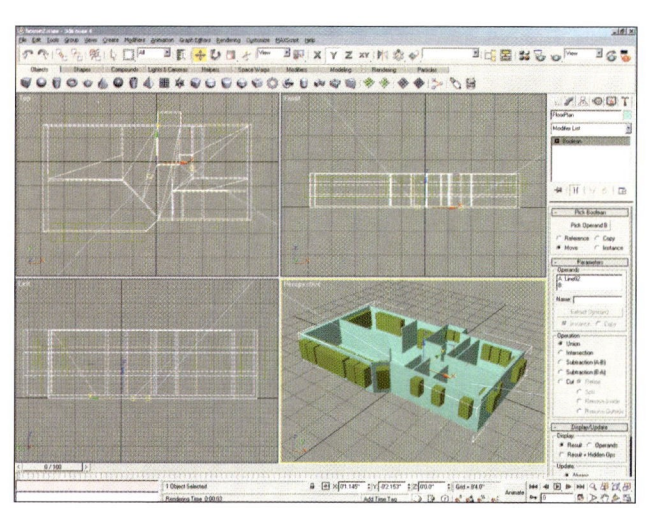

Chapter 3 Architecture Fly-Through | 51

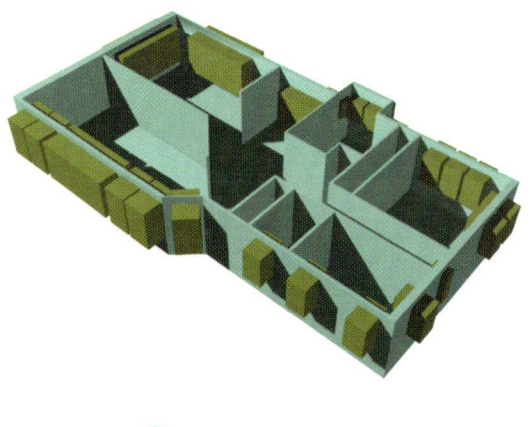

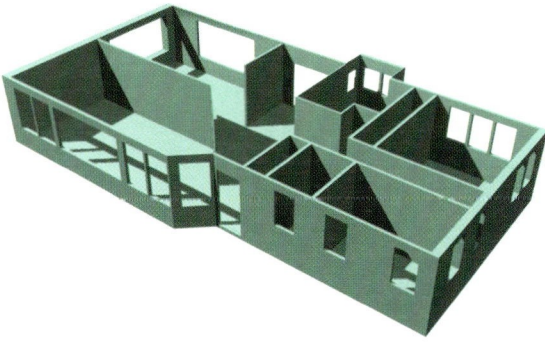

[3.10–3.12] The house with the extruded doors and windows is now ready for the real doors and windows to be added. You can even add blinds if you want!

[3.9] The extruded house with walls and the Boolean doors and windows ready for subtraction.

Note

Framing Windows The level of detail that you use in your Boolean operations is up to you. In this particular example, one subtraction was used to make the windows; however, if you used two or three subtractions while gradually increasing the window sizes, the windows would take on a framing effect. Note, adding subtractions will introduce more polygons to the overall model size, which results in slower animation.

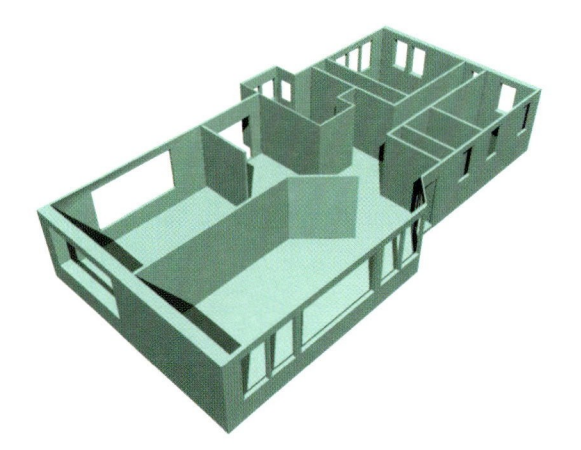

[3.13–3.14] The house with its windows and shades ready to be installed, and the lights ready to be set up.

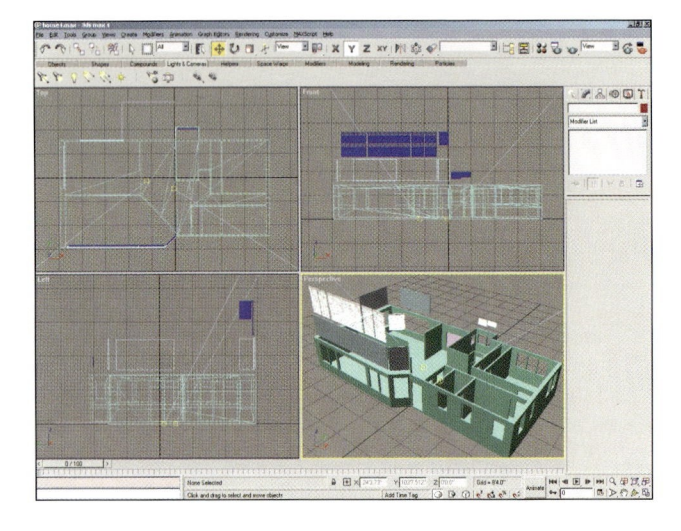

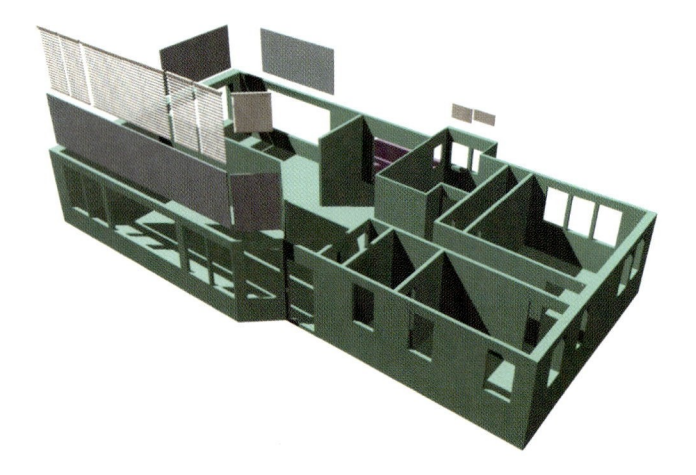

Next, you get to add more detail and realism to the model. You can add glass and blinds to Boolean windows, and doors can be added. The glass is simply a rectangle that is drawn in the top view; then it's extruded to meet the length of the window hole **[3.13–3.14]**. Later the glass's opacity can be adjusted and a reflection map can be added.

Now that we have designed and built the 3D house model, extruded the walls, added the doors and windows, and then ended the finishing touches, it is time to add more realistic details to the house, such as lights and textures. First, we'll name the models.

Naming Models

Depending on what you build your 3D models for (video, games, and so on), you may or may not be in the habit of naming them descriptively. It is a good idea to use descriptive names. Unlike 3ds max, where you can always find your model, Shockwave refers to models by name, which makes it difficult to find them if they aren't named properly. If you modeled a scene with twenty or more copies of boxes, and you didn't name the boxes, you will end up scrolling through a long list of very similarly named objects. This makes determining which object to attach your script or behavior to difficult.

You can avoid this by consistently naming your models to identify them easily **[3.15]**. For example, you might name a door with the name "door." This is simple enough. You will also need to name the camera from your 3D application. In

3ds max, exporting the camera view to Shockwave 3D is as easy as selecting the camera's viewport, and then exporting while that view is selected. Shockwave creates a default camera or cameras for you, but placement of them is usually orthographic and useless, unless you position them manually. It's much easier to set up the camera and then name it in 3ds max (or another application), rather than in Director.

Lighting

After you've named the models, you are ready to add lighting. Lighting is used to add realism, emotion, color, and depth. Unfortunately, Shockwave 3D doesn't currently support shadows from lights, which is a huge part of portraying a realistic model. Regardless, you still have color and position to work with, which can both be utilized to create a more realistic effect [3.16].

Lights can be set up in either 3ds max or in Shockwave via the Property Inspector window. 3ds max is easier to use in terms of placement and the control of your lights. You can see exactly where lights are being positioned and what they are pointing at in 3ds max. Thus, it is the recommended method.

Lights are placed inside and outside the house. The outside lights are placed at a considerable distance from the house to simulate the effects of the sun. A secondary fill-light is placed to fill in the dark shadow areas, but the secondary light is only about half as bright. One of the lights (whichever you choose) is the sun and is tinted slightly yellow in color, and the fill light is tinted slightly blue.

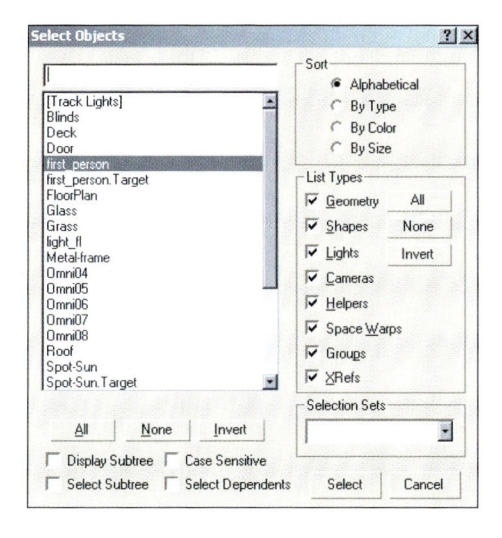

[3.15] Make identifying your models easy by naming them appropriately and consistently.

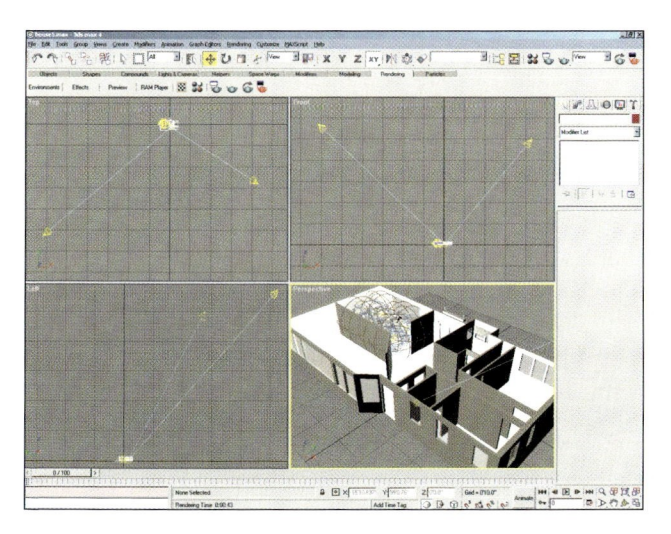

[3.16] Internal and external lights are used to make this scene more realistic.

[3.17] The completed lighting of the house from 3ds max.

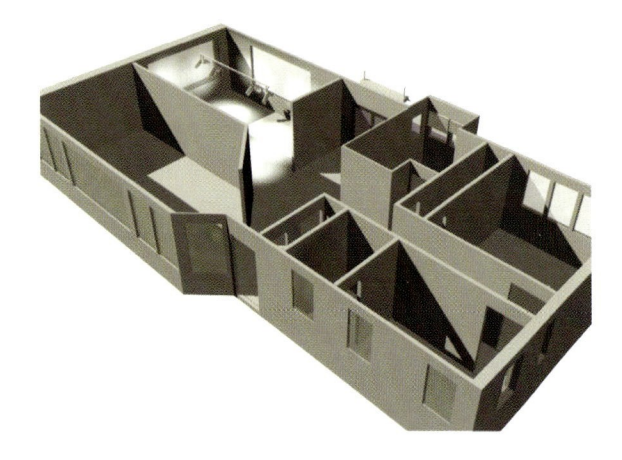

[3.18] Attenuation, glows, and rays are active in this example from 3ds max.

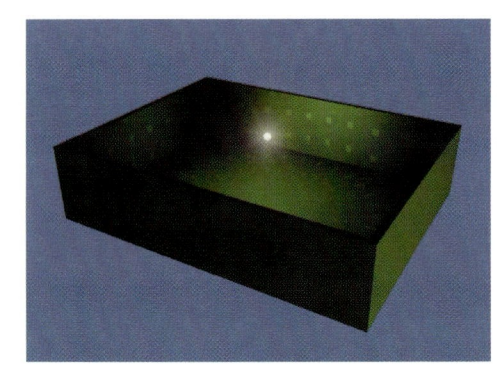

[3.19] Shockwave 3D currently doesn't support shadows, attenuation from 3ds max, and effects such as glows, rays, or lens flares.

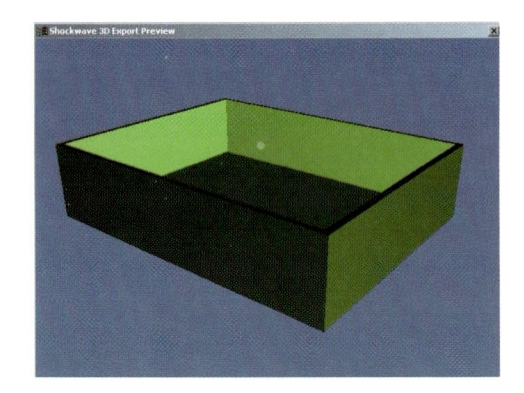

Inside the house, the track lighting is covered with omni lights that have specific attenuation parameters. Currently, Shockwave 3D doesn't support the attenuation of lights. I've added them, hoping that someday Macromedia will add this feature. Notice the huge difference between the attenuated lights in 3ds max **[3.18]** versus the lights in Shockwave 3D **[3.19]**. My 3D scenes are set up to take advantage of the attenuation feature in 3ds max.

> **Note**
>
> **Attenuation** Shockwave doesn't support the attenuation setting that is exported from 3ds max, but it does have its own internal Lingo attenuation that can be used. The attenuation Lingo function is a property that indicates the constant, linear, and quadratic attenuation setting that either spotlights or omni lights can have. You need to have skills in Lingo in order to use this example.
>
> This statement sets the attenuation property of the light named HouseLight to the vector (.5, 0, 0), darkening it slightly.
>
> ```
> member("HouseWorld").light("KitchenLight").attenuation =
> ➥vector(.5, 0, 0)
> ```
>
> This setting will darken the attenuation of the light named KitchenLight inside the Shockwave 3D member named HouseWorld.

Remember that lights are CPU-intensive, and Shockwave 3D only supports eight of them at a time. The more you add, the slower the navigation around your scene becomes. Use lights sparingly.

Texture Mapping

After the lighting is set up, texture mapping can be added. I prefer to set the mapping after I have set the lighting parameters, so that I can see instant feedback. Texture mapping adds considerable detail to your models, and Shockwave 3D supports them well. Note, you should not use any of the texture placement settings from 3ds max's Material Editor. Shockwave doesn't support these texture settings. To place and adjust texture mapping, use the UVW mapping tools from the Modify tab.

In the Material Editor for this scene, I used glass, wood, and grass textures to enhance the scene [3.20]. The glass is for the windows and has the following settings:

> The RGB color setting for the ambient and diffuse are 238, 239, and 255.
> The RGB settings for the specular are 229, 229, and 229.
> 2-sided is enabled.
> Opacity is 35%.
> The specular level is 82%.
> The glossiness is 38%.
> In the Maps tab, the meadow1.jpg texture is added to the reflection channel with a 15% value.
> The texture is named "glass" and is applied to all the windows in the house.

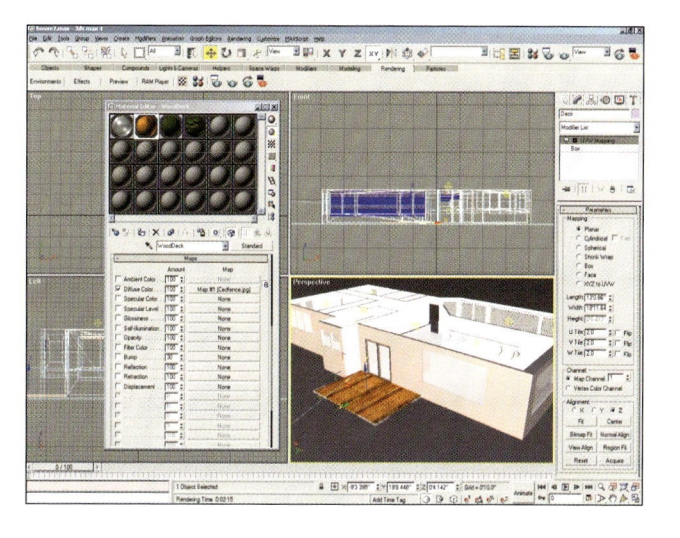

[3.20] Textures are added to our model to enhance its realism.

The deck in the back of the house uses the following texture settings:

> In the Maps tab, the cedfence.jpg texture is added to the diffuse channel with a 100% value.
> Opacity is 100%.
> The specular level is 15%.
> The glossiness is 62%.

The texture is named "WoodDeck" and applied to the deck by dragging it to the model. The UVW mapping modifier is added to the deck, the mapping type is set to planar, and the UVW settings are set to 2.0 with the texture aligned to the z-axis.

Shockwave 3D

[3.21] The house with the final textures applied.

[3.22] The texture of the lawn is more realistic. Also note that a roof can be added as an option. It can be partially transparent, or animated.

The final texture used is the grass texture, which is applied to the area surrounding the house. Following are the settings for the grass:

> RGB is not used.

> In the Maps tab, the grass2.jpg texture is added to the diffuse channel with a 100% value.

> The specular level is 10%.

> The glossiness is 10%.

The texture is named and then applied to the large plane surrounding the house. The UVW modifier is applied, the mapping type is planar, and the UVW settings are set to 8.0 with the mapping alignment set in the z-axis. With the UVW setting set to 8.0, the grass texture starts to tile **[3.21–3.22]**. This normally undesirable effect takes on the characteristic of mowed grass that has track lines. I think this actually makes the grass look more realistic.

Setting Up the Camera

The last thing that we need to set up in 3ds max is the camera. The camera is going to be the view point that your Shockwave 3D movie is going to use—thus, the angle that your users are going to see from the scene. Notice that the camera is set up right outside of the door of the house [3.23]. I picked a targeted camera simply because targeted cameras are quicker when pointing at your subject matter.

The camera focal length should be adjusted to accommodate the scene that you are building. For example, this scene [3.23] uses a camera angle that has a FOV (field of view) of 85 degrees. This FOV may seem extreme, but the result is a camera view that achieves what the human eye might see. I always recommend that you use higher FOV settings. Human eyes each see at about 50 degrees; thus, given our pair of eyes, you should use FOV settings that are between 50 and 100.

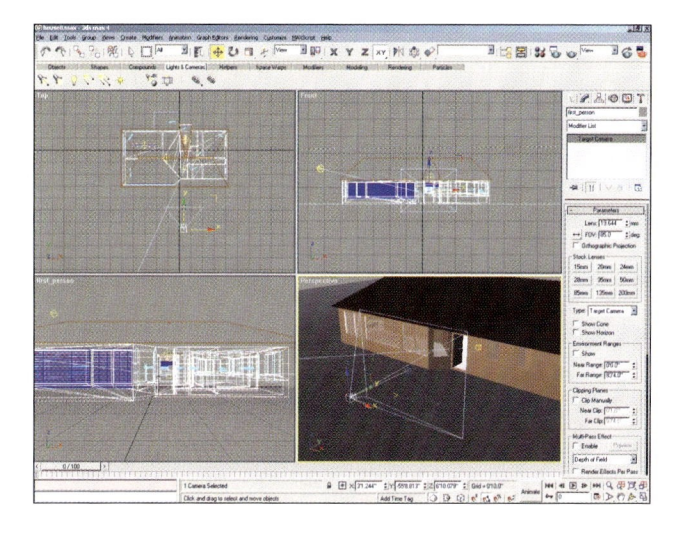

[3.23] Make sure you adjust the camera's height or z-axis to make it work the same way a human's eyes do.

Exporting Options

Now that all of your settings are complete, you are ready to export the completed scene to Shockwave 3D. The Shockwave 3D file format is called the .W3D file. You must have the right plug-in to make the exporter work correctly. There is no workaround for the plug-in; you must have it to write the .W3D file because it is the only method of getting your 3D data into Director. If you have 3ds max, you can get the plug-in from Discreet at **http://www.discreet.com/products/3dsmax/** or off the CD-ROM that comes with this book. For 3ds max users, the plug-in goes into the Plugins folder. Make sure you install the correct version of the plug-in that matches your application version.

If you have any problems with the exporter, you can reset the exporter's preferences and delete the sw3d_exp.cfg file from the 3ds max Plgcfg folder.

Character Studio 3.0.2 is the only version of Character Studio 3.0.x that will work with the exporter. Using other versions of Character Studio 3.0.x may cause random functioning or crashes.

[3.24] The Shockwave 3D exporter is found in the Export dialog pull-down menu.

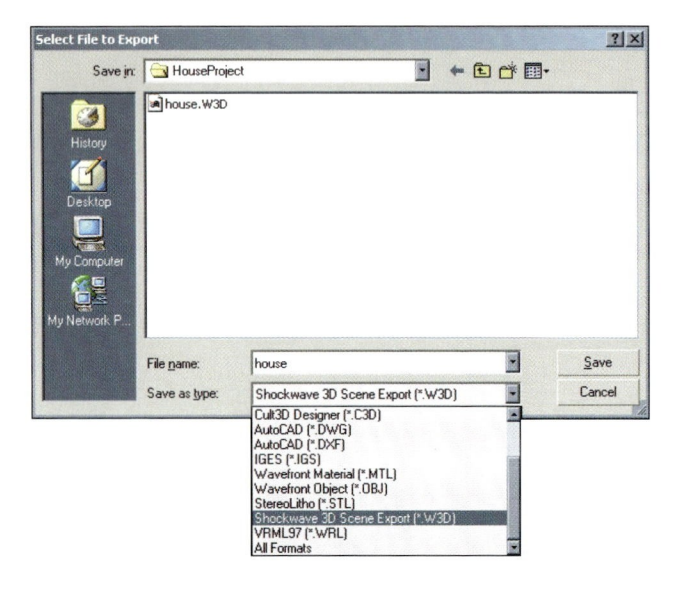

[3.25] There are a lot of options you can choose from when exporting a Shockwave 3D file.

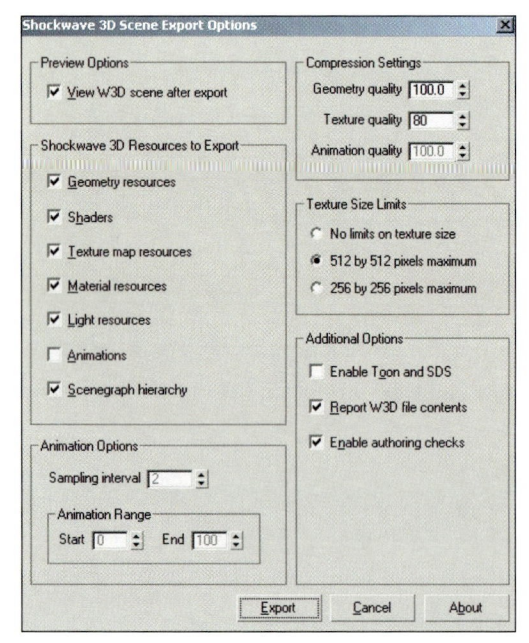

With the plug-in, you should be ready to export the house scene. To launch the exporter from within 3ds max, select the File menu, then select Export, and choose Shockwave 3D Scene Export (*.W3D) as your export type. A Directory box should appear **[3.24]**.

Name your scene and export it. Then, you will get the Shockwave 3D Scene Export Options dialog window **[3.25]**.

There are a lot of options to choose that will determine how your Shockwave 3D movie looks, functions, and animates. These settings will also determine the quality and speed of your file(s). I cover these options in great detail, as they are a very important part of creating your Shockwave movies.

The Export Options window is broken up into six sub-windows, which are as follows:

> Preview Options
> Shockwave 3D Resources to Export
> Animation Options
> Compression Settings
> Texture Size Limits
> Additional Options

Each sub-window includes options, as noted in the following tables.

Preview Options Window	
View W3D Scene After Export	When this option is checked, you will get a window that shows you what your Shockwave 3D scene is actually going to look like in Shockwave, after you export it. You can spin this view around with your mouse, or you can hold down a modifier key (such as Shift, Alt, or Ctrl) to zoom in, dolly, and so on. The Preview window will always show your entire scene, including the resources that you have disabled for export, except the Geometry Resources option.

Shockwave 3D Resources to Export Window	
Geometry resources	When this checkbox is enabled, your 3D models are exported into your .W3D file. Meshes and any bones for the meshes are exported as well. If this option is deselected, the Preview window will be completely black. The only reason you would not make this active is because you can export 3D models, shaders, textures, and animation as separate .W3D files. Then, you can use Lingo's `loadfile` command to put them back together in Director. The Lingo you use to load .W3D contents is as follows: `member(whichCastmember).loadFile("myName",FALSE ,FALSE)` See your Lingo manual for more specifics about the `loadfile` command.
Shaders	This option determines the rendering type that is exported to your file. This option should be enabled in conjunction with texture map resources and material resources. Shockwave 3D does not see the difference between shader types, such as Blinn, Phong, or anisotropic. The only shading types that are supported are Blinn and Phong, and they are exported as Gouraud shading. Shockwave 3D shaders are used to point to the location of texture maps and materials. If you leave this option off, your models will be invisible, because they have no shading information. You can use Lingo later to attach shaders to these models, and they will magically reappear.

continues...

Shockwave 3D Resources to Export Window *(continued)*	
Texture map resources	With this option enabled, the textures that you apply in your 3D application will show up on your models. If you deselect it, your models will not contain textures when loaded. After the export, you can use Lingo to assign the textures to the models if you want. This is useful for a billboard sign, for example, that you might want to have different textures.
Material resources	The material data option should almost always be active. It determines if materials are exported with your W3D file or if they are stripped out. The only time that you wouldn't use this is if you are exporting a series of bones as keyframed animations, which require new materials.
Light resources	This option determines if your lights are exported or not. You always want this option turned on (the default), except for when you are exporting animation, geometry, or texture data separately. Remember, you can only have a maximum of eight lights, and each light results in a noticeable performance decrease, so you should use them wisely.
Animation	You probably assumed that this option exports the animation in your scene. Animation data is sampled at every frame, and then compressed into a streaming format. You may find that there are times when you only want to capture parts of your animation or sample the animation steps less than once per frame. This is where you would change the sampling interval and animation range. If, for example, you have a 100-frame animation sequence and you set the sampling interval to 2, then Shockwave would look at every other frame to determine the motion. Straight-line motion can handle high sampling intervals where curved motion needs smaller intervals to be accurate.
Scenegraph hierarchy	This option contains the parent-child hierarchy among all of the objects, including geometry, lights, groups, and cameras. Always select this option when you are exporting an entire scene. The only time you should deselect this option is when you are exporting libraries of either animation or texture data.

Animation Options Window	
Sampling interval	The Sampling interval setting determines the accuracy at which your animation is played back. If you set it to 1, every frame of your animation is sampled, and your animation looks as close to the original as possible. If you set the sample to 2, every other frame is sampled and saved into the .W3D file. The higher the number, the less accurate the animation becomes.
Animation range	The animation start and end range allows you to specify which portions of your animation you want to save into the .W3D file. You can, for example, have a 3ds max file that contains 500 frames of animation and export out five different .W3D files with each having 100 frames of the animation.

Compression Settings Window	
Geometry quality	This setting determines how true to the original model you stay. 100 is the maximum quality, and it has the least file savings compared to a lower value.
Texture quality	This setting determines how applied textures look. The compression method used for textures is JPEG, so there is substantial file savings if you lower this setting. I would recommend a setting of 50% for starters, since this helps reduce your overall file size. **Note** **Value Ranges** The three compression values range from 0.1 to 100.0. The higher the value, the less compression is applied to your model. The less compression is applied, the more realistic the original source model will appear, including texture and animation. The values for compression are measured in percentages, not linear values from 1 to 100. Thus, doubling the values does not double the quality.
Animation quality	This setting is used to determine how much information of your keyframes is saved. Low numbers can yield a jerky animation playback, but they also yield smaller file sizes.

Texture Size Limits Window

There are three options for texture size limits—No limit, 512×512, and 256×256. No limit uses the original source size of the texture you applied and can result in substantially larger files. 512×512 and 256×256 reduce your textures to these respective sizes; then you can apply any texture quality compression before saving it into the .W3D file.

> **Note**
>
> **Sampling Interval Versus Animation Quality** The difference between the Sampling interval and Animation quality is that the Animation quality setting is a compression function that is performed on the animation. The Sampling interval looks at your animation sequence and saves every other keyframe, for example. If it is set at two, then the Animation quality setting compresses those samples.

Additional Options Window

Enable Toon and SDS	While in Director, the Toon modifier allows you to shade the entire Shockwave 3D scene, just like a cartoon. There are several options with this setting that have different results, from black-and-white sketches to full-color cartoons. The SDS is a modifier that adds detail to your models by subdividing the surfaces into smaller polygons and triangles. If you are planning on using the SDS modifier in Director, you must first enable this option.
Report .W3D file contents	Enabling this setting results in an Error dialog box after the export is complete. It's a good idea to keep this enabled. It will show you error messages, such as, "Wrong shader type" or "Unsupported texture mapping used." If you receive these errors, you will have to correct the problem in 3ds max, and then export again.

As you can see, the exporter has several options and can be thought of as a Control Panel for converting 3ds max files into the Shockwave's streaming .W3D format, which is no small task. You will find that even small, numerical changes in the exporter options can create significant differences in the final Shockwave 3D file. Because of this, I suggest you experiment with different versions of your exported 3D scenes. You want to find that perfect blend of quality and performance.

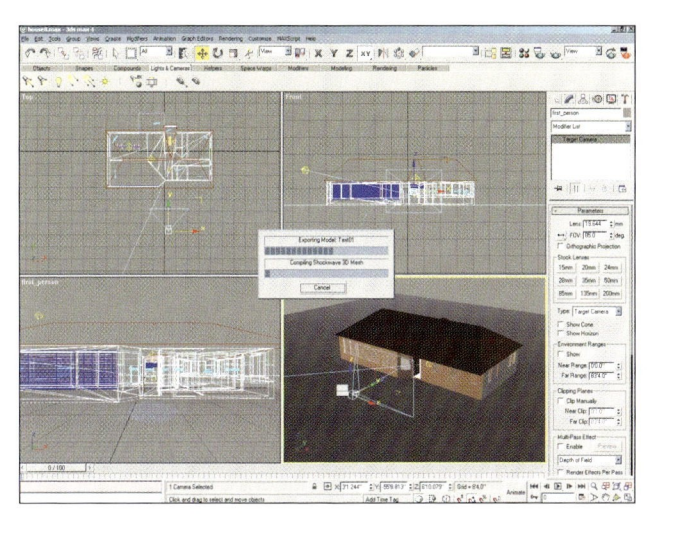

After you determine your options and compression setting, select Export, and the exporter will construct the mesh for your objects. A dialog box, the Preview window, appears [3.26].

[3.26] The Shockwave 3D exporter in action.

This window enables you to examine the 3D scene's content [3.27]. You can rotate, zoom in or out, or spin around in the scene. This preview shows you exactly what your scene will look like in Director, in Shockwave, and on the web. If you are unhappy with the quality, appearance, or animation that you see in this Preview window, you will need to correct it in 3ds max, and then export the scene again.

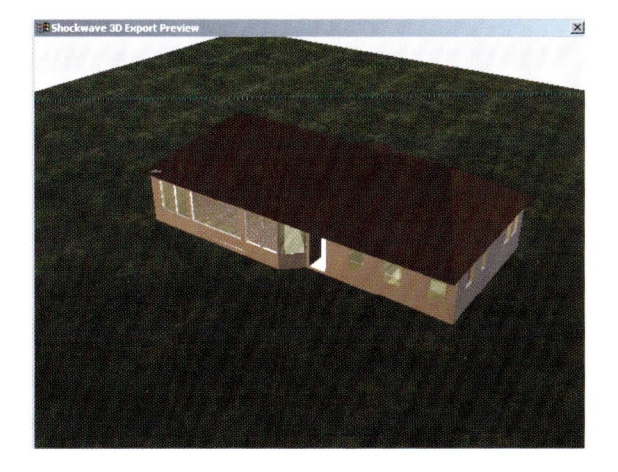

[3.27] Use the Preview window to examine your scene.

A Piece of the Pie

The Pie Chart window [3.28] opens after you close the Shockwave 3D export Preview window. The Pie Chart window gives you a way to examine your content. In a sense, the Preview window represents the right side of the brain, and the Pie Chart represents the left side of the brain. The Pie Chart window gives you a complete breakdown of your file contents by size. You can see how large the final Shockwave file is in addition to the individual files.

[3.28] Use the Pie Chart Preview window to examine your scene in more detail.

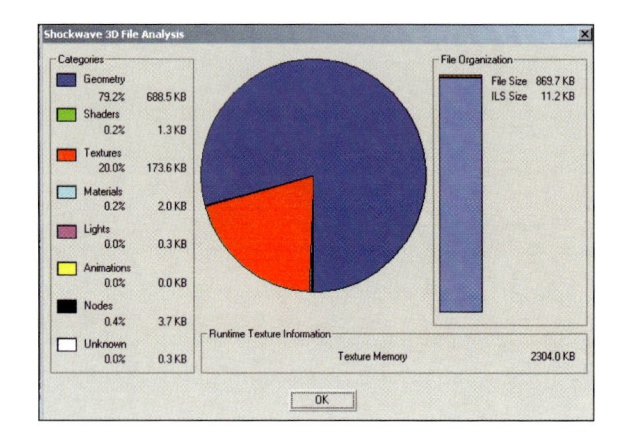

As you can see [3.28], the final size of the house .W3D file is 869.7K, and 688.5K of the total (or 79.2%) makes up the geometry in the scene. The textures account for an additional 20% taking up 173.6K. If you were trying to target the file for a specific size or if you wanted to achieve the smallest file size possible, you can increase the compression (lower the number) on the textures. This would make the files smaller and the total file size would also decrease.

Notice that the texture memory is 2304.0K. This is the amount of RAM that is necessary for the target machine to display the textures correctly. This isn't a large amount by most standards, but can easily cause "out of memory" errors in a browser that doesn't have much RAM allocated to it, especially if you use too many textures in your Shockwave 3D movie.

In practice, it's a good idea to create textures that are as small as possible either by size reduction or JPEG compression. Your users will thank you for it when your movies load faster.

Note

Crashing Exporters There is no trick to debugging the exporter. It is just like a Boolean. That is, the software usually works or it doesn't work. I have run into issues with the exporter that I will share with you in an attempt to alleviate the frustration you might experience on your projects.

Often, the exporter crashes for no apparent reason. On second attempts, it suddenly works. Random crashes are rare, but they do occur. Luckily, I have never lost data because of a crash.

The exporter has also crashed on me when I accidentally gave textures or materials the same names. This took some considerable debugging to figure out. Because 3ds max has no problem with duplicate texture names, I couldn't figure out that Shockwave's exporter does have a problem with it. The exporter crashed during the mesh building process and reported an error message that says, "I'm crashing now." It gives you a dialog box that lets you choose OK or Cancel! Believe me, I've tried to cancel the crash to no avail. The lesson here is that you shouldn't duplicate file names for textures and materials.

There has been one other situation in which the exporter crashed, and I had to forcibly quit the application. I was trying to test for a size limit for a mesh with a three million-polygon model that had mesh smoothing and seven lights on it. Needless to say, it crashed and I had to reset the exporter's preferences by deleting the sw3d_exp.cfg file from the 3ds max Plgcfg folder.

Save your debugging strength for Director—you'll need it.

Working in Director

In this section, you'll learn how to work in Director. You'll learn the importance of the size of your .W3D files, how to set up the score, how to handle visibility and color issues, and finally, how to add Lingo.

File Size Considerations

In this example, the .W3D file consumes a majority of the Director movie's size. This means that the .W3D file size is what you should be concerned with, even before you import it into Director. If it's too large, your users will have an overall bad experience viewing your movie. The movie will take a long time to download, and it might not play smoothly, especially if your viewers don't have hardware-accelerated OpenGL or DirectX type video cards.

The first thing to remember is that when you "get information" (in Macintoshes) or view properties (in Windows), ensure that you are viewing the network file size, not the file size on disk. Although it's usually not a considerable difference, it's best to use accurate information for posting next to the movie, so that users know what they will have to endure in terms of download times [3.29].

Another disadvantage of having a large file is that the majority of Internet users are not on a broadband connection; thus, a 1 megabyte file's download can take a long time. It can become an obsession to see just how small you can get a .W3D or Shockwave 3D file. I tell you about more file-saving tips later in this chapter. First, we'll set up the movie.

Score Setup

After you have imported your .W3D file and any additional assets into Director, you can lay out the score. If you prefer, you can use the house.dir file on the CD-ROM accompanying this book. This file represents a simple movie that has three necessary frames to run the entire movie [3.30].

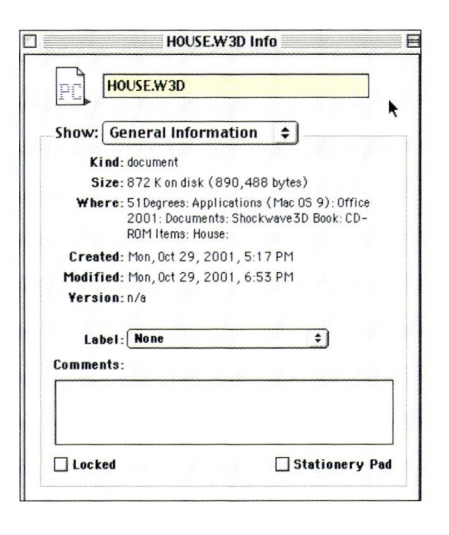

[3.29] The download size for this file is 890K, not 872K. Try to make every K count.

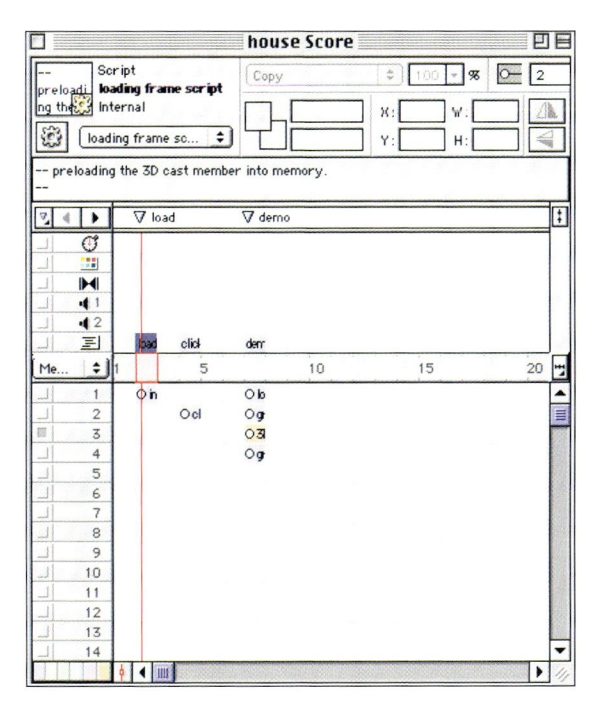

[3.30] The three frames that this movie uses are for preloading, waiting until the user is ready, and displaying the .W3D movie and interface.

I recommend that you never use the first frame of the score. This isn't a Shockwave 3D tip, but a general rule when working in Director. Director performs a lot of pre-tasks before loading the movie, such as general script initiations for sounds, windows, and video. When Director or runtime versions of your movie, such as DCRs or projectors, have assets in the first frame, you can sometimes run into inconsistencies and erratic behavior when you start the movie. I recommend that you always put sprites in frame 2, and treat frame 2 as if it is frame 1. However, if you need to run initialization scripts, putting those scripts in frame 1 is fine.

Color and Visibility

When you place your .W3D castmember into the score, you will notice a lag as Director pauses for a few seconds to process the Shockwave 3D castmember and load it into memory. The lag time occurs during any time that your playback head is moved off the Shockwave 3D castmember frame and then back on to it again. This delay can become considerably annoying at times because the program appears to hang briefly. You can also get this lag when you are trying to add behaviors to Shockwave 3D castmembers.

To avoid the lag time as you navigate the score, place your Shockwave 3D castmember in the score, and then position it on the stage where you want it to go. Now, go back to the score and turn off the visibility of the channel that contains your Shockwave 3D castmember. You don't need it to be visible to add behaviors and scripts. Now, you can scrub the playback head around the score to navigate without it pausing and hanging over the Shockwave 3D member [3.31].

Another tip is to color your Shockwave 3D member in the score, using the color chips in the lower-left corner of the score. This helps you quickly identify where in the score your castmember is.

Redrawing Issues

When visibility is turned on for a castmember, and you move that member to the stage, redraw issues occur. I have seen these same redraw issues occur in projectors and web browsers, where you have no control over it, because it is occurring outside of Director. This is a Shockwave 3D bug that Macromedia has to resolve in the future.

Another good reason to turn off the visibility of your Shockwave 3D member is because leaving it on can result in some "redrawing funkiness" that is present in Director after an image is redrawn in Director.

[3.31] Turn off the visibility of the channel that contains your Shockwave 3D sprite for better score performance.

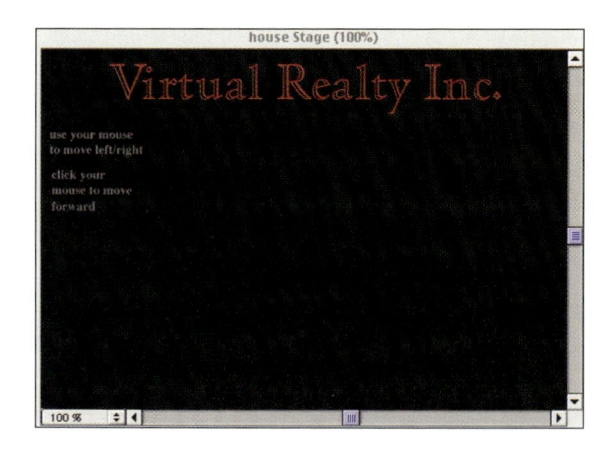

To simulate this problem, add your Shockwave 3D castmember to the stage. Then, move the Stage window to another location. The Shockwave 3D sprite does not want to update the image when the Stage window moves [3.32].

In my opinion, there is currently no ideal work-around for this bug. You can make the redrawing problem go away by turning off the Direct to stage option in the Property Inspector window; however, when you do this, your Shockwave 3D movie is drawn in screen buffer layers, and other castmembers in the score can pass on top of the Shockwave 3D sprite. This causes such a substantial slowdown in the redrawing of the Shockwave 3D sprite that it becomes useless. It's reminiscent of the days when Director's QuickTime functionality was first added to the application. You had the ability to turn off the Direct to Stage function for the QuickTime sprite, but the number of frames per second playback would drop from 24 to approximately 4, making the QuickTime movie useless. However, today you can do this with QuickTime sprites, and the performance isn't as bad as it used to be. Hopefully, redrawing sprites will get better with future improvements.

The real issue is that these redrawing artifacts occur in projectors and browsers. This is bad, because you can't turn off the Direct to Stage option for performance reasons, and you can't let your user move the window around or scroll without causing this redrawing problem. I recommend that you simply stay away from the projector option that lets your movies be in their own window (show title bar). As for working in Director, your only options are to turn off the Shockwave 3D visibility or open and close the stage window and use other windows as "giant erasers" to wipe the screen clean.

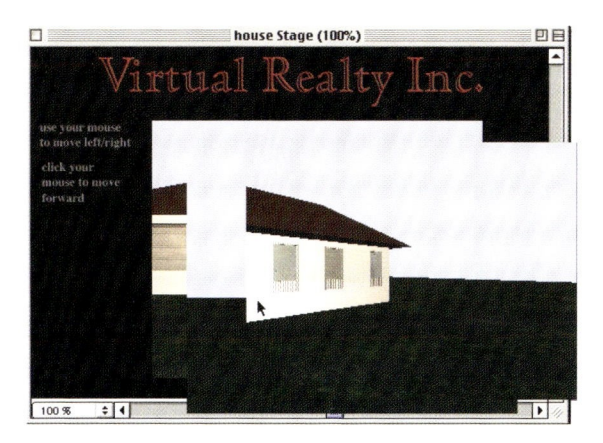

[3.32] Moving your stage with a Shockwave 3D sprite can cause redraw issues.

Adding Lingo

Yes, it's Lingo time. This movie contains Lingo examples that are either simple or difficult. There is no "middle ground" with these scripts. If you open the house.dir movie from the CD, you will see in the cast that there are four scripts—members 19, 20, 21, and 23. Number 23 is the most difficult if you are new to Lingo.

Each piece of Lingo preloads the Shockwave castmember into memory, waits for the user to continue, pauses the movie in the frame that the Shockwave castmember is in, and finally, performs a form of collision detection known as *ray casting*.

The first script that handles the preloading is a frame script. The script should be added to one of the Score window's frame script channels. It looks like this (remember, these scripts are on the CD accompanying this book as well):

```
property p3dMember

on beginSprite (me)
  p3dMember = member("3D")
  p3dMember.preload()
end beginSprite

on exitFrame (me)
  if (p3dMember.state <> 4) then
    go to the frame
  else
    p3dMember.resetWorld()
    go to the frame + 1
  end if
end exitFrame
```

Member number 19 is a script that preloads the Shockwave 3D castmember into memory (RAM) before it starts playing. The script looks for your Shockwave 3D castmember by name, not by sprite number. Because it looks for the name, be careful. If you copy the script word-for-word, don't forget to use the name of your Shockwave 3D castmember instead of the one in the script, or change the name to 3D.

Before talking about the details of this script, I want to mention Thomas Higgins. Thomas is the author of the scripts in this movie, and he is the author of many movies located at **http://www.directordev.com/**. Thomas is an employee of Macromedia, and I want to extend my appreciation for his help with this demonstration and his contribution to the book.

```
---- Preload Shockwave 3D member into memory script ----

property p3dMember  -- reference to the 3D member

on beginSprite (me)
  -- stores the 3D members name for reference
  p3dMember = member("3D")
  -- starts the preloading of the castmember
  p3dMember.preload()
end beginSprite

on exitFrame (me)
  -- check the member's state; is it loaded or not?
  if (p3dMember.state <> 4) then
    -- if it's not loaded, then hold on current frame
    go to the frame
  else
    -- reset member's world
    p3dMember.resetWorld()
    -- if it is loaded then step to next frame
    go to the frame + 1
  end if
end exitFrame
----
```

The next script that is used in the movie simply pauses it until the user is ready. After the movie has been preloaded, you don't want it to instantly start playing, because the user might not be ready. This script waits until the user clicks on the screen before advancing to the next frame to play the Shockwave 3D movie you just preloaded.

```
-- This script holds the playback head on a given
-- frame until the user clicks anywhere on stage.
--

on exitFrame
  -- hold on current frame
  go to the frame
end exitFrame
```

```
on mouseDown
  -- step to the next frame
  go to the frame + 1
end mouseDown
```

There is one additional frame script that is used to pause the Director movie on the frame that the Shockwave 3D cast-member is playing on:

```
on exitFrame
  -- hold on current frame
  go to the frame
end exitFrame
```

The next Lingo script is attached to the Shockwave 3D sprite and controls the navigation and collision of your camera. It's a very intuitive use of ray casting. (This script is also on the CD.)

What the ray casting script does is project a ray (or think of it as a vector) from the camera in the direction that the camera is moving. The camera has a sphere surrounding it that is invisible. If the camera is moving forward, a ray is being projected forward to determine the distance the camera is from an object in front of it [3.33]. If the ray being projected or cast from the camera is shorter than the distance the camera is to the sphere, the camera is close to the object, if it isn't colliding with it. The script then sets the camera's position back to the path the ray was being cast. This gives the impression that your camera has collided with an object and bounced back off of it.

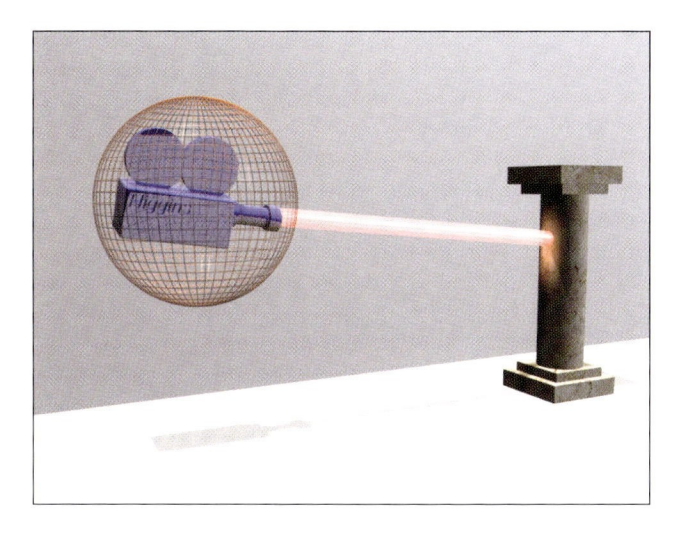

[3.33] Ray casting is used to determine the camera's distance from an object. A result of ray casting is shown here.

Following is the ray casting Lingo and an explanation of what it is doing.

These are the properties that get initialized for the script. Properties are similar to variables or global variables depending on the programming language you are familiar with:

```
property pMember          -- 3D member used by this sprite
property pSprite          -- reference to this sprite
property pMouseDown       -- user is pressing the left mouse button
property pRightMouseDown  -- user is pressing the right mouse button
property pCamera          -- the sprite's camera
property pCameraSphere    -- the sphere used to surround the camera
property pCamAnimFlag     -- introduction animation is running?
property pCamAnimInfo     -- perform an introduction animation
```

The `beginSprite` handler fills the properties with their functions and any necessary data. It also creates the sphere around the camera and a light that the camera carries with it:

```
on beginSprite (me)
-- initialize properties
  pMember = sprite(me.spriteNum).member
  pSprite = sprite(me.spriteNum)
  pMouseDown = FALSE
  pRightMouseDown = FALSE
  pCamera = sprite(me.spriteNum).camera
  pCamAnimFlag = TRUE
  pCamAnimInfo = [#initT: pCamera.transform.
  ➥duplicate(), \
                  #finalT: pMember.camera
                  ➥("first_person").transform.
                  ➥duplicate(), \
                  #count: 0]

  -- create the camera's bounding sphere
  mr = pMember.newModelResource("camera_sphere",#sphere)
  mr.radius = 7.5
  pCameraSphere = pMember.newModel("camera_sphere",mr)

-- create a light to carry with the camera
  camLight = pMember.newLight("camera_light",#point)
  camLight.color = rgb(170,170,170)

-- make the sphere and light children of the camera
  pCamera.addChild(pCameraSphere,#preserveParent)
  pCamera.addChild(camLight,#preserveParent)

-- register the camera for the timeMS event in order to
➥perform the intro animation if any
  pCamera.registerScript(#timeMS,#animateCamera,me,
  ➥0,50,51)

-- register the member for regular timeMS events in
➥order to respond to user input and resolve camera
➥"collisions"
  pMember.registerForEvent(#timeMS,#controlCamera,
  ➥me,2500,50,0)
end beginSprite
```

These mouse handlers switch the Boolean state for the property. If the mouse is down the `pMouseDown` property is TRUE, for example:

```
on mouseDown (me)
-- update the mouse down property
  pMouseDown = TRUE
end mouseDown

on mouseUp (me)
-- update the mouse down property
  pMouseDown = FALSE
end mouseUp

on rightMouseDown (me)
-- update the right mouse down property
  pRightMouseDown = TRUE
end rightMouseDown

on rightMouseUp (me)
-- update the right mouse down property
  pRightMouseDown = FALSE
end rightMouseUp
```

The `animateCamera` handler is used to animate the camera automatically over time:

```
on animateCamera (me)
-- increment the internal counter for the animation
  pCamAnimInfo.count = pCamAnimInfo.count + 1
```

```
-- determine the interpolation percentage
  pctg = 100.0 × (pCamAnimInfo.count / 50.0)

-- if pctg is greater than 100 end animation sequence
  if (pctg > 100) then
    pctg = 100
    pCamAnimFlag = FALSE
  end if

-- determine the new interpolated camera transform
  t = pCamAnimInfo.initT.interpolate
➥(pCamAnimInfo.finalT,pctg)

-- apply that transform to the camera
  pCamera.transform = t
end animateCamera
```

This `controlCamera` handler is what controls the movement of the camera for each of the four directions. It also controls the collisions with objects:

```
on controlCamera (me)

-- respond only if the intro camera animation is
➥completed
  if not(pCamAnimFlag) then

-- CONTROL THE LEFT/RIGHT ROTATION OF THE CAMERA
-- if the shift key is *not* down then follow the mouse
-- to adjust left right looking
    if not(the shiftDown) then

-- check for the mouse locH wrt the sprite loc
      deltaH = the mouseH - pSprite.locH

-- calculate rotation value to apply
      rotn = -(deltaH/165.0) * 4.0

-- apply that rotation
      pCamera.rotate(pCamera.worldPosition,
➥vector(0,0,1),rotn,#world)
    end if

-- CONTROL THE FORWARD/BACKWARD MOVEMENT OF THE CAMERA
-- if the left mouse is down then move the character
➥forward
    if pMouseDown then
      pCamera.translate(0,0,-2.5)
    end if

-- if the right mouse is down then move the character
➥backward
    if pRightMouseDown then
      pCamera.translate(0,0,2.5)
    end if
```

The following part of the script controls the collisions of the camera with the walls or other objects. This casts rays forward or backward depending upon movement, and it will also cast rays to the left and to the right. For each ray that is cast, the script will verify that the distance to the nearest model exceeds the camera's bounding sphere radius; if the distance is less than the bounding sphere's radius, move the camera out of the collision state in a direction perpendicular to the intersected model's surface.

```
    -- cast one ray fwd/bckwrd depending upon which
➥mouse button is down
    case (TRUE) of

-- left mouse down, cast ray forward
      (pMouseDown):
```

```
        -- cast ray
            tList = pMember.modelsUnderRay
            ➥(pCamera.worldPosition,-pCamera.transform.
            ➥zAxis,#detailed)

        -- if there are models in front of the camera, check
        ➥for collisions
            if (tList.count) then
                me.checkForCollision(tList[1])
            end if
    -- right (control+) mouse down, cast ray backward
        (pRightMouseDown):

        -- cast ray
            tList = pMember.modelsUnderRay
            ➥(pCamera.worldPosition,pCamera.transform.
            ➥zAxis,#detailed)

        -- if there are models in front of the camera, check
        ➥for collisions
            if (tList.count) then
                me.checkForCollision(tList[1])
            end if
        end case

    -- cast a ray to the left
        tList = pMember.modelsUnderRay
        ➥(pCamera.worldPosition,-pCamera.transform.
        ➥xAxis,#detailed)

    -- if there are models in front of the camera, check
    ➥for collisions
        if (tList.count) then
            me.checkForCollision(tList[1])
        end if

    -- cast a ray to the right
        tList = pMember.modelsUnderRay
        ➥(pCamera.worldPosition,pCamera.transform.xAxis,
        ➥#detailed)

    -- if there are models in front of the camera, check
    ➥for collisions
        if (tList.count) then
            me.checkForCollision(tList[1])
        end if
    end if
end controlCamera


on checkForCollision (me, thisData)
    -- grab the distance value
        dist = thisData.distance

    -- if distance is smaller than bounding radius, resolve
    ➥collision
        if (dist < pCameraSphere.resource.radius) then

    -- get distance of penetration
        diff = pCameraSphere.resource.radius - dist

    -- calculate vector perpendicular to the wall's surface
    ➥to move the camera
        tVector = thisData.isectNormal * diff

    -- move the camera in order to resolve the collision
        pCamera.translate(tVector,#world)
        end if
end checkForCollision
```

This script controls the navigation for the Shockwave 3D sprite. After the script is attached to your sprite and the movie is started, the cursor position relative to the Shockwave 3D sprite determines the rotation of the camera, even if your cursor isn't rolled over the Shockwave 3D sprite. So, for example, if your cursor is off the screen to the right, your camera will be turning to the right inside your Shockwave movie. Be aware of the functionality, because at some point, your movie will need to explain to your users how to navigate.

With the script controls in order, it's time to test what you have completed.

Testing—"Test Early, Test Often"

A wise man named John Dowdell once taught me to "test early and test often." I must admit that this is one of the best pieces of advice I have ever received. Testing your project long before it is due is essential and shows the difference between someone who is playing with Director and someone who is using Director in production or in a contract environment where there can be no errors, such as when Director is your source of income!

In this house example, or in any Director movie, you typically know where your target playback platform is going to be—on the Internet, a CD-ROM, a DVD, or a projector. Because you know way ahead of time what your target delivery device or platform is, you should start building beta versions of your completed project right away. You will discover idiosyncrasies, bugs, and errors much earlier, allowing you to correct them and allowing you to take them into consideration *while* building your movie.

Note

QA (Quality Assurance) Another thing that I learned the hard way is that multimedia technologies almost always work on the cutting edge. They use the extreme features of computers making the multimedia engineer not just someone who programs, but someone who must find results while walking on the edge. Slipping can be a painful lesson, which I'm sure you don't want to visualize. When I worked for Macromedia, I assisted a consulting firm that over-sold the capabilities of Director and Shockwave to a large Japanese auto maker. They jumped into development with no QA (Quality Assurance check) or testing only to find out at the end of the project that what they were trying to do was impossible. They lost a million-dollar account.

Although Director and Shockwave 3D are both great technologies, being able to finesse out of them exactly what you want to achieve takes a professional mindset and the knowledge to master computers. I hope this experience is enough motivation to get you to build a projector of your current project right now, and to test it.

For the house.dir movie, the target playback platform is the Internet and a projector. After the castmembers have been imported, moved into the score, and the scripts have been attached, the movie should be exported for testing as a projector and then published to test within the browser **[3.34]**. The following sections show you how to test the movie in a projector and on the Internet.

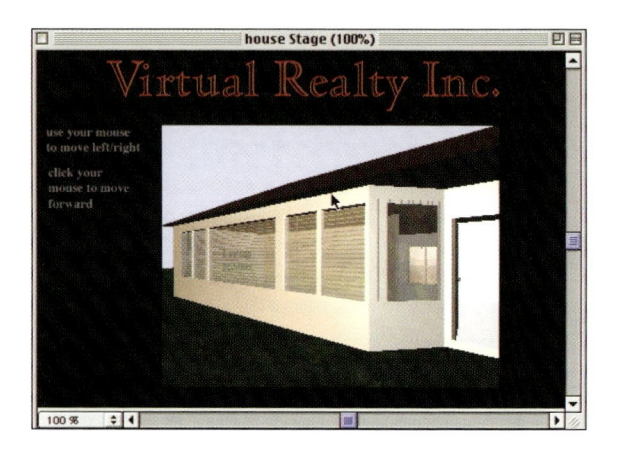

[3.34] Your score window should resemble something this.

Projector Testing

Export the movie as a projector [3.35].

After the projector has complied, you should adjust the memory that is allocated to the projector. Boosting the memory higher is what I typically do while I'm testing projectors and Shockwave movies to give the movie extra RAM [3.36]. Then, as each successive build is created, I lower the RAM a few megabytes at a time.

On the Macintosh, your projector or browser's memory has to be manually adjusted. To do this, find the icon of the projector or the browser (not the alias), and then choose Get Info on the

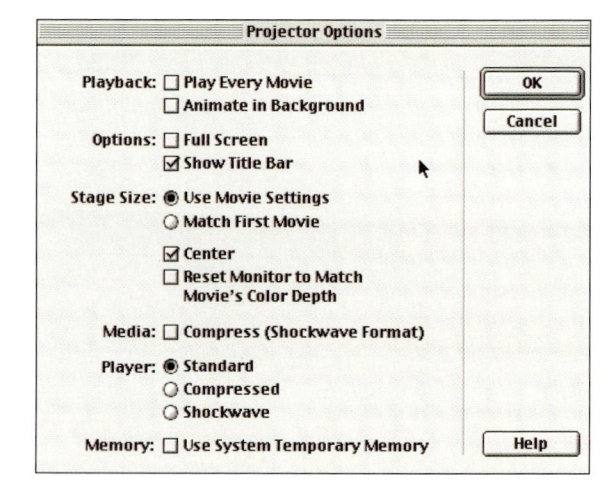

[3.35] Export your movie as a projector for testing early.

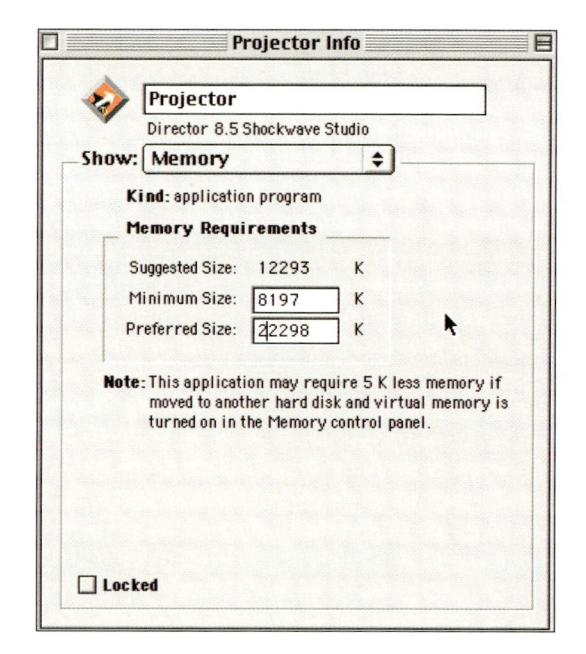

[3.36] Increase the memory allocated to the projector.

application. You can also do this using the keyboard combination Command-I. Start by adding 10 megabytes (or 10,000K) to the preferred size text field.

After the memory is increased, start the projector to see if everything is functioning the way you planned. In this version of the house, exporting with the projector setting Show title bar causes the redrawing problems that I discussed previously. Note that this problem would not have been caught if we hadn't tested the movie as a projector.

Web Testing

Running a Shockwave movie in a browser is the hardest place to get perfect results; thus, extra testing is necessary. Movies run slower because of the additional overhead of running in a browser. When the Shockwave movie is in a projector, that projector is running on top of the operating system, but in a browser, the browser is running on top of the operating system and the Shockwave playback is handled by an additional plug-in. To complicate this scenario, the movie might not be present on the computer but could be streaming over a 56K connection.

After you publish your movie [3.37], Director should compact your file, save a .DCR for you, write the HTML file, and then launch that HTML file in your browser for testing. If you don't see a graphic [3.38], then you might not have the latest version of the Shockwave browser plug-installed. You can get it from the Macromedia site at **http://www.macromedia.com/shockwave/**.

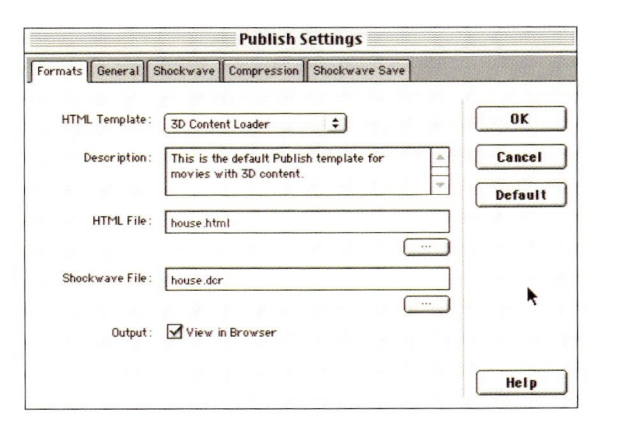

[3.37] The 3D content loader is fine for testing published content.

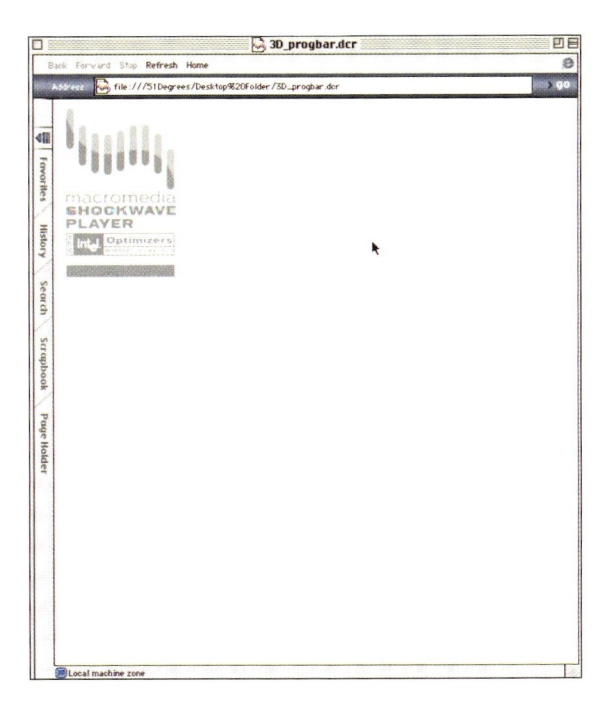

[3.38] The new Shockwave 8.5 plug-in loading.

[3.39] The graphics explain how to navigate your movie. These have to be cleaned up before you are "officially done" with your movie.

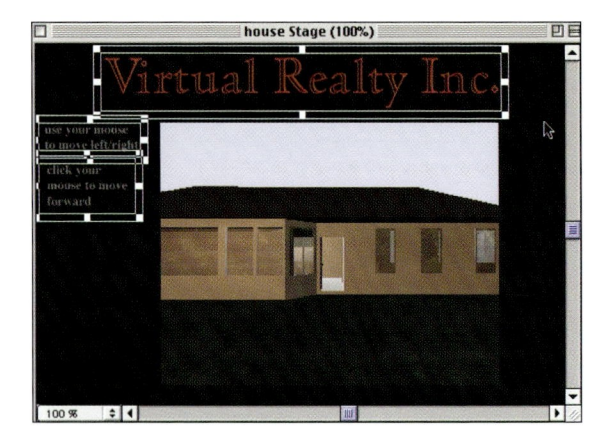

[3.40] Removing Xtras can help make your projectors smaller, but it puts the burden of downloading on your users.

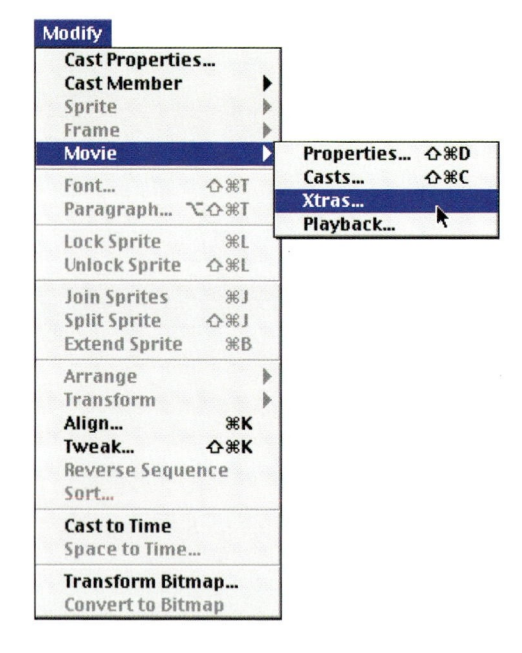

What you should be looking for when you are testing your movie in the browser is speed! If your movie takes a long time to load when the file is local, then consider what it's going to be like for someone who has to download it. If your movie is large, you can preload members and use the Lingo Frameready command to test to see if the content has loaded.

If you have the capability, you should upload the movie to a web server and time the download times while it's downloading and streaming. This is the only way to get a true result of what the experience is going to be like for your users.

If your movie passes the test of running in a projector and a browser, you are done. You are done as long as you are not going to make Lingo changes and you do not want to swap out the Shockwave 3D castmember for a replacement. Now, you can complete the Xtra work, clean the graphics **[3.39]**, and export your movie. The following sections describe how to take care of these loose ends.

Xtra Embedding

Because Shockwave 3D is an Xtra in Director, you have to decide how you want it to load when the projector or Internet version of your movie starts playing.

You have two options for Xtra delivery. You can embed the Xtra into the movie or you can request that it be downloaded automatically.

If you want the projector to be completely self-contained and if you want it to work on a computer with no Internet connection, then you definitely want to ensure that the Xtra is included inside the projector [3.40]. Clicking the Include in Projector checkbox (located in the Xtra window) makes this happen [3.41]. The only drawback to this option is that it also makes your projector larger. The more Xtras you include, the larger the projector.

If file size is a concern, then you can exclude your Xtras from the projector and use the Download if needed option, which is located in the Xtra window. This option isn't very elegant, as it prompts the user to download the required Xtra if it is not already installed on his computer. It does work, so use it if you need to make your projector smaller.

The Download if needed option makes the movie prompt the user to download a required Xtra if it is not installed in the user's system. The Xtra is downloaded from the location specified in the Xtrainfo.txt file and permanently installed in the user's system. My recommendation is to leave the Xtras installed in the projector and make up the savings another way if possible.

Graphic Dithering

Another way you can squeeze out more file savings is through graphic dithering in the Paint window. Any graphics that you add to your Director movie are usually in 24- or 32-bit color. These images are a waste of space.

You should go through the castmembers and dither the graphics down to at least 16-bit color [3.42]. For the house movie, the castmembers were reduced to 16-bit to save space, and you can't see the difference unless you are typesetting in Directory, and you have a sharp eye. Another way to save some space is to use the Quickdraw tools (Command-7 for Macintosh and Ctrl-7 for Windows) to create shapes and text instead of importing another bitmapped graphic from Photoshop, for example. The Quickdraw castmembers are very small, and in fact, their castmember sizes are shown in bits, not in K!

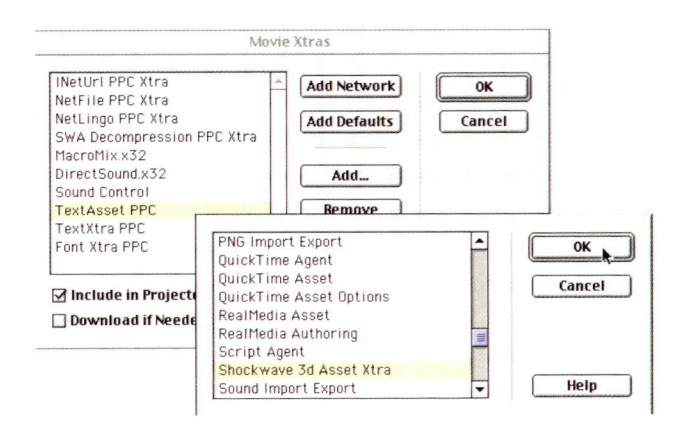

[3.41] Add the Shockwave 3D Xtra to your projector.

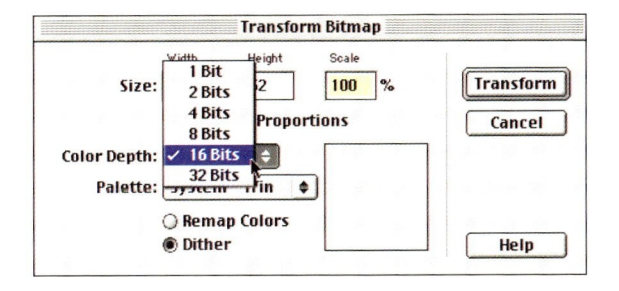

[3.42] Change the color depth to save tons of space!

Completing the Movie

If you are happy with the dithering of castmembers, save the movie and create your projector or .DCR file. If you are not going to change anything, choose Save and Compact from the File menu. Saving and compacting ensures that the data in the movie is properly ordered and that any redundant data is deleted from the movie. This is absolutely necessary.

Now you should have a perfect .DIR file, ready to be converted into a .DCR through publishing, a Macintosh projector, or a Windows projector. If you want to create a .DCR, the publishing templates work well. There are even templates that will put up a loading progress bar for your users as your movie is being streamed.

If you are going to create a projector, you have a few options. You can save your movie in its own window by turning on the Show title bar option. However, your users could potentially run into the redraw problem. Or, you can choose the Full screen option. This will put your movie in a fixed window hiding the rest of the background.

For the smallest projector possible, you will want to turn on the Compress Shockwave format to the media option and set the player to Shockwave, which is found in the Projector Options window. I must warn you, however, that this will give you a very small projector at the expense of increased startup time. If the user doesn't have the Shockwave player already installed, he will have to endure a download. For the house movie, a standard projector is about 5 megabytes, where a Shockwave player version is about 2 megabytes. Although this is a good amount of file savings, the expense might not be something that your audience is willing to endure. Standard projectors are always my choice; I then try to make up the size by using a third-party compression program, such as Stuffit or Zip.

Now that you have completed a movie, it's time to learn about physical interactions in Havok…

CHAPTER

4

■ **In This Chapter**

Storyboarding the Car Simulation, 80

Constructing the 3D Environment, 81

    Textures, 85

    Lighting the Scene, 86

Physics Time, 87

    Rigid Body Collection, 88

    Setting the Model's Physical Properties, 89

    Friction, 91

Speeding Up Simulations, 92

Testing and Exporting Your Scene, 93

    Exporting in Shockwave, 94

    Texture Warning, 96

    The Pie Chart, 96

In Director, 97

    The Havok Behaviors, 97

Importing the .W3D File and the .HKE File, 107

Playing God, 110

Exporting the Movie, 111

Creating a Cross-Platform File, 111

What About Lingo?, 112

Wreaking Havok

Havok (**http://www.havok.com**)© has created an amazing physics library, which is sold to third-party developers who want to create real-time, interactive scenes and games that incorporate physics. The Havok system is a powerful way for you to create interactive worlds and Shockwave 3D movies that contain real, physical interactions between your models. Havok's code enables the extremely realistic car-driving games for Playstation, Nintendo, and other game platforms. The physics interactions are based on how real objects interact in the real world.

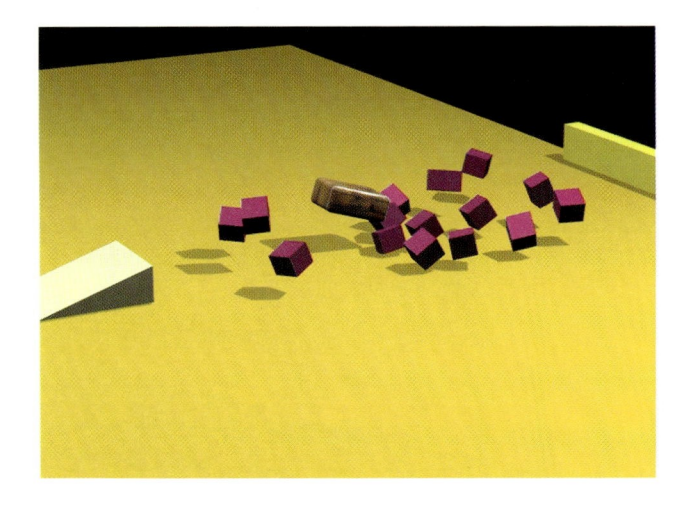

The Havok system automatically applies gravity to your world. In addition, your models are automatically given collision detection. In other words, objects colliding in the game are doing so the same way that they would if they operated in the real world. Speed and direction are accounted for in these interactions.

These simulations are the tip of the iceberg. I know what you are thinking, "Sounds too good to be true," or "It's probably difficult to integrate into Director." I assure you that this is not the case. The Havok physics engine is included with Director 8.5 and it's already installed on your machine waiting to be used. In addition, the Havok real-time scene creator is a free install for 3ds max 3 or 4 users. The 3ds max installers are included on the CD-ROM that accompanies this book.

This chapter shows you how to design your own driving simulation. You will drive a car in your own fictional world. In this chapter, I use 3ds max 4, the Havok physics plug-in for 3ds max (called Reactor in the release version), and Macromedia Director 8.5 to help you develop the car simulation. In this chapter, and in the next chapter, we'll follow a procedure for building the model (or, in this case, the simulation). First, we'll storyboard it, then we'll construct it, and finally, we'll add features, such as lighting and friction. You'll discover that wreaking Havok on your simulations is a good thing.

Note

Reactor   Note that the free version of Havok for 3ds max (included on the CD-ROM) is called Havok, but in the screen shots throughout this chapter, you will see the name Reactor. This is because Reactor is the shipping version of the Havok physics libraries sold by Discreet. The free Havok plug-in is essentially the evaluation version of Reactor. The Reactor evaluation demo, or Havok, is limited to 100 frames of animation, but this is only a 3ds max limitation. After you create your scene in 3ds max, you can export it to Director where there is no limitation on what you can do. For more information on Reactor, go to **http://www.discreet.com/products/reactor/**.

Storyboarding the Car Simulation

Just like anything that you plan to do in Shockwave 3D, I recommend that you start with a simple sketch. You need to storyboard or sketch your models first, especially when you are creating Shockwave 3D content with Havok. There are so many physical interactions in these models that you can easily become sidetracked. Without a sketch or plan, you will likely get stuck in planning mode.

In this sketch [4.2], you see a plane with some boxes and a ramp. This scene is made from very generic primitives to speed the production. The simplicity of the shapes is in no way going to compromise the complexity of the physical interactions that we will be initiating in Shockwave 3D.

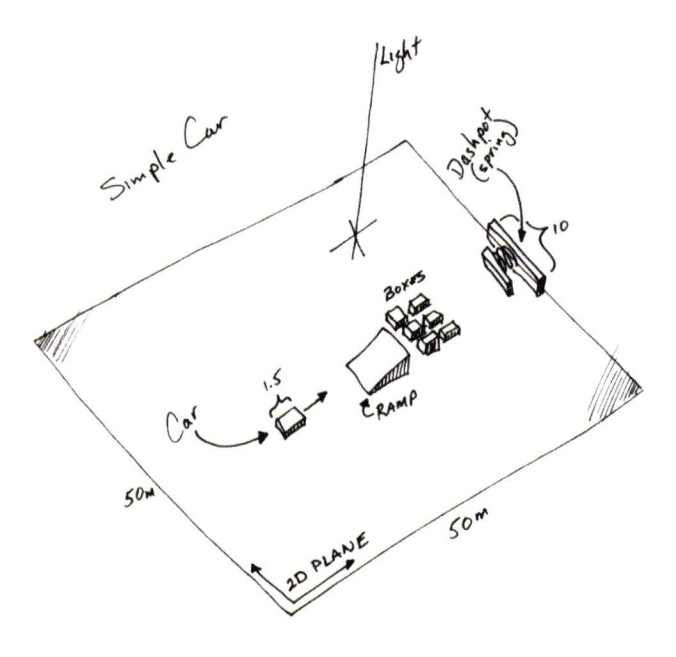

To create this scene, we are going to use 3ds max. My current version is 4.2. The CD-ROM that accompanies this book includes the source files for this chapter in version 4.2. In 3ds max, we will need to first create the 3D models in our scene as close to our napkin sketch as possible.

[4.2] The sketch of the 3D scene that includes the car and a ramp.

Constructing the 3D Environment

The completed scene that we are going to construct will show a zoomed-back point of view that closely resembles the sketch [4.3]. You can make variations to the scene after you complete the initial layout if you like. Here, I'll show you how to construct the initial layout.

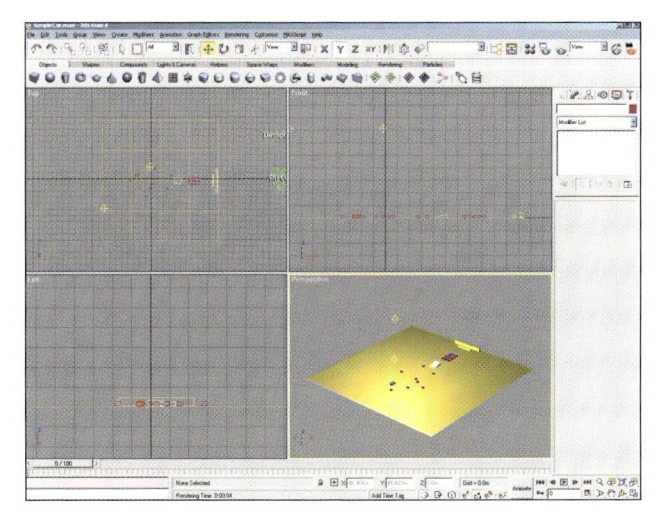

To create this scene, we must first create a plane. This plane is not a 3D box or a 3D box with no height, but it's a simple 2D plane. In 3ds max, you create planes using the Plane tool located under the Objects tab. This plane is the ground for our entire scene; therefore, it's the surface that the car drives on, and the surface on which other objects come to rest. Because the plane isn't going to be big, there is the possibility for driving off the world. With the Plane tool, set the length and width of the plane to 50 meters.

[4.3] The completed scene.

[4.4] The bar of soap, or the object that will become the car.

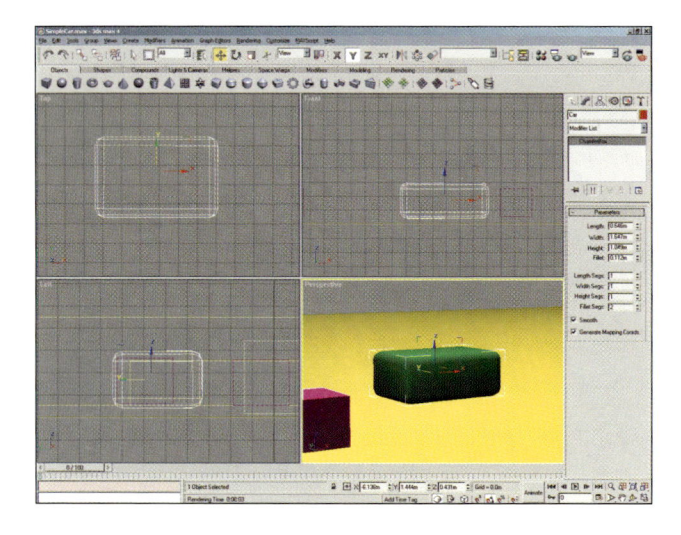

[4.5] The high-performance bar of soap that eventually becomes the car.

Next, we are going to create the car, which is going to be a super, high-performance chamfered box, or if you prefer, a bar of soap [4.4]. If you mathematically calculate the power to the weight ratio, this box will go from 0 to 60 in less than a second!

> **Note**
>
> **Rounded Corners** The reason that I recommend that you use the chamfered box is because it has rounded corners. This isn't for visual appeal; it's so that the front of the car can easily drive over other objects.

Create a chamfered box with a length of 0.6, a width of 1.6, and a height of 1.0. Give it a filet of 0.1. Both smooth and generate mapping coordinates are active for later use. The chamfering creates a scoop or ramp-type of lip on the front of the shape, allowing the block to hit and go over objects rather than hitting them and flipping over end to end. The final result of the car now represents a high-performance bar of soap [4.5].

After you have created the soap bar, you can create the boxes. These are going to represent objects that the car can drive into showing off the physics engine. The boxes can be any size or any shape because the physics engine doesn't calculate the weight of objects based on size. (I'll explain more about the physics engine's calculations later.)

Create a 3D box that is almost perfect with a length of 0.6, a width of 0.6, and a height of 0.5. Next, duplicate the box (use the Shift and drag method) and spread the copies around your plane [4.6]. I distributed the boxes in a pattern of 3×5 with extra space (almost the length of one cube) between each of them. Feel free to scatter other random boxes around your plane too. Remember that the more objects you introduce to the scene, the more taxing the scene becomes in terms of CPU usage.

Notice that the cubes are lifted slightly off the floor [4.6]. This is necessary when constructing Havok scenes, because we want the cubes to have an invisible collision-tolerance force field surrounding them. When the physics engine is activated, the field is used to determine if the cubes are touching one another or other objects [4.7].

If your objects are touching (that is, the collision tolerance of one object overlaps another object), when you activate the Havok system, the objects will instantly push each other away from each other. This is just like two (in this case, fifteen boxes) magnets pushing each other apart.

The next object that you'll create is the ramp. The ramp is a simple extrusion of a line. Draw a line using the Poly-line tool that has roughly the same shape as the front view of the soap bar object. Then, extrude the line using the Extrude tool located under the Modeling tab. Set your extrusion depth to 2 meters [4.8].

The placement of the ramp in relation to the ground plane is not as important as the placement of the boxes. This is because the ground plane and the ramp are going to be fixed, unmovable objects. This means that you don't really have to

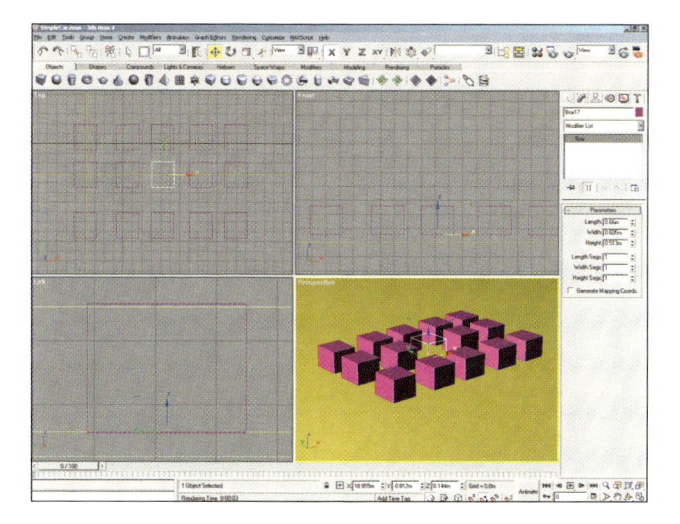

[4.6] Creating the boxes.

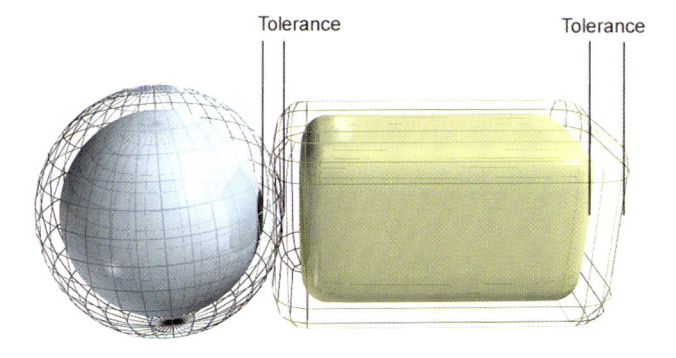

[4.7] The collision-tolerance force field surrounding the objects.

[4.8] Constructing the ramp.

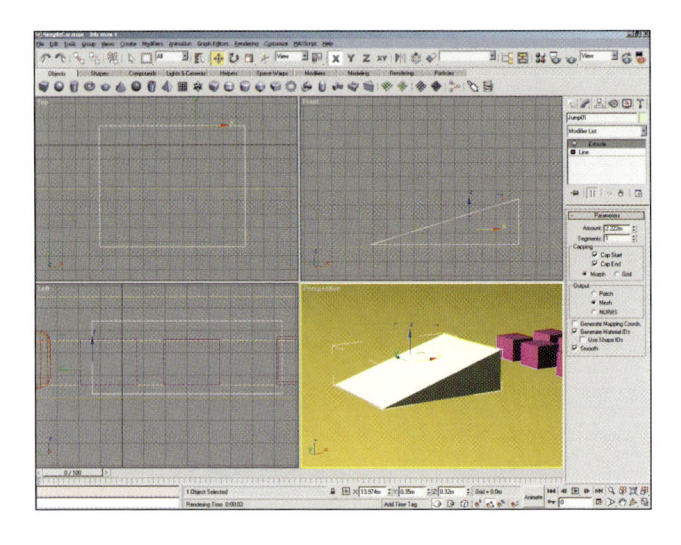

[4.9] The completed ramp in the scene.

worry about the collision tolerance around the ramp. This isn't to say that they can overlap! There is a big difference between overlapping objects and overlapping objects' collision tolerances. Don't worry, you'll set the object properties soon, and this will start to make more sense. Part of the process of modeling is to analyze your "worlds" for these types of problems.

Note

Overlapping Objects and Havok When constructing scenes that use the Havok system, you cannot have overlapping objects. Objects that overlap are considered to be interpenetrating, and the Havok system basically ignores them by leaving them out of your simulation.

The only ramp placement that you have to worry about is ensuring that the ramp isn't positioned too high above the plane so that the car can't drive on to it. You should also place your ramp close to the blocks so that the car can jump on to them, giving your scene a destruction factor that will be fun to watch **[4.9]**. If you place the ramp too close to the boxes, the car will fly over them, but if you place it too far away, the car will fall short of the boxes.

Next, build the rams. The rams are two rectangles that are interconnected by a spring. The larger rectangle is an immovable object and the smaller rectangle moves as if it is connected by a strong spring to the larger rectangle. Having an object drive into a springy ram is fun. The effect is similar to a ball that is bouncing around in a pinball game.

First, create two rectangles. The smaller rectangle settings are 5.0 for the length, 0.5 for the width, and 0.5 for the height. The larger rectangle has a length of 10.0, a width of 0.5, and a height of 1.0.

After you create the rams, position them in relation to the blocks and the ramp [4.10]. The position shown here prevents objects from flying out of the world when the car jumps the ramp.

The same rules apply for positioning the rams. They can't overlap any other objects, and the small ram needs to be positioned slightly above the plane because it is going to be a moveable object [4.11]. The larger ram can be set much closer to the ground plane because it is not moveable.

Now that we have completed the geometrical shapes, we can add textures to them. The following section describes how to do this.

Textures

Texturing is the process of either mapping a picture (.jpg, .bmp, and so on) to your 3D shapes, or mapping procedural shaders to the shapes. Shockwave 3D doesn't support procedural shading. A texture can be applied in a number of different ways. The car is box-shaped, so textures are applied using box mapping. Planar shapes would use planar mapping, spheres use spherical mapping, and so on.

> **Note**
>
> **Texture Tools** Remember that Shockwave 3D does not support the texture adjustment and mapping tools in the Material Editor window. If you need to adjust the mapping type, you have to apply a UVW modifier to your geometry first.

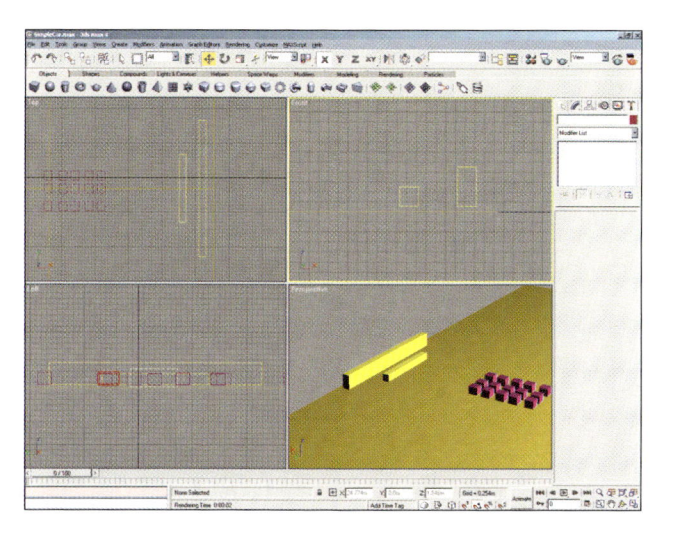

[4.10] The rams prevent objects from flying out of the 3D world.

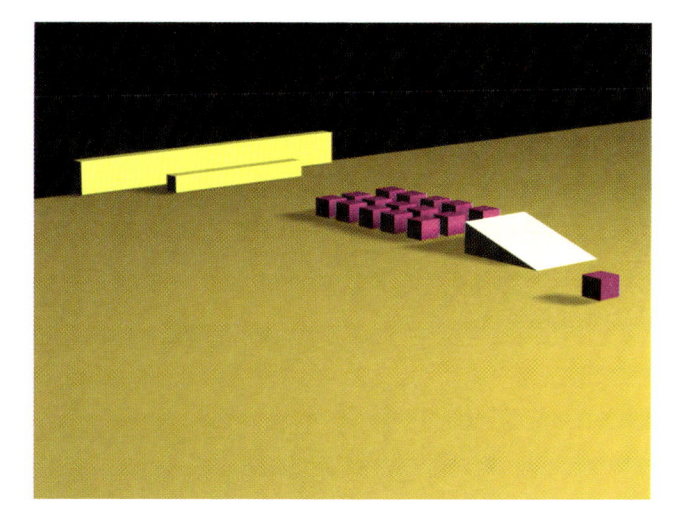

[4.11] The completed rams positioned within the scene.

[4.12] Applying texture to the car.

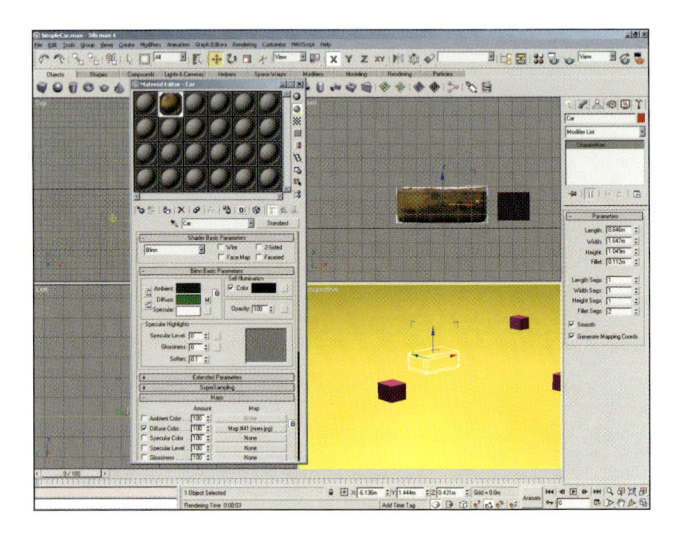

[4.13] Texture mapping has been applied to the soapbox car.

In this example, only the car is going to get a texture map applied to it **[4.12]**. In 3ds max, go to the Material Editor and pick an empty slot. Click on the button to the right of the Diffuse color chip to open the Mapping window. When you apply a bitmap image, it will replace the colors in the Diffuse channel with this image. The image selected for the car is the mars.jpg that can be found in your 3dsmax\Maps\Space directory.

Next, apply the material to the car and make the texture visible in the scene. Because the mars.jpg is already a complex pattern, you don't need to use a UVW mapping modifier. UVM modifiers are only necessary when accurate texture placement is necessary, but they are a superfluous step when they aren't needed. Your car, or soapbox, is now texture-mapped **[4.13]**.

If you don't want to complete the texture mapping on your own, you can load it from the CD-ROM.

Lighting the Scene

It's time to add some lights. There is nothing that can make your 3D scene more realistic than well-done lighting. Lighting is an art form of its own. There are people whose only job is to light the scenes that animators create. Poorly done lighting can make your 3D scenes look like flat 2D sketches. For Shockwave, 3D lighting is important in that it sets the tone of your scenes. You can adjust color, position, and the type of lighting, but you can't use shadows. This means that your scenes can reflect mood and emotion, but not realistic-looking shadows. For the car scene, we need to use lighting so that the car's view is well lit.

> **Note**
>
> **Digital Lighting** If you are interested in exploring lighting in more depth, I highly recommend *[digital] Lighting & Rendering* (New Riders Publishing, 2000). You can visit the author's web site at **http://www.3drender.com/**.

In this scene, I decided to use two omni lights for an even, global lighting effect. You can use any type of light. For example, spotlights can be used to produce various effects, making the scene more challenging to the car's driver, as it creates dark spots where the driver can't see the driving plane.

The omni lights in this scene are placed above the plane in opposing corners of the scene. One light's multiplier is set to 1.0 and the other is set to .75. If both lights are set to 1.0, the effect appears too harsh for the scene. Both lights are assigned the RGB color of 255, 253, 243 to simulate a slight yellowish tint, such as the sun's light **[4.14]**. After you finish the lights, you are ready to activate the Havok rigid body system.

Physics Time

The scene we created will now begin to take shape. In addressing the physical nature of the scene, it is given gravity, and the objects in the scene are given properties, such as mass, friction, and elasticity.

If you don't know much about physics, don't fret. Havok does most of the hard work for you. However, you should understand how the scale of the world in this scene and its objects affect the final look.

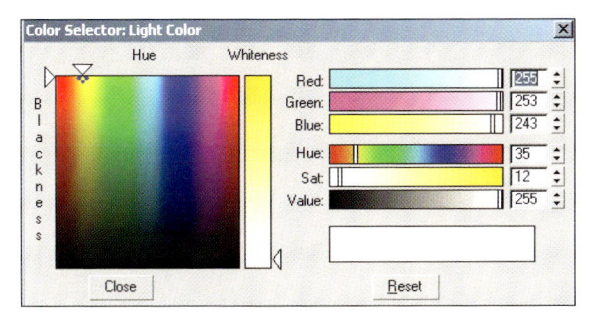

[4.14] Light color and setup.

The scale of objects in relation to the unit scale of your Havok engine will determine if your simulation looks real or not. Havok doesn't care what the units of measurement you use are; it just wants the numbers to be consistent. Always be consistent! If, for example, you are working in meters, then make sure that gravity is set to a value that is in meters (if you want earth-like gravity, then use 9.8 meters/second squared). If you prefer to work in inches, then you need to specify the quantities in inches.

Keep in mind that these units of measurement are going to dictate rates of gravity as well, which is another reason to remain consistent; otherwise, your objects will have varying rates of gravitational pull. For example, if you create a cube with a size of 100 units, but you don't specify gravity in inches, the cube will still fall at the same speed (even though you now think of it as being about seven feet in length on each side). If gravity is set to 9.8 units, the physics engine is effectively simulating a gravitational pull of 9.8 inches per second (this is less than the moon's gravity). For example, the cube is 100×100×100 meters, and gravity is 9.8 meters/second, squared. The cube falls too slowly. Then, you change the measurements to inches. The cube is now 100×100×100 inches, but nothing has actually changed, because gravity is now 9.8 inches/second, squared. When you convert gravity to inches, the gravity is set to 386 inches/second, squared. The cube now falls at the expected speed.

The Havok physics engine always works with dimensionless units. It is up to you to keep the numbers consistent and convert values to the correct units as necessary. To complicate matters, the Havok engine is designed to be most accurate when it is handling numbers that are closest to the value of 1.0 (values such as 1,000,000 and 0.000001 are not effective).

Therefore, in your scenes, when creating objects that are 1×1×1 in size, it is more useful to work in meters than centimeters or kilometers, because you will generally be simulating objects larger than an orange and smaller than a building. This is why the physics engine works with meter scales by default.

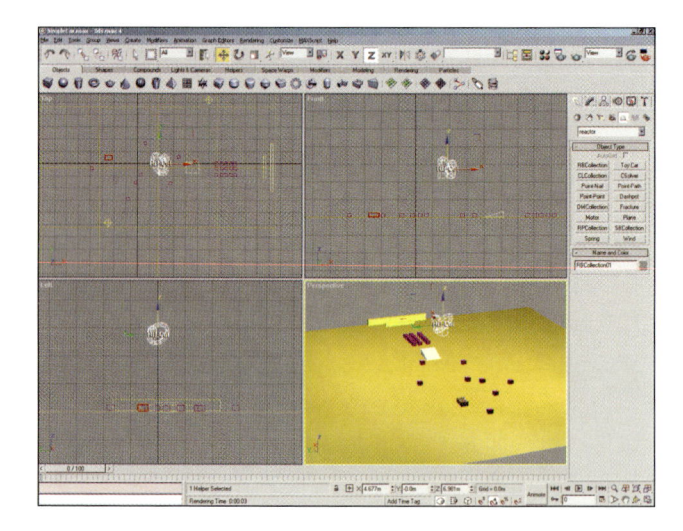

Note

Measurements of Gravity

1 inch = 0.0254 meters

Gravity in inches = 9.8/0.0254, which is equivalent to 386 inches/second, squared

[4.15] The rigid body collection.

Rigid Body Collection

To add the Havok engine to your scene in 3ds max go to the Create tab, then use the Helpers button to pull-down either the Havok or Reactor option. This brings up the Object Type button collection where all the Havok features are accessed. We are going to add a rigid body collection [4.15] to the scene. The button you press is called RBCollection. To add it to the scene, click the button, and then click any place in the viewport. This adds an unusual wireframe object to your scene. This is nothing more than a visual indication that you have added a rigid body collection to your scene. This object does not render and doesn't export out as a piece of geometry. Place it where it won't get in your way.

Next, you need to add the objects in your scene to the rigid body collection. Essentially, you are going to group all your objects under the RBCollection. To do this, click on the rigid body object in your viewport to select it, and then go to the Modify tab. The RBCollection01 object should be selected. Click the Add button.

This brings up the Select rigid bodies window [4.16] where you can add all the objects by clicking the All button and then clicking Select.

If you add additional objects to your scene, they will *not* be included in the physics simulation unless you repeat this process, adding each newly created geometrical piece. In other words, if you add new models, they will show up in 3ds max and they will show up in your Shockwave 3D file; however, they will not be part of the physics scene. The car will drive through these objects as if they were invisible. Don't forget to add all your objects before initializing the simulation process!

Setting the Model's Physical Properties

Now that the models have been added to the rigid body collection, each one needs to be assigned physical properties. These properties, such as mass, will tell the physics engine how to treat the objects in the world.

The physics system applies gravity to the objects. The mass that each object has determines how heavy it is in the scene, how fast it falls to the ground (Havok simulates being on the earth's surface), and how hard it is to move when it's hit by another object.

Objects that have higher mass settings obviously weigh more than those with less mass, *except* for objects that have a mass setting of 0.0. Objects whose mass is 0.0 are considered to be fixed, immovable objects. This means they are in the scene and objects can run into them, but the objects will bounce off of them. Zero-mass objects are not affected by gravity. Because of this, it makes sense that our ground plane has a physical mass setting of 0.0. Because we want the car to drive on it, we don't want it to fall, and we don't want it to move.

To set the plane's mass to 0.0, click the plane, go to the Utilities tab menu, and select Havok. Then, open the Properties tab to view the Physical properties setting. Set the plane's mass to 0.0 (also the default).

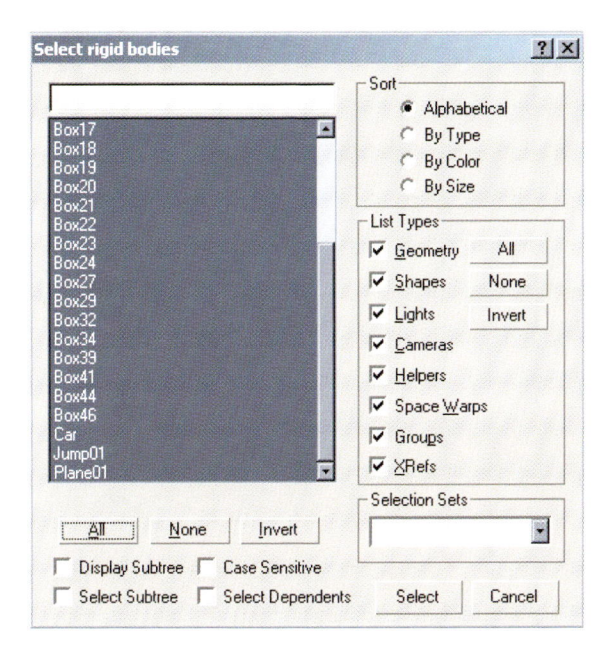

[4.16] The Select rigid bodies window is where you add your scene's objects.

> **Note**
>
> **Finding the Havok Button** If you do not see the Havok button in the Utilities tab menu, you might need to click the More button, and then choose Havok from the list of additional tools that can be added to the Utilities window.

Under the Properties tab, there are choices for Convex or Concave. I explain the difference between these settings later. For now, set the plane as an oncaveobject by selecting the Use Mesh option under the Concave section of Simulation Geometry.

[4.17] Applying mass to the car.

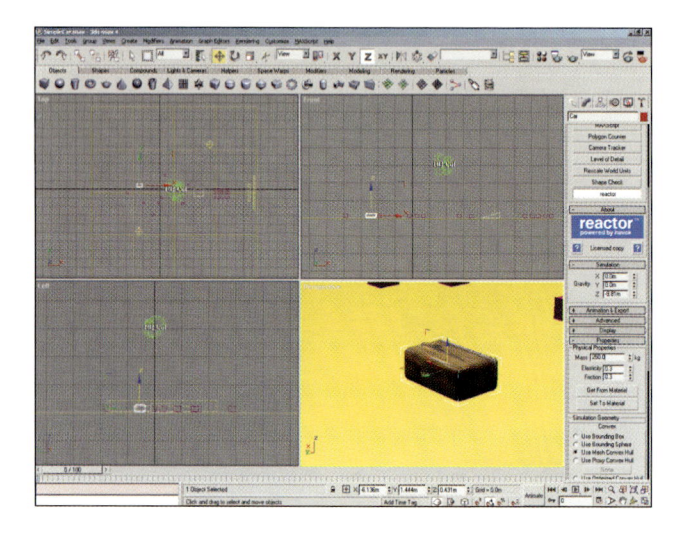

[4.18] Setting the mass for multiple objects.

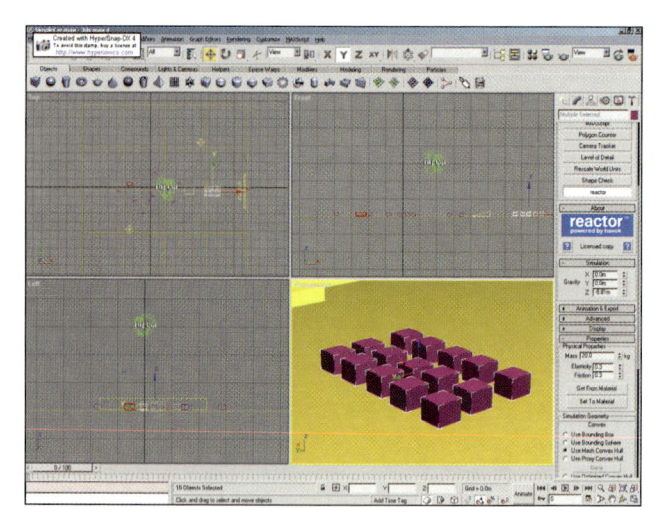

The car is the heaviest object in the scene so that it can inflict the most damage if other objects collide with it. If, for example, there is a cube in the scene that has a higher mass setting than the car, running into it would likely cause the car to flip over, ending your Havok wreaking days.

Select the car in your viewport, then go back to the Properties tab and set the car's mass to 250.0 **[4.17]**. Leave the car as a convex object.

Now, select the same Mass property settings for all the boxes in the scene. The boxes' mass shouldn't be as heavy as the car's. Give them a mass that is a tenth of the car's mass. A setting of about 20 kilograms is appropriate. You can experiment with different settings. If you do, this point in the process is the best time to do so.

If you want to set several objects (such as the boxes) with the same mass, you can control and click (or drag and select) them at one time, and then type in one setting in the Mass properties field **[4.18]**.

Select and set the ramp object's mass to 0.0. The ramp, like the ground plane, is an immovable object. Don't change any of the Convex or Concave settings.

Select the smaller ram and give it a mass of 50.0. Finally, select the larger ram and give it a mass of 0.0. Now that the mass of object is set, you can assign friction settings to each object.

Friction

Friction isn't just that tense feeling you get during the holidays when you are at your relatives' house talking about politics or about the relatives who aren't there. It's much more than that.

In the Properties setting under mass, there is a friction setting. This setting determines how "sticky" your objects are. Let's get the college textbook out for this explanation. Basically, there are two types of friction—static and dynamic. Static friction is friction between objects that are at rest, and dynamic friction is friction between objects that are in contact with each other but also moving, such as a car's tire and the road.

Friction is a physical quantity that prevents surfaces from sliding off one another; it is a force that can hold stacked boxes together [4.19]. During any collision, a specific amount of energy (motion and power) is lost because of the friction coefficient you set in the Properties Setting dialog. For example, if you lower the friction number to 0.1 for the car in this scene, it will appear as if it's driving on ice. If you raise it to a setting such as 0.75, it will appear as if the car is driving through sand.

The default setting of 0.3 is appropriate for this demonstration; however, I recommend that you experiment with this setting to see how dramatically it can change your scenes. Two more settings in the Properties dialog are the Convex and Concave. We explore these next.

[4.19] Friction holds the rock to the board, but only to a point!

Convex Objects Versus Concave Objects

In the Havok system, your objects are classified as either convex or concave. The textbook definition of a convex object states that any two points inside the object always result in a straight line whenever a connection is made between the objects inside of the object. Convex objects are spheres, cylinders, boxes, cones, and so on [4.20]. If an object is not a convex it is concave. A concave object is an object that generally has a hole in it, such as rings. In terms of the physics engine, concave objects are the slowest to simulate because of their double-sided collision nature.

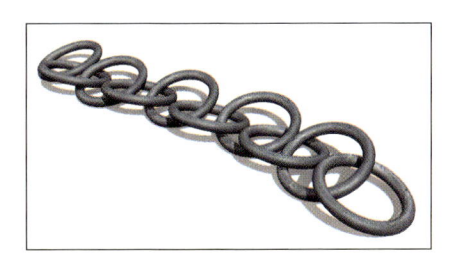

[4.20] A chain is an example of a concave object.

Speeding Up Simulations

Imagine that you want an object to collide with a teapot. That teapot is a complex shape for the physics engine to "monitor" for collisions. Compare the shape of a teapot to a cube, and you can visualize the difference between the two shapes. The complexity of the teapot adds to the physics engine's math routines, which slows down the simulation. There are two ways to get around this.

The first method is to use a display proxy. A proxy is simply an object that is referenced by the physics engine. Consider a box that is see-through, and inside of it is a realistic car shape [4.21]. The more realistic car is the display proxy for the simple box. What this does is allow the physics engine to simulate the collision with a basic shape while showing a display of the more complex car instead. You do have to ensure that the box surrounding the car isn't too large, because the collisions will then happen before the car reaches the object.

The second method of speeding up your Shockwave 3D scene involves a great little trick. For this, you don't use a display proxy, but you switch the more detailed model for the simulation model just before you export the model. For example, let's say you have two models—one is a cube, and the other one is a complex car model. Both models are in the same X, Y, and Z position in the scene. The cube is added to the rigid body collection, and it is given mass just as a normal object. The cube's name is cube01, and the car is named car_model. Now comes what I call the "which hand is it in" switch. Export the .HKE file from the Havok exporter. (To learn how to do this, read the following section.) Remember that the .HKE file references the cube01 model. Now, delete cube01 from your scene, and rename the car_model to cube01. Then, export the Shockwave 3D .W3D file. The Havok system simulates a cube while the Shockwave 3D system displays a more complex car model!

The advantage to using this method is improved performance from the Havok physics engine. If you use a model of a car, Havok has to calculate the complex curves and angles that the body and tires have when determining collisions. However, if you are using a cube, the calculations are much simpler, translating into increased performance.

Now that you've built your scene, you can test and export it. The following section tells you how to do this.

[4.21] A proxy of a car and block.

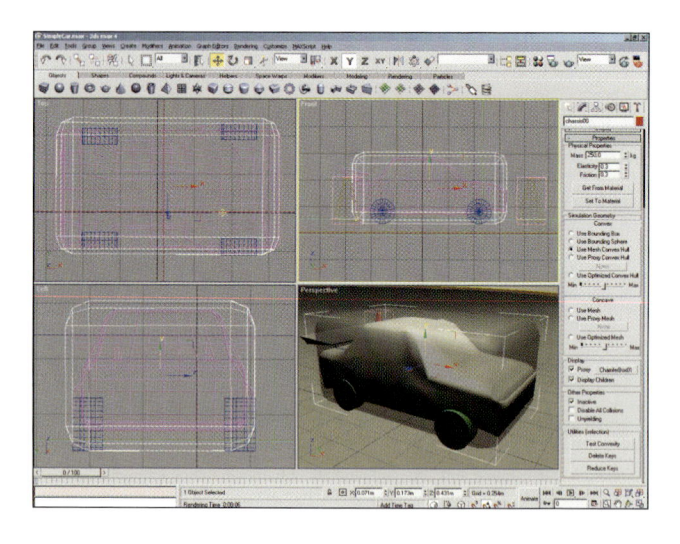

Testing and Exporting Your Scene

Before you export the .HKE file, you need to test the scene to ensure that there are no overlapping geometries and to ensure that the objects have been included in the rigid body collection. This is a quick and easy process.

At the Havok display section, click the Preview in window button. This brings up the Havok display window and shows you the items that are included in the rigid body collection. You can preview the collisions and the gravity of your scene [4.22].

By going to the Simulation menu and choosing Play, the gravity will be applied to the objects and they will begin to fall and settle to the plane. If the plane falls, then its mass setting of 0.0 is wrong also, if any of your objects blow apart like a bomb then they have overlapping collision tolerances. You will need to go back to those models and move them slightly away from one another or you can alter the collision tolerance setting for your entire scene in the Havok Advanced rollout. When you are finished playing with your world, you can just close the window. Remember this window does nothing more than apply gravity; you can't drive the car yet.

Some times, you will make small changes to your scene, such as adding or deleting objects. In these cases, you still need to test your scenes to make sure there are no errors in it. Instead of using the Preview in window option, you can use the Analyze World option [4.23]. This button is found in the Havok Advanced rollout. When you click this button, it tests your world for various errors, such as gravity overlapping objects.

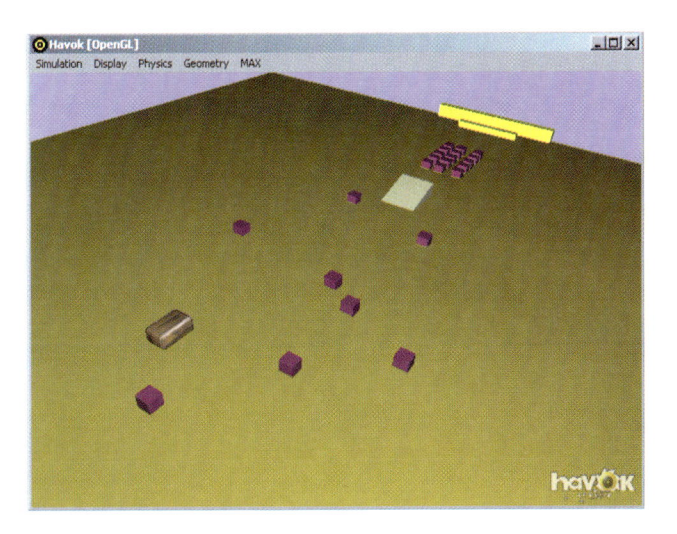

[4.22] Havok's Preview window.

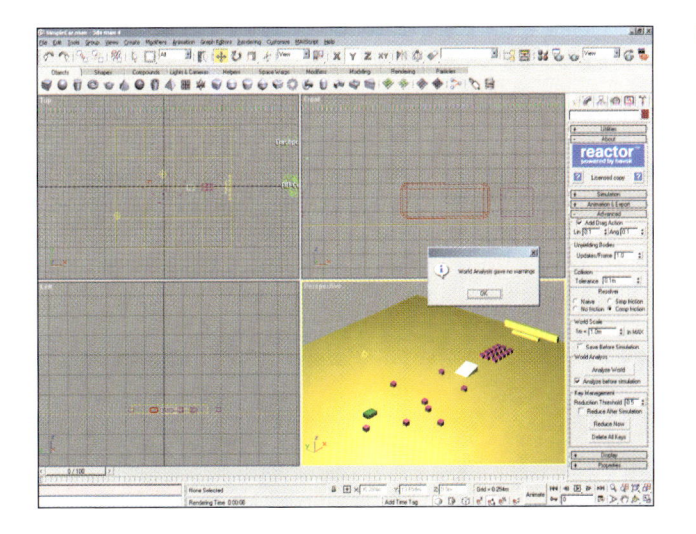

[4.23] A world with no warnings according to the Analyze World option.

It's a good idea to use the Analyze World option whenever you make significant changes to your scene or just before you export the scene to an .HKE file.

After everything is tested and works, the scene is ready for export. In order to export a Havok scene as a Shockwave 3D file, we have to export two separate data files. We need to export a Havok .HKE file that contains the physics information for the scene (the left-brain file), and then we need to export a separate Shockwave 3D .W3D file that contains all the visual data (the right-brain file).

To export the .HKE file, simply go to the Havok Animation & Export rollout tab and click the Export to File button. Make sure the Binary option is selected and that the Export Display Information box is not active. In the File Dialog window, save and name the file (choose any name). Remember where you save it, as you will have to import it into Director soon.

Exporting in Shockwave

If you are reading this book linearly, then you should already know how the Shockwave 3D exporter works. You can skip ahead if you already know how to export. Otherwise, the first step you take is to set up the Perspective view to start your Shockwave 3D movies in Director.

> **Note**
>
> **Before You Export** The last viewport you select in 3ds max will be the way your Shockwave 3D movie will start. Make sure to set up your camera and select that camera's viewport before performing the Shockwave 3D export.

In Director, we are going to attach a camera-tracking behavior that zooms in and follows the car as we drive it. Thus, the more you zoom back in the Perspective window, the more the camera zooms into your scene. Make sure that your Perspective view port is selected before choosing Export from the File menu [4.24].

In the Shockwave Export dialog, I recommend naming your file to closely resemble the name you gave the .HKE file [4.25]. For example, if your .HKE file is named simplecar_1.hke, name the file simplecar_1.w3d.

You will likely end up creating several modifications of your files; thus, your desktop will get cluttered with files.

After you name the file, you will see the Shockwave 3D Export window and the export options [4.26]. Here, you can turn off the Animations option and select the texture size in the Texture Size Limits section.

The texture that was used for the car was so complex that a low setting of 256×256 won't hurt the quality, but it will help improve redraw performance in Director.

When you see the Shockwave Preview window, and it looks like the 3ds max Perspective viewport, you've succeeded in exporting the scene. Check the Preview window [4.27] to ensure that your objects are in the scene and that everything is laid out the way you wanted it to be, and then close the window to check for any warnings.

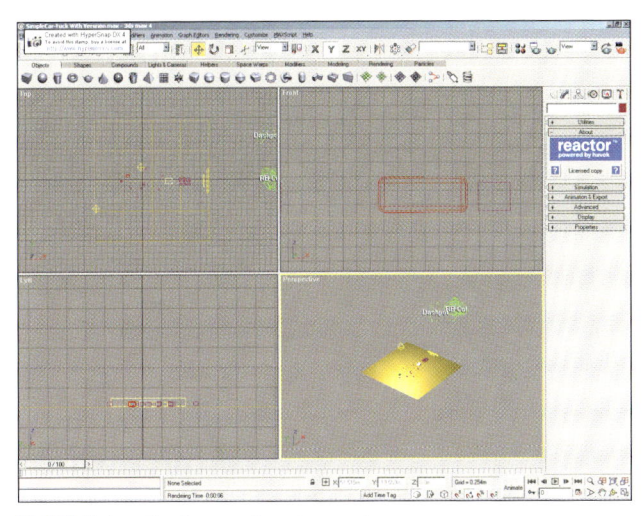

Chapter 4 Wreaking Havok | 95

[4.24] Set up the Perspective view port.

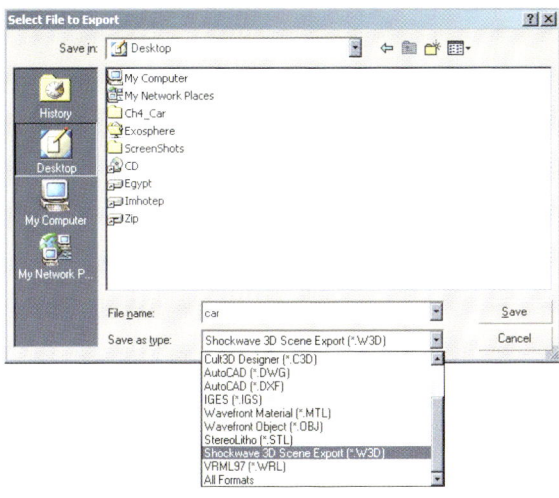

[4.25] The Shockwave Export dialog.

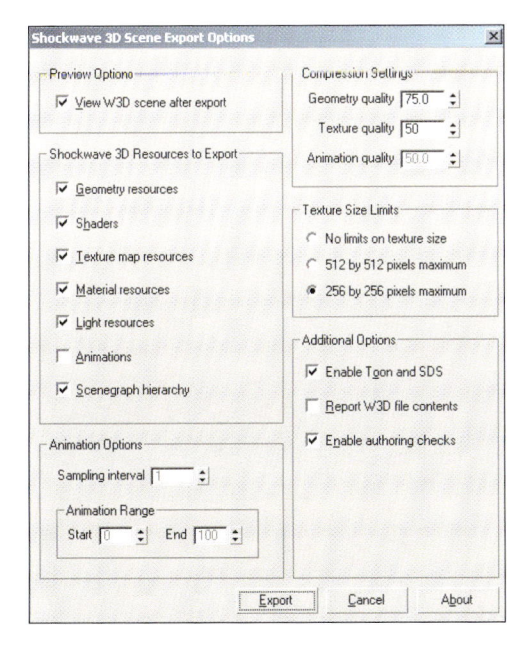

[4.26] Export options.

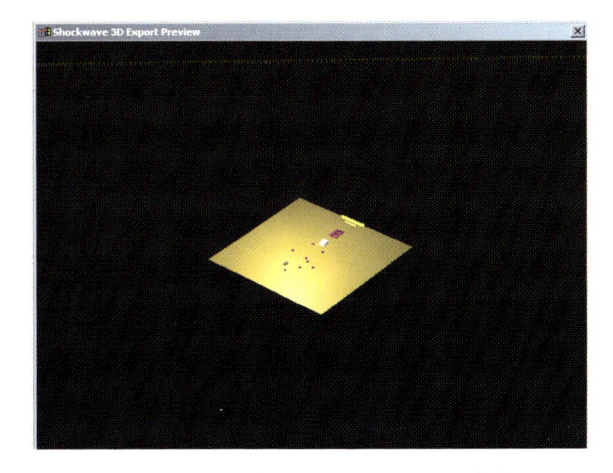

[4.27] The scene in the Shockwave 3D Preview window.

[4.28] The Shockwave 3D warning window.

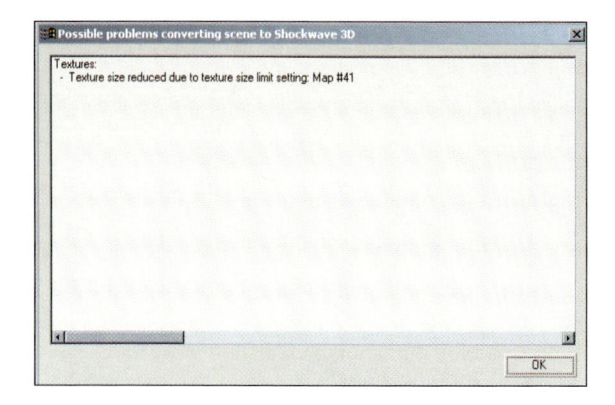

[4.29] The pie chart.

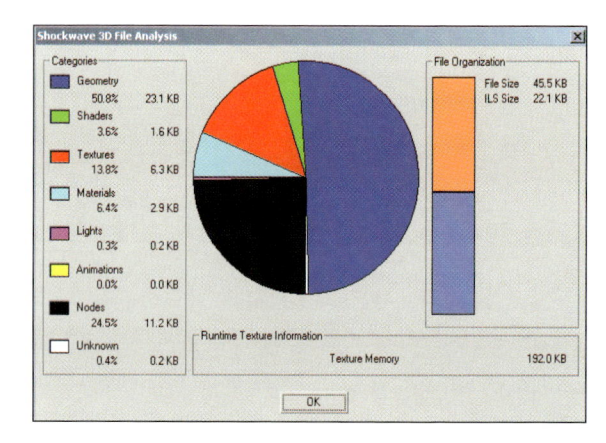

Texture Warning

When you close the Preview window, you might receive a Possible problems converting scene to Shockwave 3D dialog [4.28]. This window warns you about any problems that are encountered during the conversion from 3ds max to Shockwave 3D.

In this case, the warning is negligible. The exporter is just warning us that it has reduced the texture applied to the car to 256×256, as we specified for it earlier. When you close this window, the Shockwave 3D File Analysis window appears. This window contains the pie chart, which is discussed in the following section.

The Pie Chart

The pie chart is used to evaluate what objects are taking up the most space in your scene. In the Shockwave 3D File Analysis window, you can see that the geometrical shapes in our scene are taking up the most space in the Shockwave 3D file [4.29]. However, even though the models are 50% of the file size, they still only account for 23.1K of space, which isn't that much in terms of file size. In fact, with a total file size of only 45.5K, this movie would work well as a web-streaming movie at any connection speed. Remember, however, that we haven't added any code or interface elements in Director yet. The following sections discuss how to do this.

In Director

Finally, you've made it to Director. For this demonstration, you will use custom behaviors that were written specifically for driving a car. Havok has already created the behaviors for you and they can be found at **http://www.havok.com/xtra** or on the accompanying CD-ROM.

You should (if you haven't done so already) install the new behaviors before starting this project. To do so, follow these steps:

1. Find the behaviors on the CD-ROM or download and decompress them from the web site.

2. Ensure that Director isn't running. Find your Director folder (or directory), and then find and open the Libs folder. You will place the Havok folder in the Libs folder. You should find two files in the Havok folder—Control.cst and a Setup.cst. These files contain the behaviors for this chapter and for other types of Havok controls you might want to use in the future.

3. After you have added the Havok behaviors to the Libs folder, they are installed. Close all of your folders, and start Director. Then, open the Behaviors library, and you should see the name Havok in the list of behaviors [4.30]. These behaviors add several types of controls to your Shockwave 3D castmembers.

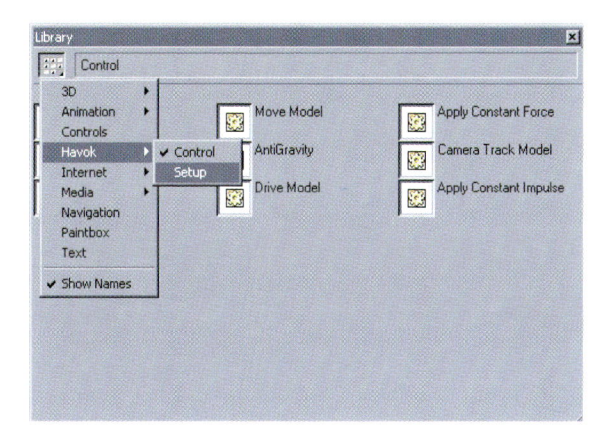

[4.30] The new Havok behaviors.

The Havok Behaviors

This section gives you a quick overview of the Havok behaviors you just added. This section can serve as a reference. I start by explaining what each of the new behaviors is for and what you can do with them. Then, we'll add the behaviors to the car. If you'd like, you can skip this section and go to the next section.

The new Havok behaviors are divided into two categories—seven are setup behaviors and six are control behaviors. The setup behaviors are used for manual construction of an empty Shockwave 3D scene and the activation of the physics engine. The control behaviors are used for adding functions and interactivity to a scene. I start by explaining what the setup behaviors do.

SETUP BEHAVIORS

This table contains the behaviors in the Havok library. These behaviors act on objects in your scene.

Make Fixed Rigid Body

The Make Fixed Rigid Body behavior [4.31] creates a new 3D object in your customized Havok scene that is immovable. Its options are:

Which model   This pull-down menu lets you pick the existing model in your scene that you want the behavior to be attached to.

Restitution   Accepting numerical values, this option controls the return to or restoration of a previous state or position (default = 0.3).

Friction   Accepting numerical values, this option determines the strength of the force that holds objects together.

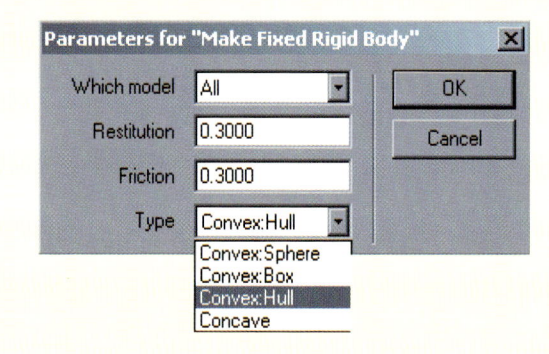

[4.31] Create a fixed, 3D object with this behavior.

Type   The types are Convex: Hull, Convex: Sphere, Convex: Box, and Concave.

Make Linear Dashpot

The Make Linear Dashpot behavior [4.32] creates a dashpot between two objects that already exist in the scene. A dashpot can be thought of as similar to a spring. Its options are:

Name   Lets you type a name for the dashpot for referencing later.

Model A   A pull-down menu that lets you pick the first model that the dashpot is attached to.

Point A   A 3D vector that points to the place on model A that the dashpot is connected to.

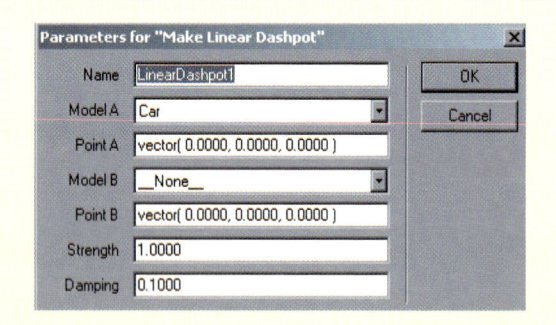

[4.32] A linear dashpot can simulate a spring-like connection between two of your objects.

SETUP BEHAVIORS (continued)

Make Linear Dashpot (continued)

Model B A pull-down menu that lets you select the second model that the dashpot is attached to.

Point B A 3D vector that pins the dashpot to model B.

Strength A numerical value that determines how hard the spring pushes on objects that hit it.

Damping A numerical value that determines how quickly the dashpot is restored to its original shape.

Make Movable Rigid Body

The Make Movable Rigid Body behavior [4.33] creates a new 3D object in your customized Havok scene that can be moved by other objects and is affected by gravity. Its options are:

Which model This pull-down menu lets you pick the existing model in your scene that you want the behavior to be attached to.

Restitution Accepts numerical values and controls the return to or restoration of a previous state or position (default = 0.3).

Friction Accepts numerical values and determines the strength of the force that holds objects together.

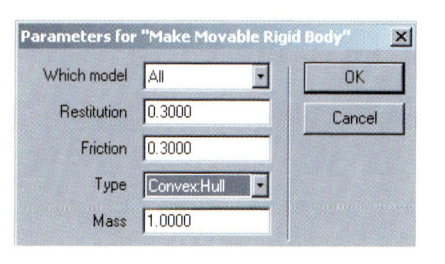

[4.33] Create objects that are movable in your scene.

Type Convex: Hull, Convex: Sphere, Convex: Hull, and Concave.

Mass A numerical value that determines the weight of the object in the scene.

Make Spring

This behavior [4.34] creates a spring between two objects, both of which already exist in the scene.

Name This option lets you enter a name for the spring for referencing later.

Model A A pull-down menu that lets you pick the first model that the spring is attached to.

Point A A 3D vector that points to the place on model A that the spring is connected to.

continues...

SETUP BEHAVIORS (continued)

Make Spring (continued)

Model B   A pull-down that lets you select the second model that the spring is attached to.

Point B   A 3D vector that attaches the spring to model B.

Rest Length   A numerical value that determines the fixed length of the spring. This setting determines the distance between model A and model B when they are at rest.

Elasticity   A numerical value that controls the flexibility that the spring has and how hard the spring pushes back on the objects that collide with it. Increase the value proportionate with the damping setting for realistic spring effects.

Damping   This value controls how long it takes before the spring returns to its resting length.

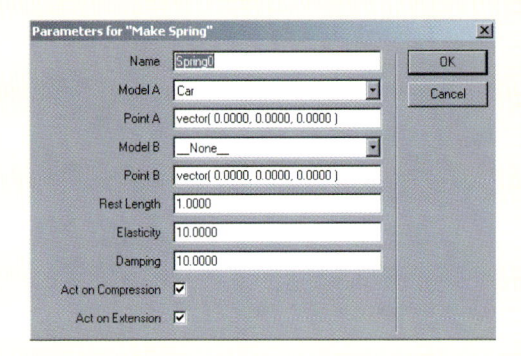

[4.34] Connect a fully functional spring between two of your objects.

Act on Compression   This checkbox lets you turn the spring push on or off.

Act on Extension   A checkbox that allows you to turn on or off the pushing force when the spring is no longer resting.

Havok Physics (HKE)

Havok Physics (HKE) is the physics behavior that links the simulation engine to the Shockwave 3D sprite [4.35].

Which Havok Cast Member   With this setting, you can select the imported HKE file you are using.

Time Step   This setting specifies how far forward the physical world is advanced on each animation frame. For example, the car demonstration is set to run at 60 frames per second, which equals a time step of 1/60 of a second. This translates closely into 0.0167 in decimal units.

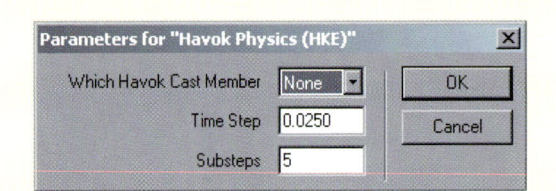

[4.35] This behavior links your HKE file to the Shockwave 3D engine inside Director.

Substeps   The Substeps parameter indicates how many additional steps the Havok engine will split the time step into.

SETUP BEHAVIORS (continued)

Make Angular Dashpot

The Make Angular Dashpot behavior [4.36] creates an angular dashpot between two objects that already exist in the scene. An angular dashpot can be thought of as similar to a spring except spiral rather than linear in nature.

Name Lets you type a name for the dashpot for referencing later.

Model A A pull-down menu that lets you pick the first model that the dashpot is attached to.

Model B A pull-down menu that lets you select the second model that the dashpot is attached to.

Rotation Axis The axis in which the force is applied.

Rotation Angle The angle at which the rotational component of a transform is calculated.

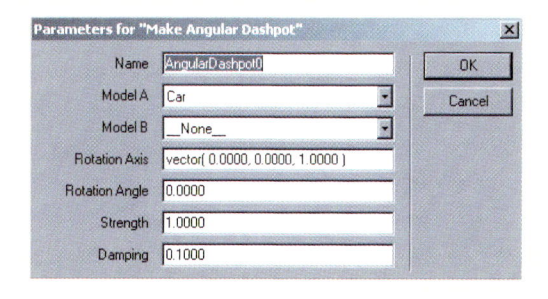

[4.36] Use the Make Angular Dashpot behavior to create angular dashpots between objects in your scene.

Strength A numerical value that determines how hard the spring pushes on objects that hit it.

Damping A numerical value that determines how quickly the dashpot is restored to its original shape.

Havok Physics (No HKE)

Havok Physics (No HKE) behavior is the physics behavior that links the simulation engine to the Shockwave 3D sprite [4.37]. This behavior is used when writing your own Shockwave 3D movie from scratch using Lingo. The options are:

Which Havok Cast Member The custom text or HKE file to be used can be selected from this drop-down list.

Tolerance Determines how close objects can be to one another before they are have collided. Smaller numbers let objects get closer to one another.

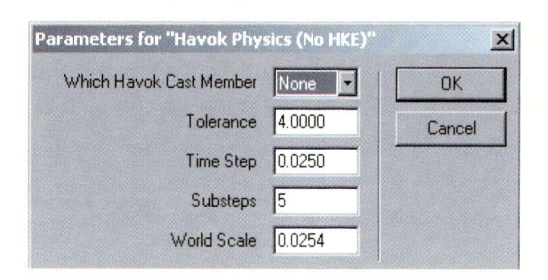

[4.37] Attach your custom physics engine with this behavior.

continues...

SETUP BEHAVIORS *(continued)*

Havok Physics (No HKE) *(continued)*

Time Step   The Time Step specifies how far forward the physical world is advanced on each animation frame. For example, our car demonstration is set to run at 60 frames per second, which equals a time step of 1/60 a second. This translates closely into 0.0167 in decimal.

Substeps   The Substeps parameter indicates how many additional steps the Havok engine will split the time step into.

World Scale   This option determines the scale of the gravity component in relation to the objects created.

CONTROL BEHAVIORS

This table contains the behaviors in the Havok Control library. These behaviors act on objects in your scene.

Set Gravity

The Set Gravity behavior [4.38] allows you to determine the vector for the gravity in your scene. (The vector, of course, indicates both direction and velocity.) With this behavior you can pick the direction gravity pulls and how hard it pulls.

Gravity   This is a 3D vector whose normal gravity equals: 0.0, 0.0, −9.81.

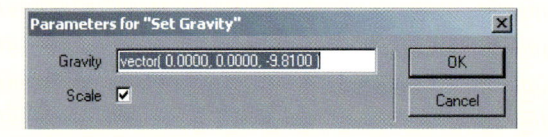

[4.38] Control the pull of gravity in your Shockwave 3D scene with this behavior.

Scale   This checkbox helps scale the gravity function in relation to the size of your objects.

Push Model

The Push Model behavior [4.39] applies a force with a specific strength to an object of your choice in the scene.

Which model   This option lets you pick the model in the scene that the force will effect.

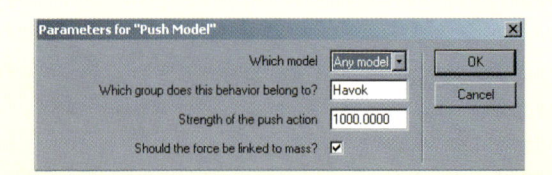

[4.39] Apply a force to any model in your scene.

CONTROL BEHAVIORS *(continued)*

Push Model *(continued)*

Which group does this behavior belong to? This is a text field that lets you name the group associated with the effect.

Strength of the push action A numerical value, this represents how hard the model is pushed.

Should the force be linked to mass? The Link to Mass option determines if the pushing effect is stationary pushing the model away, or if the pushing force is continuous, such as the force of a rocket engine pushing a rocket.

Rocket Model

This behavior [4.40] attaches controls to an existing model that allow you to control it like the space ship in the Asteroids video game, except in 3D. For this behavior to function well, gravity should be low or off. Note that this behavior can be found on the CD-ROM accompanying this book.

Which model This option lets you pick a model in the scene to apply the behavior to.

Thrust Power Thrust Power sets the force of the push applied to the model. The Thrust Power should be a factor of the object mass and the gravity.

Turning Speed This sets how fast the model can spin around.

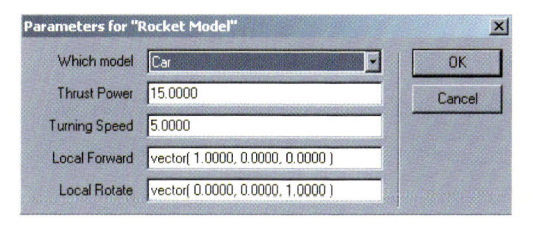

[4.40] Fire your models just like rockets.

Local Forward This is a 3D vector that sets the forward motion of your model.

Local Rotate This is a 3D vector that determines the spin axis that your model turns around.

Move Model

The Move Model behavior [4.41] allows you to move any model in your scene with a trigger effect. You can attach this behavior to a cube, for example, then attach a mouse left trigger effect and click and drag models around your scene.

Which model Lets you pick the model the behavior affects.

Which group does this behavior belong to? The group name the behavior is affected by.

continues...

CONTROL BEHAVIORS *(continued)*

Move Model *(continued)*

Strength of the mouse spring If the mouse is used, the object is attached to the mouse with a spring. The setting determines the strength that the model is bound to the mouse.

Damping of the mouse spring The is how quickly the object comes to rest when the mouse is holding the object.

Should the spring be linked to mass? Determines if an attached spring releases this model when it pushes, or if it is attached permanently to the model.

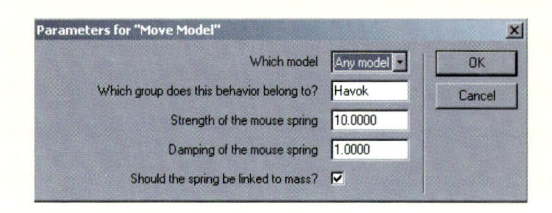

[4.41] Grab and move any model in your scene with this behavior.

AntiGravity

AntiGravity is a simple behavior **[4.42]** that allows you to pick either all objects or a specific object that the gravity in the scene stops effecting.

Which model This is a pull-down menu that lets you choose your model or models that gravity will not affect.

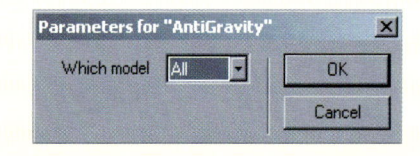

[4.42] You can turn off gravity on select models with the anti-gravity behavior.

Drive Model

The Drive Model behavior **[4.43]** will allow you to drive a model around the scene like a car. It is the behavior that we will be using for the scene that we created in this chapter. Note that this behavior is on the CD-ROM accompanying this book.

Which model Lets you pick the model to apply the behavior to.

Maximum Speed Controls the speed of the object in relation to its mass.

Maximum Turning Speed Controls how fast the car can spin in a turn.

Acceleration A value in relation to the model's mass that controls the speed that the model can move from a resting position.

CONTROL BEHAVIORS (continued)

Drive Model (continued)

Reverse Acceleration This option works the same way as the Acceleration option, except that it's used for backing up, not moving forward.

Handbrake Power Controls the drag force applied to the rear of the model.

Turning Controls how far the object turns at each given time step.

Grip Controls the friction applied between the model and the ground or the object the model travels on.

Aerodynamic Drag Applies a simulated wind to the model.

Local Forward A 3D vector that assigns the front direction to the car model.

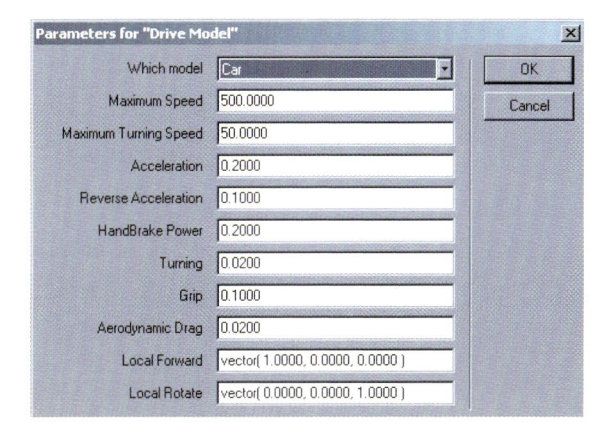

[4.43] Turn any model into a car that you can drive with this behavior.

Local Rotate A 3D vector that picks the axis that the car spins around.

Apply Constant Force

This behavior is similar to the Push Model behavior, except that you cannot stop the force once it has been activated **[4.44]**.

Which model This option lets you pick the model to apply the force to.

Force A 3D vector that specifies the direction and magnitude of a force for your model(s).

Angular Force? A checkbox that lets the force curve in a spiral simulating a torque or a motor.

Scale This sets the force relative to the world's scale.

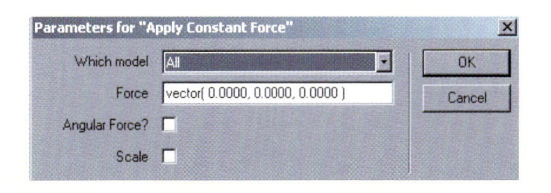

[4.44] This behavior can apply a force to your models to push them around your scene continually.

continues...

CONTROL BEHAVIORS (continued)

Track Camera Model

This behavior attaches the Shockwave 3D sprite camera to a model in the scene [4.45]. The camera can be offset to perform as a chasing helicopter or a walking person. This behavior is used in our car simulation. The options for it are:

Which model This option lets you pick the model to apply this behavior to.

Target Offset Target Offset lets you pick the distance the camera is from the target model it is following.

Camera Up Vector This option lets you set the camera's orientation in the scene.

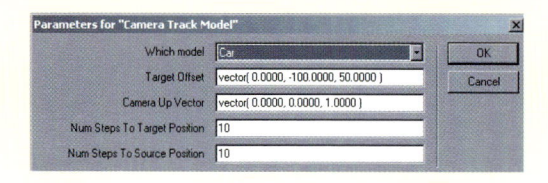

[4.45] With this behavior, a camera automatically follows your models as they move.

Num Steps to Target Position This option sets the rate at which the camera zooms from its starting point to the tracking point of the model.

Num Steps to Source Position This sets the rate at which the camera zooms back to its original starting point.

Apply Constant Impulse

This behavior will apply a force to your model similar to the thrust of a rocket engine [4.46].

Which model This option lets you choose which model to attach the behavior to.

Impulse With this option, pick the 3D impulse direction the model will travel in your scene.

Angular Impulse? With this option, choose a force that will cause you model to spin, simulate torque, or move straight.

Scale This sets the force relative to your world's scale.

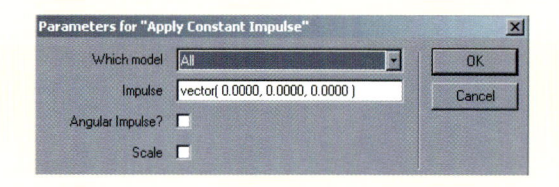

[4.46] Shoot your models like a bullet with this behavior.

Importing the .W3D File and the .HKE File

Now, let's get back to the car demonstration and the scene we constructed. The following sections describe how to complete the car demonstration inside of Director. To get started, we first need to get the Shockwave 3D and Havok files imported into Director, and then we will install and configure the necessary behaviors.

In Director, go to the File menu and select Import. Locate and import the .W3D and .HKE files that you exported from 3ds max, and import them into the Cast window. Or, for a faster method, you can right-click your mouse in the Cast window. A pop-up menu appears where you can select Import [4.47]. (On the Macintosh, control-click to the Import menu.)

Now, move the Shockwave 3D castmember onto the stage. In the example [4.48], the castmember (on the stage) is scaled to be larger. In this example, the car scene can be scaled larger because it is not that complex (640×480 was used).

You should experiment with different sizes to gain the best performance level from your computer. If you make the scene too large, playback performance suffers.

Next, a Go to the frame Lingo script is added to the score to prevent the movie from stopping while the Shockwave 3D sprite is playing. For our example, the script is put into frame 10 [4.49].

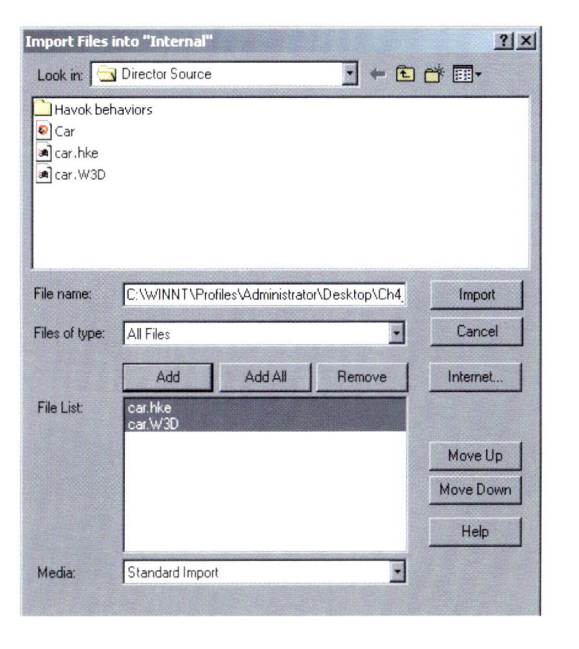

[4.47] The standard Import dialog window.

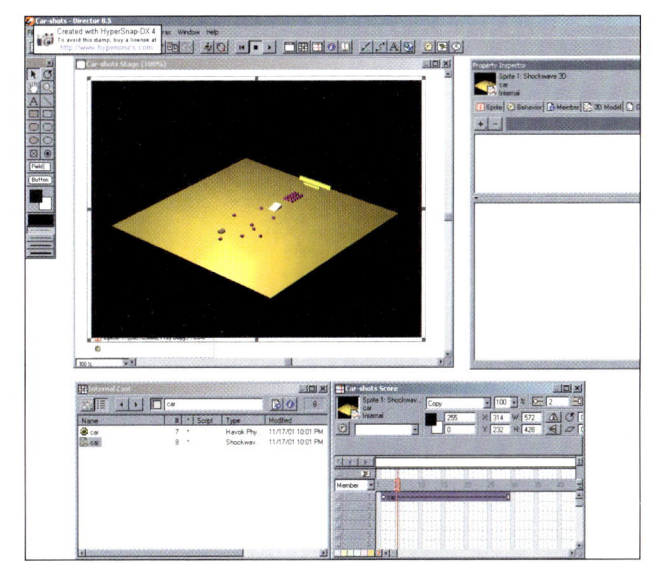

[4.48] Scale the Shockwave 3D sprite on the stage.

[4.49] Add a "go to frame" script in the score.

[4.50] Attach the HKE behavior to your imported .HKE file.

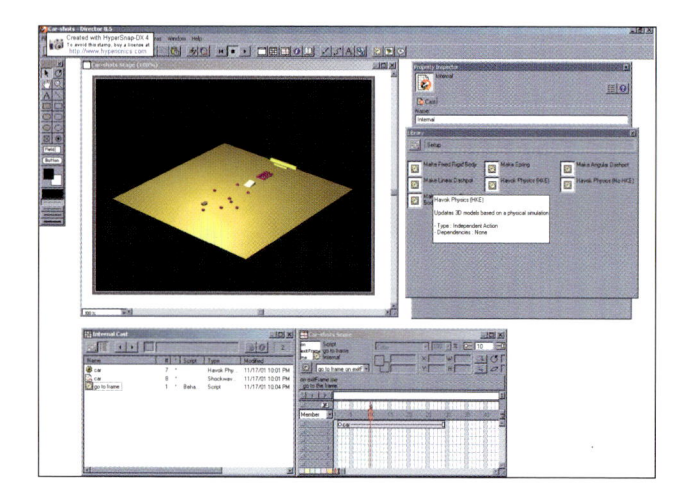

[4.51] Select the physics .HKE file in your cast.

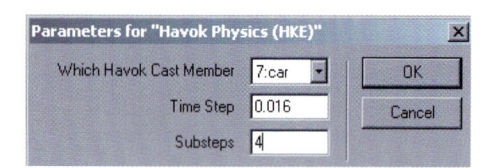

Note

Give Director Some Breathing Room Form the habit of not putting anything into Channel 1 of your score to allow Director additional overhead when loading itself into ram.

Open the behaviors' Library window and select the Havok collection. Open the Havok, Setup collection. Here, drag the Havok Physics (HKE) behavior into your Internal Cast window [4.50].

Drag the HKE behavior from the Internal Cast window onto the Shockwave 3D sprite that is on the stage. This brings up a dialog [4.51]. This behavior is used to link the Shockwave 3D car with the Havok .HKE file that was exported from 3ds max. This behavior also simultaneously installs the physics engine.

In the pull-down menu for this dialog box, make sure that the car .HKE file is selected. Then, set the time step to 0.016 and the sub steps to 4. Then, click OK.

With a Time Step setting of 0.016, the Havok simulation is set to run at 60 frames per second. In Director, you will need to set the tempo of the movie to 60 FPS to match the Time Step setting. I recommend that you put a 60-frame per second tempo setting in the Tempo channel of the Score window. This ensures that your movie is running at 60 FPS each time you start the Director movie.

Now, the physical world is working and has been linked to the display. The animation is ready to be played. Clicking the Play button will cause the Shockwave 3D movie to react as gravity is applied; however, you are so far away that it is hard to see anything. Let's attach the other behaviors to complete the scene.

From the Havok behavior library, drag the Drive Model behavior to either the Cast window or directly on to your Shockwave 3D sprite. This brings up the Drive Model properties. The behavior's default settings are fine. Ensure that the Which model option is set to Car; otherwise, you could end up driving one of the cubes instead of the car.

The Drive Model behavior assigns the arrow keys as the controls for your car. Up controls acceleration, Down acts as the brake, Left turns the car left, and Right turns it right. The spacebar is assigned as a handbrake that you can use to slide the car. The keyboard settings can be changed in the Property Inspector window; however, you will have to know the ASCII keyboard command for the keys you want to re-map.

The entire movie is now completely functional, the car is drivable, and the collisions and interactions are in operation. The only problem is that the camera is far away from the action.

By attaching the Camera Track Model behavior, we can make the camera follow your car wherever you drive. Drag the Camera Track Model behavior onto your Shockwave 3D sprite and give it the following settings:

> Which model: Car
> Target Offset: vector (−900.0, −100,0, 175.0)
> Camera Up Vector: vector (0.0, 0.0, 1.0)
> Num Steps to Target Position: 10
> Num Steps to Source Position: 10

Now, when you rewind and play your movie, the camera will zoom into a hovering position just above and to the right of your car [4.52].

The camera attempts to stay in the same position, above the car, as the car is being driven. That is, it will attempt to keep this exact same position relative to the car, just as a chase plane view would do. Try to drive the car, and run it into the bumper on the other side of the ramp [4.53].

If the car drives off the plane, or if it flips over and you can't recover it, you'll have to restart the simulation. The simulation will restart from the current position and the camera will restart at the position it was in when the car stopped.

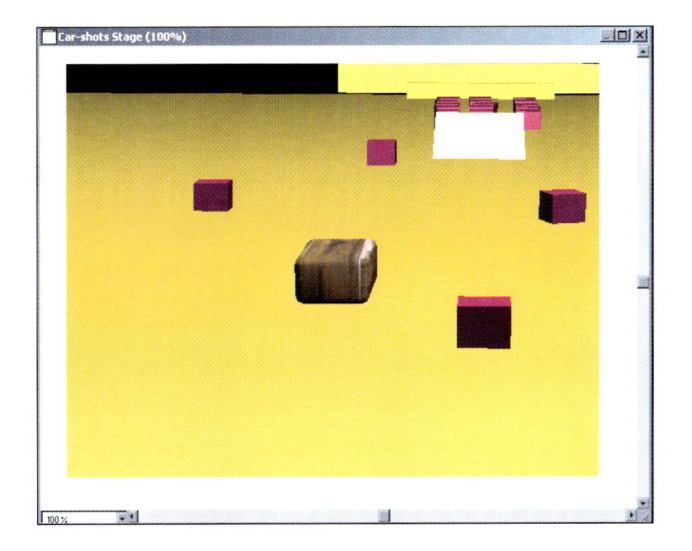

[4.52] You are ready to cause some Havok.

[4.53] The camera will now follow you as you drive.

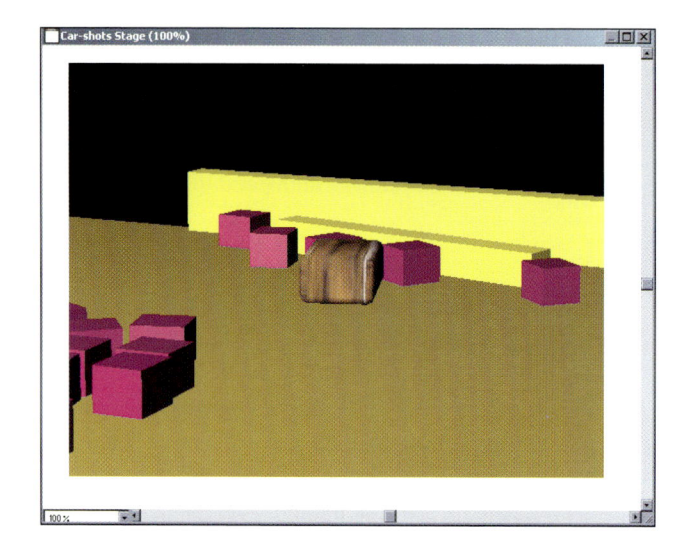

[4.54] Use the Reset World button if you get lost while you are driving.

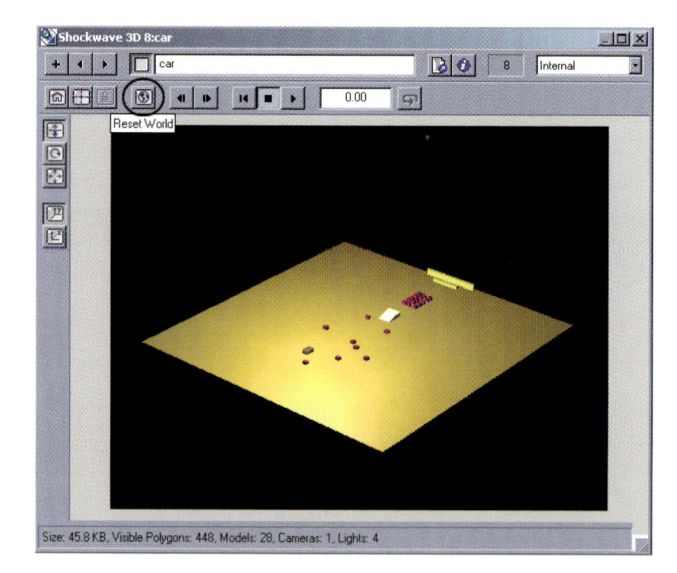

If, however, you want to reset the world to the original starting point (what you exported out from 3ds max), you will need to open the Shockwave 3D castmember and click the Reset World button [4.54].

Playing God

With the simulation complete, you could compile the movie into a Shockwave .DCR file or save it as a projector. However, I'm going to show you one last behavior that will let you interact with the movie with the mouse. The interactions allow you to "play God" by controlling the scene.

Open the Behavior library again and go to the Havok control to apply the Move Model behavior to your Shockwave 3D sprite. Give the behavior the following settings:

> Which model: Any model

> Which group does this behavior belong to?: Havok or any name

> Strength of the mouse spring: 10.0

> Damping of the mouse spring: 1.0

> Should the spring be linked to mass?: Checked

Now, attach a Mouse Left behavior from the 3D Triggers library. In the Mouse Left parameters window, make sure that you choose Group Havok, Move Model from the Select a group and its action settings. The Move Model behavior should be the only one in your library unless you have added others to Director.

Now, when you run the movie, the camera should zoom in on the car. The car is drivable by the arrow keys and you can now use the mouse to click and drag (or toss) any object in the scene. Any object that has a mass setting of 0.0 is not moveable, however.

Exporting the Movie

The movie is almost ready to be exported. Save and compact your movie, then check the publishing settings for publishing a .DCR file. The publishing settings are personal preferences.

The only option that I recommend you set is the Display Progress Bar option [4.55]. Enabling it shows your audience the estimated time it will take for downloading the movie.

If you plan to make a projector out of your movie, I would recommend that you save and compact your file, then use the following settings for the projector (if you have specific project needs, feel free to change these settings):

> For the Options section of the Projector Options, I recommend that whenever possible, you use the Full Screen option. There are re-drawing issues with Shockwave 3D when the window is dragged around the screen. By using the Full Screen option, you prevent users from dragging the window around revealing this issue.

> For the Player options, I recommend using the Standard player whenever possible. Choosing this option doesn't compress the movie and helps the projector start faster, which the user will appreciate.

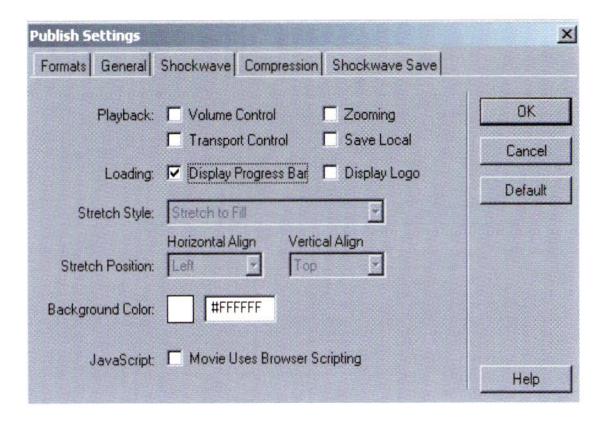

[4.55] The Publishing Settings options.

Creating a Cross-Platform File

If you plan to create a cross-platform version of your movie, you must first be fortunate enough to own a second computer and another copy of Director Shockwave Studio before you can accomplish this. On the Macintosh and PC (Windows), Director writes a binary, cross-platform file that will go over a network through an email server, or onto a zip disk with no translations or conversion problems. Thank Macromedia for some snazzy engineering on this one.

The only thing that you have to do is name your files with the dot-three extension if you plan to move the file from a Macintosh to the PC world. It's a good habit to name your Director movies with the DIR extension, as shown in the following: *filename*.DIR. You never know when the files will end up on a PC.

If you are going from a PC to a Macintosh, there is no necessary file naming or conversion to perform, as the Macintosh

OS can read PC files. You need to make sure that your Extension Manager does not turn off the Control Panel's File Exchange.

A Windows Director movie can then be copied directly to the desktop using a PC-formatted zip disk, CD-ROM, or floppy disk.

After your file is on the opposite platform, your car.dir movie will function properly; however, you should copy the Havok behaviors off the CD-ROM and install them in the Libs folder here. You'll want to use the behaviors on both platforms.

What About Lingo?

I specifically avoided using Lingo in this chapter to illustrate to you that you can create compelling, interactive movies even if you don't know much about Lingo. If you are itching to learn new Lingo, you will find it ahead!

CHAPTER 5

In This Chapter

Havok Cast Member Lingo Property Reference, 114

Havok Cast Member Lingo Function Reference, 117

Rigid Body Lingo Property Reference, 126

Rigid Body Lingo Function Reference, 132

Spring Lingo Property Reference, 135

Spring Lingo Function Reference, 136

Linear Dashpot Lingo Property Reference, 137

Linear Dashpot Lingo Function Reference, 138

Angular Dashpot Lingo Property Reference, 139

Angular Dashpot Lingo Function Reference, 140

Havok Lingo Reference

Havok.com, Inc. (© Copyright 2000/2001) provided the material for this chapter [5.1]. This chapter is meant to serve as a reference chapter. Many thanks go to the team at Havok for letting me distribute this information to the Shockwave 3D community. More information can be found at **www.havok.com/xtra**.

Remember the No .HKE Havok behavior? This chapter is the Lingo reference for that behavior. If you are a Lingo programmer, you can use commands to custom write your own Shockwave 3D movies from scratch, and you can give life to those 3D worlds using the Havok physics library. Outlined here, with slight modifications to give the material context, is the Lingo property reference library. For more information on Havok, visit them at **http://www.havok.com**.

Havok Cast Member Lingo Property Reference

You can access the properties discussed in the following sections through the Havok castmember. The Havok term in each property description indicates that you must access the property through a Havok Xtra castmember. It does not mean that the actual word Havok is part of the syntax. In the example code, the variable Havok is an instance of the Havok castmember, as shown in the following:

```
havok = member(havokCastMemberNumber)
```

The following sections include the properties, their appropriate syntax, the commands used to access them, and descriptions and examples of each.

havok.initialized

Syntax   `havok.initialized`   **Access**   Get

Description   This property returns the current state of the physical simulation.

Example   The following fragment of Lingo checks the simulation state before either initializing or stepping it:

```
if not havok.initialized then
    havok.initialize( member("scene"))
else
    havok.step( 0.025, 5 )
end if
```

havok.tolerance

Syntax   `havok.tolerance`   **Access**   Get

Description   This property holds the simulation's initial collision tolerance. See `havok.initialize()` under the Havok Cast Member Lingo Function Reference section for more information on collision tolerances.

Example   The example Lingo displays the current tolerance value:

```
put havok tolerance
-- 0.1
```

havok.scale

Syntax   `havok.scale`   **Access**   Get

Description   This property holds the current scaling factor for the simulation. See `havok.initialize()` under the Havok Cast Member Lingo Function Reference section for more information on simulation scale.

Example The following piece of Lingo displays the current scaling factor:

```
put havok.scale
-- 0.0254
```

havok.timeStep

Syntax havok.timeStep   **Access** Get/Set

Description This property holds the current time-step factor for the simulation. Time-step factor represents the amount of time that the physics simulation advances with each call to `havok.step()`. See `havok.step()` under the Havok Cast Member Lingo Function Reference section for more details.

havok.subSteps

Syntax havok.subSteps   **Access** Get/Set

Description This property holds the current number of substeps used by Havok during each call to `havok.step()`. See `havok.step()` under the Havok Cast Member Lingo Function Reference section for more details.

havok.simTime

Syntax havok.simTime   **Access** Get

Description This property holds the total physics time that has elapsed since the beginning of the Havok simulation. For example, the total number of time steps × time step.

havok.gravity

Syntax havok.gravity   **Access** Get/Set

Description This property holds the current force of gravity for the simulation. You specify gravity display units, so you need to be careful when setting it up. If using a scale factor of 1.0 (in meters, for example), then gravity should be (0, –9.81, 0) to act appropriately (this assumes that a positive Y is up).

Example The following Lingo example displays the current gravity before changing it:

```
put havok.gravity
-- vector( 0, 0, -386.22 )
havok.gravity = vector( 0, 0, -100 )
put havok.gravity
-- vector( 0, 0, -100.0 )
```

havok.rigidBody

Syntax havok.rigidBody   **Access** Get

Description This property is a list of the rigid bodies in the simulation.

Example The following piece of Lingo adds an anti-gravity force to all objects in the system:

```
repeat with i = 1 to havok.rigidbody.count
  havok.rigidBody[i].applyForce( -havok.gravity )
end repeat
```

havok.spring

Syntax havok.spring   **Access** Get

Description This property is a list of the springs in the simulation.

Example The following Lingo sets the rest of the length of the springs in the simulation to 10:

```
repeat with i = 1 to havok.spring.count
havok.spring[i].restLength = 10
end repeat
```

havok.linearDashpot

Syntax havok.linearDashpot   **Access** Get

Description This property shows a list of the linear dashpots in the simulation.

Example The Lingo sets the damping of the linear dashpots in the simulation to be 0.5:

```
repeat with i = 1 to havok.linearDashpot.count
havok.linearDashpot[i].damping = 0.5
end repeat
```

havok.angularDashpot

Syntax havok.angularDashpot   **Access** Get

Description This property shows a list of the angular dashpots in the simulation.

Example The following Lingo sets the damping of all the angular dashpots in the simulation to be 0.5:

```
repeat with i = 1 to havok.linearDashpot.count
havok.angularDashpot[i].damping = 0.5
end repeat
```

havok.collisionList

Syntax havok.collisionList   **Access** Get

Description This property returns the current collision list. This list is made up from zero or more sub-lists containing individual collision information. This information includes the names of the colliding bodies, the world position of the contact point, and the contact normal.

Example The following Lingo displays the current list of collisions within a physical simulation:

```
put havok.collisionList
-- [["BallWhite", "DisplayFelt", 83.6288, 2.1487,
15.0180, 0.0000,0.0000, 1.0000]]
```

havok.deactivationParameters

Syntax havok.deactivationParameters   **Access** Get/Set

Description This property is a list of two frequencies that simulations use to deactivate low-energy objects. Simulations check objects at regular intervals to decide whether or not they should be deactivated. To make deactivation more aggressive, raise the frequencies. To make it less aggressive, lower them. A deactivated object is removed from the physical simulation, and therefore, it takes no CPU time. It is still involved in collision testing, but purely in the case when objects hit it and reactivate it.

The property's two frequencies are short- and long-range deactivation parameters. In both cases, they refer to a time period during which the behaviors of the simulated objects are monitored. The short-range frequency selection specifies a time period during which Havok attempts to deactivate objects that move by very small amounts or not at all, and is typically 1/20th of a second. At times, objects are effectively at rest and should be deactivated, but due to the current time step or numerical error, they jitter. In such cases, the short-range, non-aggressive deactivator fails, as the objects are moving too much to be considered inactive. The long-range test is more aggressive but acts over a longer time period (typically, 10 seconds).

To turn off deactivation, either long-range or short-range, set the appropriate parameter to 0. To make either the short- or long-range deactivation more aggressive, increase the frequency value (a value of 60Hz when simulating with a frame rate of 60Hz is the most aggressive possible).

Example   The following Lingo displays the current frequencies used for deactivations. The default short frequency is 2 Hz (1/2 of a second period). The long frequency default is 0.1 Hz (10-second period):

```
put havok.deactivationParameters
-- [2.0000, 0.1000]
```

havok.dragParameters

Syntax   `havok.dragParameters`   **Access**   Get/Set

Description   This property is a list that contains the linear drag coefficient and the angular drag coefficient, respectively. The drag force is applied to oppose the motion of a rigid body and is applied equally to the bodies in a Havok simulation. At high values, the drag can nearly instantaneously oppose motion. A reasonable value for these is [0.1, 0.1].

Havok Cast Member Lingo Function Reference

You can access the following functions through the Havok castmember.

havok.initialize()

Syntax   `havok.initialize(W3DMember)`,
`havok.initialize(W3DMember, tolerance, worldScale)`

Description   You can create physical information for the Havok simulation in two ways. The first method for creating physical simulation information is through a modeling tool. The modeling tool that you use must support exporting .HKE files. You can import the .HKE file as a movie castmember using the File, Import menu options. .HKE files already contain world scaling information and tolerance (as specified within the 3D modeler), so you do not have to supply this value when initializing.

The second method for creating physical information is directly from the models within a 3D scene. In this case, you must create a blank Havok cast member using the Insert, Media Element, Havok Physics Scene menu option. It is very important that you establish the scale of the physics scene from the start. Internally, the Havok physics simulation employs the metric system (the default unit is meters). A W3D castmember may be created in any number of world units (meters, inches, feet, user, generic). The Havok Xtra interface can work with the same units as this W3D castmember. However, in order to perform the proper simulation, the Havok Xtra must know the correspondence between the display (3D scene) units and the simulation units.

You must provide a world-scaling factor when initializing the physical simulation. For example, if you designed a scene using inches, then you would supply a scaling value of 0.0254 (1 inch = 0.0254 meter). Be aware that any values in the scene, such as gravity, rest length of springs, and so on, are interpreted as scene units rather than internal physics units. That means that a real-world gravity value of 9.81 meters/second-squared, would have to be set as 386.22 inches/second-squared if you are working in inches.

You must also provide a collision tolerance parameter [5.2]. This tolerance is used to determine when objects are touching (for example, it determines if they are closer than the tolerance). In general, higher collision tolerance values yield more stable simulations. However, setting too high a value could lead to noticeable gaps between stacked objects. Thus, it is

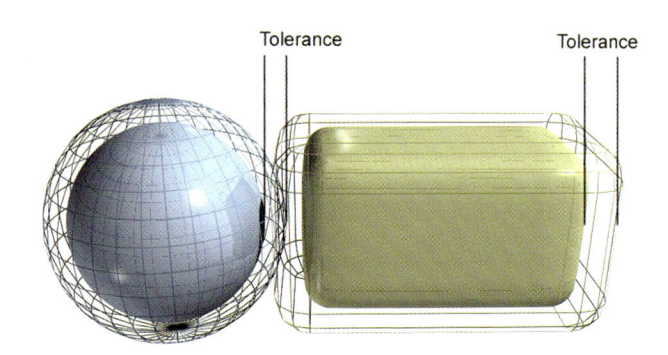

[5.2] The invisible collision-tolerance field that surrounds objects.

recommended that you set the collision tolerance to the highest value at which it does not visually affect the scene.

For example, if a scene consists of many objects in a room (crates, tables, chairs, and so on), a tolerance of around 0.1 m should be fine. However, if the objects in the scene are dice on a table, a smaller tolerance, such as 0.01 m or less, is preferable. If the objects are cars or buildings, a higher tolerance applies, and so on. If no value is supplied, then the default tolerance of 0.1 is used. As a general rule of thumb, set the tolerance value close to 10% of the scaling factor used in the simulation.

Example The world scale in the following example is set to 0.0254, as the scene was constructed in inches (i.e., 1 meter × 0.0254 = 1 inch), and the collision tolerance is set to 4.0 inches.

```
havok.initialize(member("MyScene"), 4.0, 0.0254)
```

> **Note**
>
> **Collision Tolerance** Collision tolerance is a value measured in scene units. That means that the scaling factor affects its actual value. `havok.initialize()` must be the first Havok function called or other Havok functions will have no effect on the scene.

havok.reset()

Syntax `havok.reset()`

Description This function resets the current physical simulation to its initial state. This is only appropriate for physical simulations initialized from an .HKE file where a `reset()` call reverts the entire scene back to the state defined in the .HKE file. A physical simulation not using an imported .HKE file has an initial state that contains no rigid bodies.

havok.step()

Syntax `havok.step()`, `havok.step(TimeIncrement)`, `havok.step(TimeIncrement, NumOfSubsteps)`

Description This function steps the physical simulation by the time increment and uses the specified number of sub-steps to super sample and splits that interval into smaller units. This function is usually called for each frame to advance the physics simulation by a small time period. To pause the simulation, simply refrain from calling `step()`. To achieve an approximate real-time performance, you should step the simulation according to the frame rate of the movie. For example, for a Director tempo of 60 frames per second, you should step the world 0.0167 seconds each frame (or, 1.0 / 60).

Example This steps the simulation by 0.0167 seconds (60 updates per second) with four internal sub-steps:

`havok.step(0.0167, 4)`

> **Note**
>
> **Absolute Frame Rates** The frame rate specified in Director is not necessarily the actual frame rate at which the movie plays. It depends on how long it takes Director to render the movie. To achieve true real-time performance, you need to keep track of elapsed absolute time. The number of sub-steps gives display-independent control over the accuracy of the simulation. You should always try to step the simulation with `NumOfSubSteps` being equal to 1, because it is the fastest.

Often, numerical instability results. For example, this can happen with large stacks. Increasing the number of sub-steps causes the simulation to make a number of passes over the simulation for each call to `step()`. This gives more accurate results, but it does so at the cost of additional CPU overhead.

havok.shutdown()

Syntax `havok.shutdown()`

Description This function stops the current simulation and removes it from memory.

> **Note**
>
> **`havok.shutdown()` Versus `shutdown()`** Be careful not to confuse `havok.shutdown()` with Director's `shutdown()` function, which attempts to shut down your computer.

havok.rigidBody()

Syntax havok.rigidBody(RBName)

Description This function queries the physical simulation for a rigid body of a given name. If it finds the rigid body, it returns a reference for it. You can use this to alter properties and call functions on rigid bodies.

Example The following Lingo looks for a rigid body and then sets its position to the origin of the world:

```
rb = havok.rigidBody(model.name)
rb.position = Vector(0.0, 0.0, 0.0)
```

havok.deleteRigidBody()

Syntax havok.deleteRigidBody(RBName or RBIndex)

Description This function removes a rigid body from the physics simulation giving the rigid body a name or index.

Example:

```
havok.deleteRigidBody( "WhiteBall" )
```

havok.makeMovableRigidBody()

Syntax havok.makeMovableRigidBody(modelName, mass), havok.makeMovableRigidBody(modelName, mass, isConvex), havok.makeMovableRigidBody(modelName, mass, true, type)

Description This function creates a movable rigid body with a specified mass greater than zero (specified in kilograms) from a model of name modelName, and adds it to the simulation. The optional Boolean flag, isConvex, indicates whether the new rigid body is to be convex or concave. The default is convex. In addition, if you specify the type of parameter to be convex (for example, true), you can then construct a bounding sphere (#sphere) or axis-aligned box (#box) rather than the default convex hull. It is easier and faster to use convex geometries to resolve collisions, so you should use them whenever possible. A convex body is one where a line drawn from its inside to the outside can only cross the object's boundary one time. Convex objects cannot have holes, hollows, or loops such as a teapot's handle [5.3]. Concave geometries have no geometric restrictions, but their collision resolution is much more complex and slower as a result [5.3].

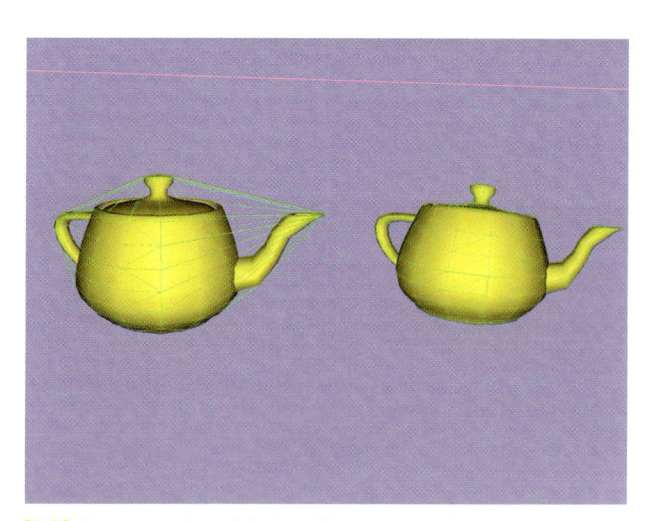

[5.3] Representation of the invisible convex and concave surrounding fields.

Example   The following code first creates a movable rigid body, 1kg in mass, from the object called WhiteBall, and it uses a convex hull representation by default. The second line also creates a moveable rigid body of 1kg mass, but it uses a bounding sphere for the physical representation.

```
havok.makeMovableRigidBody("WhiteBall", 1)
havok.makeMovableRigidBody("WhiteBall", 1, true,
#sphere)
```

Note

Rigid Body   When you are creating a rigid body from a model, you must add the `meshdeform` modifier to the model. For example, you would use `model.addModifier(#meshDeform)`. Otherwise, the Havok Xtra cannot access the geometry of the model. The convex representation of a rigid body is called a *convex hull*. When you create a convex hull for a new rigid body, the resulting mesh is heavily dependent on the original mesh of the object. Havok does handle a lot of co-planar polygons easily, which is common in 3D elements, such as extruded text. The resulting convex hull can have many badly formed triangles that seriously degrade performance, and in some rare cases, this can cause failure of the collision detection. In these cases, you are better off using the geometry itself by creating the rigid body as concave. Alternatively, you could use a bounding box.

havok.makeFixedRigidBody()

Syntax   `havok.makeFixedRigidBody(modelName)`, `havok.makeFixedRigidBody(modelName, isConvex)`, `havok.makeFixedRigidBody(modelName, true, type)`

Description   This function creates a fixed rigid body from a model of modelName and adds it to the simulation. The optional Boolean flag, `isConvex`, indicates whether the new rigid body is convex or concave (see havok.makeMovableRigidBody). The default value is convex. Fixed rigid bodies never move, but are still involved in collision detection. These are most often used for scenery elements, such as walls.

Example:

`havok.makeFixedRigidBody( "PoolTable", false )`

Note

Creating a Rigid Body   When you create a rigid body from a model, you must add the `meshdeform` modifier to it, as in `model.addModifier(#meshDeform)`. If you don't add the meshdeform modifier, then the Havok Xtra cannot access the geometry of the model. Fixed bodies do not have mass. Mass is a property that only makes sense for objects that are free to move.

havok.registerInterest()

Syntax   `havok.registerInterest(RBName1, RBName2, Frequency, Threshold)`, `havok.registerInterest(RBName1, RBName2, Frequency, Threshold, \#LingoHandler, scriptInstance)`

Description   This function allows for the detection of specific collisions between rigid bodies and for the passing of details of the collision to a specified Lingo callback handler. The following information is passed to a callback handler in the form of a list:

> **RBName1** This is the name of the first object involved in the collision.

> **RBName2** This is the name of the second object involved in the collision. Use #all if you want all the collisions between RBName1 and every other rigid body in the scene.

> **Contact Point** This is the point of collision between the two objects.

> **Contact Normal** The object's collision direction [5.4], which is the normal of the second object at the point of collision.

> **Normal Relative Velocity (NRV)** This is the relative velocity of the two objects involved in the collision.

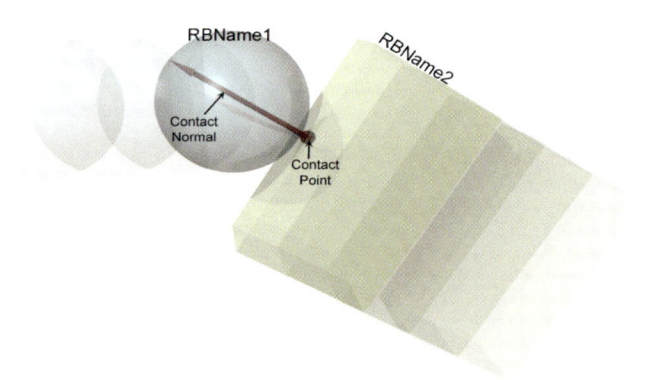

[5.4] The object's collision direction is the Contact Normal.

This value is the sum of the absolute value of the objects' velocities in the direction of the collision normal. Thus, for two spheres, each traveling at 10 m/second directly toward one another, the NRV would be 20 m/second. If you do not specify a collision handler, then collision information is simply added to a collision list, which you can access using the havok.collisionList function. If the type #all is passed in for RBName2, then any collision involving RBName1 initiates a callback. Frequency determines how often a collision is recorded. Applications that require callbacks for every collision should set a frequency of zero. The value that you set for the frequency determines the number of callbacks per second. For example, when you set the frequency at 10, you only get 10 events raised every second, which invokes the callback a maximum of 10 times each second. Threshold specifies how strong a collision must be before the Lingo callback is invoked. Threshold is defined in terms of the normal relative velocity (for example, meters per second), which is the relative speed of the objects in collision. Positive values indicate that the objects are heading toward each other.

Example The following Lingo fragment registers interest in collisions involving the rigid bodies named rb1 and rb2. When this collision occurs, the Lingo handler, collisionHandler, displays the collision point in the message window:

```
havok.registerInterest(rb1,rb2,0,0,#collisionHandler,
↪me)
on collisionHandler(me, collisionDetails)
put collisionDetails
end
```

To register interest in only collisions involving `rb1` and `rb2`, where they collide at a relative velocity greater than 10 m/second, use the following:

`havok.registerInterest(rb1,rb2,0,10,#collisionHandler,`
`➥me)`

Note

Rigid Bodies You must provide a rigid body name for `RBName1`.

havok.removeInterest()

Syntax `havok.removeInterest(RBName)`

Description This function stops collisions involving the specified rigid body being recorded.

Example

`havok.removeInterest(rb.name)`

havok.disableCollision()

Syntax `havok.disableCollision(RBNameA, RBNameB)`

Description This function disables any collision between two rigid bodies identified by their names.

havok.enableCollision()

Syntax `havok.enableCollision(RBNameA, RBNameB)`

Description This function re-enables any collision between two rigid bodies identified by their names.

havok.disableAllCollisions()

Syntax `havok.disableAllCollisions(RBNameA)`

Description This function disables any collision between the rigid body of a given name and the other objects in the physics simulation.

havok.enableAllCollisions()

Syntax `havok.enableAllCollisions(RBNameA)`

Description This function re-enables collisions between a rigid body with a given name and the other objects in the simulation.

havok.registerStepCallback()

Syntax `havok.rcgisterStepCallback(#stepHandler, scriptInstance)`

Description During each simulation step, the Havok engine may take a number of sub-steps (specified by the `havok.subSteps` property). This function allows the users to register a callback to a Lingo handler that gets called at each sub-step passing the length of time since the last sub-step. This allows behaviors to be written that are called after each step of the physics engine. This is important for behaviors involving real-world parameters.

Example The following Lingo fragment registers the step callback to the Lingo `stepHandler`:

```
havok.registerStepCallback(#stepHandler, me )
on stepHandler(me, timeStep)
put "I've been called"
end stepHandler
```

havok.removeStepCallback()

Syntax   `havok.removeStepCallback(#stepHandler, scriptInstance)`

Description   This function removes the callback to the given handler and its script instance.

havok.spring()

Syntax   `havok.spring(SpringName)`

Description   This function queries the physical simulation for the spring of a given name. If it finds the spring, it returns a reference for it. You can then use this for altering properties and calling functions on springs.

Example   The following Lingo code looks for a spring and then sets its rest length to 5:

```
spring = havok.spring( "TheSpring" )
spring.restLength = 5
```

havok.makeSpring()

Syntax   `havok.makeSpring(SpringName, RBNameA, RBNameB)`, `havok.makeSpring(SpringName, RBName, WorldPoint)`

Description   A spring is an object with a preferred rest length, which is attached to a pair of objects. When the spring is stretched or squashed, it attempts to restore equilibrium by applying a restoring force to the attached objects.

The first version of this function makes a spring between the centers of mass for two named rigid bodies. The second version of this function makes a spring between a rigid body with its name (RBName), and a world point.

Example   The following Lingo code creates a spring between the center of mass of two rigid bodies:

```
spring = havok.makeSpring("MySpring", "Box1", "Box2")
```

havok.deleteSpring()

Syntax   `havok.deleteSpring(SpringName)`, `havok.deleteSpring(SpringIndex)`

Description   This function removes the spring of a given name or index from the physics simulation, as shown here:

```
havok.deleteSpring("TheSpring")
```

havok.linearDashpot()

Syntax   `havok.linearDashpot(LinearDashpotName)`

Description   This function queries the physical simulation for a linear dashpot of a given name. If it finds the linear dashpot, it returns a reference for it. You can then use this to alter properties and call functions on linear dashpots.

Example The following Lingo code looks for an angular dashpot and then sets the damping to 0.5.

```
dashpot = havok.linearDashpot("TheLinearDashpot")
dashpot.damping = 0.5
```

havok.makeLinearDashpot()

Syntax `havok.makeLinearDashpot(DashName, RBNameA, RBNameB)`, `havok.makeLinearDashpot(DashName, RBName, WorldPoint)`

Description A linear dashpot is a heavily damped zero-length spring. It applies forces to objects when the velocities of their attached points begin to differ. Dashpots can be made stiffer than regular springs because velocities are taken into account. In addition, you can use a dashpot to attach a point on a body to a fixed point in world space. The first version of this function makes a linear dashpot between the centers of mass of two rigid bodies that are named.

The second version of this function makes a linear dashpot between a rigid body given a rigid body's name (`RBName`), and a point in world space where the other end of the dashpot is attached (`WorldPoint`).

Example This following Lingo code creates a linear dashpot between the centers of mass of two rigid bodies:

```
dashpot = havok.makeLinearDashpot
➥("MyDash","Box1","Box2")
```

havok.deleteLinearDashpot()

Syntax `havok.deleteLinearDashpot(DashpotName)`, `havok.deleteLinearDashpot(DashpotIndex)`

Description This function removes a linear dashpot of a given name or index from the physics simulation.

Example:

```
havok.deleteLinearDashpot("TheDashpot")
```

havok.angularDashpot()

Syntax `havok.angularDashpot(AngularDashpotName)`

Description This function queries the physical simulation for an angular dashpot of a given name. If it finds the angular dashpot, it returns a reference for it. You can use this to alter properties and call functions on angular dashpots.

Example The following code looks for an angular dashpot and then sets the damping to 0.5:

```
angularDashpot = havok.angularDashpot
➥("TheAngularDashpot")
angularDashpot.damping = 0.5
```

havok.makeAngularDashpot()

Syntax `havok.makeAngularDashpot(DashName, RBNameA, RBNameB)`, `havok.makeAngularDashpot(DashName, RBName)`

Description An angular dashpot is the rotation equivalent of a linear dashpot. An angular dashpot tries to align two objects so that they have the same orientation. If the objects' orientations differ, forces are applied to both bodies that push them closer to the same orientation. You can also use an angular dashpot to align a single body to an orientation in world space.

The first version of this function makes an angular dashpot between two rigid bodies given their names (`RBNameA` and `RBNameB`). The initial rotation is the zero-angle. The second version of this function makes an angular dashpot between a rigid body (`RBName`) and the reference frame. The initial rotation is the zero-angle.

Example   The following Lingo code creates an angular dashpot between the two named rigid bodies:

```
angDashpot = havok.makeAngularDashpot("My Dash", "Box1",
➥"Box2")
```

havok.deleteAngularDashpot()

Syntax   `havok.deleteAngularDashpot(AngularDashpotName)`, `havok.deleteAngularDashpot(AngularDashpotIndex)`

Description   This function removes an angular dashpot of a given name or index from the physics simulation:

```
havok.deleteAngularDashpot( "TheAngularDashpot" )
```

Rigid Body Lingo Property Reference

The properties discussed in the following sections can be accessed through a Havok rigid body that can be obtained from a Havok cast member using the following function:

```
havok.rigidBody(RBName) or havok.rigidBody[i]
```

The word `hkRigidBody` has been added in front of each property description in order to indicate that access must be made through an `hkRigidBody`. This notation is equivalent to the use of "havok" in other chapters. In the example code, the variable `rb` is an instance of an `hkRigidBody`:

```
rb = member(havokCastMemberNumber).rigidBody("Box01")
```

`RigidBody()` can take either a string name or an index number to identify the castmember.

hkRigidBody.name

Syntax   `hkRigidBody.name`   **Access**   Get

Description   This property returns the name of a rigid body. In general, this equates to the rigid body's display equivalent in the 3D scene.

Example   The following fragment of Lingo displays the name of a rigid body in the message window.

```
put rb.name
-- "Box01"
```

hkRigidBody.position

Syntax   `hkRigidBody.position`   **Access**   Get/Set

Description   This property sets or gets the position of a rigid body. Position is in the form of a Director vector object.

Example   The following fragment of Lingo sets the position **[5.5]** of a rigid body to position (2.0, 3.0, 4.0), and then displays the position in the message window:

```
rb.position = vector(2.0, 3.0, 4.0)
put rb.position
-- vector( 2.0000, 3.0000, 4.0000 )
```

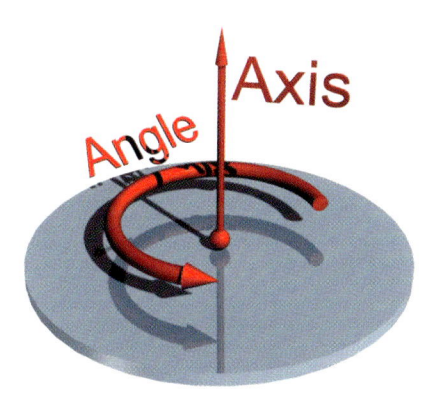

[5.5] Setting the position of the rigid body.

Note

Rigid Body Position   If you place a rigid body in a position so that it interpenetrates another rigid body, collisions between these two rigid bodies is not resolved. See hkRigidBody.attemptMoveTo() for additional information.

hkRigidBody.rotation

Syntax   hkRigidBody.rotation   **Access**   Get/Set

Description   You can use this property to set or get the rotation of a rigid body. Rotation is in the form of a Director list containing a vector object that indicates the rotation axis and a real number indicating rotation angle. Rotations use the right-hand rule (for example, point the thumb of your right hand in the direction of the axis of rotation and the fingers curl in the direction of the rotation). Angles are specified in degrees.

Example   The following fragment of Lingo script gets the rotation of a rigid body and displays it in the message window:

```
put rb.rotation
-- [vector( 1.0000, 0.0000, 0.0000 ), 90.0000]
```

Note

Resolving Collision   If you place a rigid body in an orientation such that it interpenetrates another rigid body, then collisions between these two rigid bodies is not resolved. See hkRigid-Body.attemptMoveTo() for additional information.

hkRigidBody.mass

Syntax   hkRigidBody.mass   **Access**   Get/Set

Description   You can use this property to set or get the mass of a rigid body (specified in kilograms).

Example   The following fragment of Lingo script displays the mass of a rigid body in the message window:

```
put rb.mass
-- 1.0000
```

Note

Movable Rigid Bodies   Only movable rigid bodies can have mass. If a fixed rigid body needs mass, then create it as a movable rigid body and lock its position.

hkRigidBody.restitution

Syntax hkRigidBody.restitution   **Access** Get/Set

Description You can use this property to set or get the restitution or bounciness of a rigid body. Restitution relates to an object's energy loss or gain after a collision. If an object has a restitution value of zero, then all energy is lost on collision and it does not bounce. A restitution value of 1 gives a perfect bounce. A restitution value greater than 1 means a bouncing object gains energy after each collision. Thus, a bouncing ball would reach a higher height each time it hits the floor.

Example The following fragment of Lingo script sets the restitution of a rigid body:

```
rb.restitution = 0 -- no bounce

rb.restitution = 1 -- perfect bounce

rb.restitution = 0.5 -- lose 50% of energy after each
➥bounce
```

hkRigidBody.friction

Syntax hkRigidBody.friction   **Access** Get/Set

Description You use this to set or get the coefficient of friction or stickiness of a rigid body. A value of 0 equals no friction; typical values are 0.8–1.0. Friction relates to how much force is required to move or roll one rigid body over another. If a sliding object has a friction value of zero, then it never stops sliding. In reality, there are two forms of friction: dynamic and static. Objects moving relative to each other (such as sliding) use dynamic friction. Objects at rest and stacked are held in place by static friction. The transition from static to dynamic friction is crucial to the realism of a physics simulation. It is a difficult problem to solve in general. For example, when you strike a pool ball with a cue, it initially slides over the surface of the pool table and slows due to dynamic friction. Eventually, it catches and begins to roll. Static friction takes over and maintains the contact between the ball and table converting forward momentum into torque. This causes the ball to spin or roll. The ball eventually comes to rest due to energy loss resulting from the static friction.

Havok Xtra requires only a single value of friction to be specified, but internally it fully simulates both static and dynamic friction behaviors and the transition between them.

Example The following fragment of Lingo script sets the friction of a rigid body:

```
rb.friction = 0 -- slide forever
```

Note

Friction For objects in contact you need to specify both friction parameters to get the desired result. The friction used is the square root of the sum of the squares of the friction coefficients.

hkRigidBody.active

Syntax hkRigidBody.active   **Access** Get/Set

Description You may use this property to set or get regardless of whether a movable, rigid body is active. A deactivated object never moves until struck by another object or because of a force that acts upon it.

Example The following Lingo code deactivates an object if it falls outside a specified distance from the world origin:

```
if rb.position.length > 10000 then
rb.active = false
end if
```

hkRigidBody.pinned

Syntax hkRigidBody.pinned   **Access** Get/Set

Description You can use this property to set or get regardless of whether or not a movable, rigid body is pinned in place. A pinned object never moves when struck by another object, but it may be released under Lingo control at a later point in the simulation. This is unlike an object initially created as fixed.

Example The following Lingo code fixes a movable, rigid body if it's currently movable:

```
if not rb.pinned then
rb.pinned = true -- fix body
end if
```

hkRigidBody.linearVelocity

Syntax hkRigidBody.linearVelocity   **Access** Get/Set

Description Use this property to set or get the linear velocity of a rigid body. A Lingo vector specifies the value. Linear velocity is simply the speed of the object. The magnitude of the velocity vector is the actual speed of the body, and the vector specifies the direction in which the object is moving.

Example The following fragment of Lingo script prints the linear velocity of a rigid body, which, in this case, is moving at 10 units per second in the positive Z direction.

```
put rb.linearVelocity
-- vector( 0.0000, 0.0000, 10.0000 )
```

hkRigidBody.angularVelocity

Syntax hkRigidBody.angularVelocity   **Access** Get/Set

Description Use this property to set or get the angular velocity of a rigid body [5.6]. A Lingo vector specifies the value of the velocity. The magnitude of the vector determines the speed in degrees per second, counterclockwise (CCW) about the specified axis. The normalized vector, or the unit length version of the vector, gives its axis. Thus, an angular velocity of 2.0, 0.0, 0.0 corresponds to a rotation speed of 2.0 degrees per second, counterclockwise around the positive x-axis.

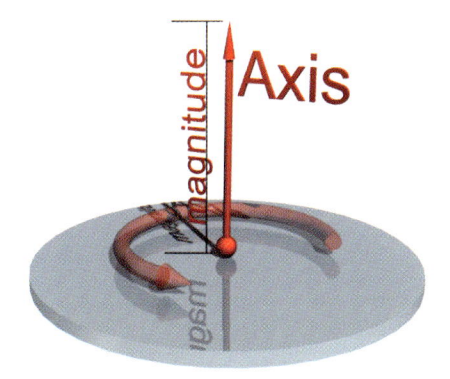

[5.6] The magnitude vector and rotation axis.

Example The following fragment of Lingo script prints the angular velocity of a rigid body.

```
put rb.angularVelocity
-- vector( 10.0000, 0.0000, 0.0000 )
```

hkRigidBody.linearMomentum

Syntax   hkRigidBody.linearMomentum   **Access**   Get/Set

Description This property is used to set or get the linear momentum of a rigid body. A Lingo vector specifies the value. Momentum is mass multiplied by velocity.

Example The following script sets the linear momentum of a rigid body:

```
rb.linearMomentum = vector(1, 0, 0) × rb.mass
```

hkRigidBody.angularMomentum

Syntax   hkRigidBody.angularMomentum   **Access**   Get/Set

Description This property is used to set or get the angular momentum of a rigid body. A Lingo vector specifies the value.

Example The following fragment of Lingo script sets the angular momentum of a rigid body:

```
rb.angularMomentum = vector(1, 0, 0) × rb.mass
```

hkRigidBody.force

Syntax   hkRigidBody.force   **Access**   Get

Description Use this property to get the current total force acting on a rigid body. The total force acting on a body depends on the forces applied through the Lingo script and the forces applied by the Havok system during simulation.

Example The following fragment of Lingo script puts the current force on a rigid body to the message window:

```
put rb.force
-- vector(15.0000, 0.0000, -9.8100)
```

hkRigidBody.torque

Syntax   hkRigidBody.torque   **Access**   Get

Description Use this property to get the current torque on a rigid body. Torque is the angular analog of force. You should apply a torque to induce a spin in an object. Torque, like angular velocity, is a single vector. The vector's magnitude is that of the exerted torque. The normalized vector specifies the axis about which the torque exerts.

Example The following fragment of Lingo script displays the current torque exerted on a rigid body in the message window:

```
put rb.torque
-- vector(0.0000, 10.0000, 0.0000)
```

hkRigidBody.centerOfMass

Syntax   hkRigidBody.centerOfMass   **Access**   Get

Description This property gives the user the offset from the model's origin to the rigid body's center of mass.

hkRigidBody.corrector.enabled

Syntax   `hkRigidBody.corrector.enabled`   **Access**   Get/Set

Description   This property enables or disables the corrector for a particular rigid body. It can be set to true or false. For more details, see the `hkRigidBody.correctorMoveTo` function.

hkRigidBody.corrector.threshold

Syntax   `hkRigidBody.corrector.threshold`

Access   Get/Set

Description   This property is used to determine how close the body is to the final destination before any reckoning occurs (see `hkRigidBody.corrector.level` for the different reckoning levels). This is measured in design units. The Havok simulation will set this to a default parameter depending on the scene. The user may wish to change it. A reasonable threshold is 0.01–0.7, depending on the design of the scene. If the threshold is too small, the corrector may go into an infinite loop (never arriving at the exact position). If the threshold is too large, the corrector may have little or no effect on the body.

hkRigidBody.corrector.multiplier

Syntax   `hkRigidBody.corrector.multiplier`

Access   Get/Set

Description   This property is used to determine how fast a rigid body will move to its destination using `hkRigidBody.correctorMoveTo`. A multiplier value of 1.0 gives one unit of time to get to the destination. With a very high multiplier, the objects may hit each other with too much force. The default for this parameter is 5.0.

hkRigidBody.corrector.level

Syntax   `hkRigidBody.corrector.level`   **Access**   Get/Set

Description   This property sets the reckoning level of the corrector. The levels are:

> - **0** Hold: never stop correcting (HOLD)
> - **1** No dead reckoning (leave, go with velocities equivalent to 0)
> - **2** Dead reckoning (set velocities)
> - **3** The 2nd order reckoning (set accelerations)

hkRigidBody.corrector.maxTries

Syntax   `hkRigidBody.corrector.maxTries`

Access   Get/Set

Description   The property is the number of attempts made to move the rigid body to its final destination during an `hkRigidBody.correctorMoveTo` (if blocked).

hkRigidBody.corrector.maxDistance

Syntax   `hkRigidBody.corrector.maxDistance`

Access   Get/Set

Description   For this property, if the difference between the current position of the body and the desired position of the body is greater than the maxDistance property, then the corrector will simply move the rigid body to its desired position.

Rigid Body Lingo Function Reference

You can access the properties in the following sections through a Havok rigid body, which you can obtain from a Havok castmember using the following function:

`havok.rigidBody(RBName)`

or

`havok.rigidBody[RBNum]`

Each entry is preceded by an `hkRigid` body tag to indicate the method of access:

`rb = member(havokCastMemberNumber).rigidBody("Box01")`

hkRigidBody.applyForce()

Syntax   `hkRigidBody.applyForce(force)`

Description   This function applies a force to a rigid body at its center of mass. A Lingo vector specifies the value of this force. An example application of applying a force would be applying the brakes in a car, which takes time to have an effect. Applying a force at the center of mass does not affect the spin of the object.

Example   The following fragment of Lingo script applies an anti-gravity force to a rigid body:

```
grav = havok.gravity()
rb.applyForce( -grav )
```

hkRigidBody.applyForceAtPoint()

Syntax   `hkRigidBody.applyForceAtPoint(force, point)`

Description   This function applies a force to a rigid body at a specified point in model space. Lingo vectors specify the value of the force and the position. Forces applied at points other than the center of mass of an object induce a torque effect, causing the object to spin.

Note

Force Point   The model space point does not have to be on or contained within the object. It works as though a lever connects the specified point to the object's center of mass and the force applies to the end of the lever.

hkRigidBody.applyImpulse()

Syntax   `hkRigidBody.applyImpulse(impulse)`

Description   This function applies an impulse to a rigid body at its center of mass. A Lingo vector specifies the value of the impulse. An example of a stopped impulse would be like a car hitting a wall, whereby the car stops immediately. An impulse, unlike a force, has an immediate effect on the velocity of the rigid body so it gives it a greater degree of control over the object.

Example   The following fragment of Lingo script applies an impulse to a rigid body straight up in the air:

`rb.applyImpulse(vector(0.0, 0.0, 100.0))`

hkRigidBody.applyImpulseAtPoint()

Syntax   `hkRigidBody.applyImpulseAtPoint(impulse, point)`

Description   This function applies an impulse to a rigid body at a specified point relative to the position of the model. Lingo vectors specify the value of the impulse and the position. Similar to forces at a point, applying an impulse at a point other than the center of mass of an object induces a torque effect, causing that object to spin.

Example   The following fragment of Lingo script applies an impulse to a rigid body in its up direction. As the impulse is offset from the object's center of mass, the body acquires an angular velocity:

```
rb.applyImpulseAtPoint(Vector(0.0, 0.0, 100.0),
➥Vector(0, 0, 5))
```

hkRigidBody.applyTorque()

Syntax   `hkRigidBody.applyTorque(torque)`

Description   This function applies torque to a rigid body at its center of mass. A Lingo vector specifies the value of the torque. The magnitude of the vector determines the size of the torque. The normalized vector gives the axis for which the torque is applied.

Example   The following Lingo script applies a torque of magnitude 10 times the mass of the rigid body inducing a CCW rotation about the positive x-axis. This effectively works just like a motor action on the object along the its local x-axis:

```
rb = havok.rigidBody("FrontLeftWheel")
rb.applyTorque(Vector(10.0, 0.0, 0.0) × rb.mass)
```

hkRigidBody.applyAngularImpulse()

Syntax   `hkRigidBody.applyAngularImpulse(impulse)`

Description   This function applies an angular impulse to a rigid body at its center of mass. A Lingo vector specifies the value of the impulse. The magnitude of the vector determines the size of the impulse. The normalized vector gives the axis for which the impulse is applied. An angular impulse has an immediate effect on the angular velocity of the object in a similar way that an impulse has an immediate effect on the linear velocity of an object.

Example   The following Lingo script applies an angular impulse of a magnitude of 100 to a rigid body. This applies a twist around the object's local z-axis.

```
rb.applyAngularImpulse(vector(0.0, 0.0, 100.0))
```

hkRigidBody.attemptMoveTo()

Syntax   `hkRigidBody.attemptMoveTo(position, rotation)`

Description   This function takes a position (vector) and a rotation (in the form of a list containing an axis and an angle, expressed as a vector and a floating-point value respectively). The function attempts to move the rigid body to a position and orientation specified by the three parameters. If the rigid body is in an acceptable physical state when repositioned, such as not interpenetrating, it is left there and the function returns true [5.7]. Otherwise, the function returns false. In both examples, the function returns false.

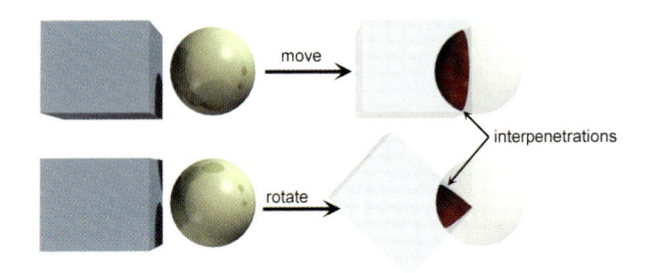

[5.7] Objects will not move if they interpenetrate with another object.

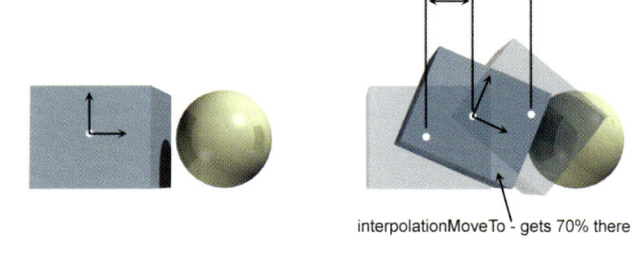

[5.8] When attempting to move an object from one point to another, the object cannot end its motion inside another object.

Example The following Lingo script attempts to position a rigid body at world coordinates (0, 0, 100) with its initial orientation:

```
m = rb.attemptMoveTo(vector(0,0,100), [vector(0,1,0), 0])
if not m then
  put "Move Failed"
end if
```

hkRigidBody.interpolatingMoveTo()

Syntax hkRigidBody.interpolatingMoveTo(position, rotation)

Description This function takes a position (vector) and a rotation (passed in the form of a list containing an axis and an angle, expressed as a vector and a floating-point value, respectively). The function attempts to move the rigid body to a position and orientation specified by the three parameters. If the rigid body is not in an acceptable physical state when repositioned, such as interpenetrating another object, it is moved back from the specified position to the first valid point along a direct path from its initial position to the specified position [5.8].

This returns a floating-point value between 0 and 1.0 indicates that the rigid body cannot move from its initial location. A value of 1 indicates that the object has been successfully repositioned where specified. A value of 0.5 means the object has been repositioned to exactly halfway between its initial position and the desired location. This value also applies to the orientation, both axis and angle.

Example This Lingo script attempts to position a rigid body at world coordinates (0, 0, 100) with its initial orientation. It then prints the result:

```
newPos = vector(0, 0, 100)
newRot = [vector(0, 1, 0), 0]
d = rb.interpolatingMoveTo(newPos, newRot)
put "Got " & (d × 100) & "% of the way there"
```

hkRigidBody.correctorMoveTo()

Syntax   hkRigidBody.correctorMoveTo(position, rotation), hkRigidBody.correctorMoveTo(position, rotation, linearVelocity, \ angularVelocity), hkRigidBody.correctorMoveTo(position, rotation, linearVelocity, \ angularVelocity, linearAcceleration, angularAcceleration)

Description   A corrector receives a desired state for a body through this function. The corrector will then attempt to bring the body to that desired state. This corrector uses impulses to get a body to a desired position. If the body's current position is greater than the maximum distance away from the desired position of the property of the corrector, the body will be moved to the desired position. The first function sets the position and rotation of the body. The second version of this function sets position, rotation, linear velocity, and angular velocity. The third version sets position, rotation, linear velocity, angular velocity, linear acceleration, and angular acceleration.

Spring Lingo Property Reference

You can access the properties in the following sections through a Havok spring, which you can obtain from a Havok castmember using the following functions:

havok.spring(SpringName)

or

havok.spring[i]

The hkSpring of each property description below indicates your means of access to them. It does not mean that the actual word hkSpring is part of the syntax. In the example code, the variable spring is an instance of an hkSpring:

spring = member(havokCastMemberNumber).spring
➥("Spring01")

hkSpring.name

Syntax   hkSpring.name   **Access**   Get

Description   This property gets the name of the spring.

hkSpring.pointA

Syntax   hkSpring.pointA   **Access**   Get/Set

Description   This property contains the position on rigid body A to which the spring is attached. The position is relative to rigid body A.

Example   The following code attaches the spring to the origin of rigid body A:

newPos = vector(0, 0, 0)
spring.pointA = newPos

hkSpring.pointB

Syntax   hkSpring.pointB   **Access**   Get/Set

Description   This property contains the position on rigid body A to which the spring is attached. The position is relative to rigid body B. If there is no rigid body B, then this point is a point in world space to which the spring is attached.

Example   The following code attaches the spring to the origin of rigid body B:

```
newPos = vector(0, 0, 0)
spring.pointB = newPos
```

hkSpring.restLength

Syntax   hkSpring.restLength   **Access**   Get/Set

Description   This property contains the rest length of the spring.

Example   The following Lingo code sets the rest of the length of the string to 10:

```
spring.restLength = 10
```

hkSpring.elasticity

Syntax   hkSpring.elasticity   **Access**   Get/Set

Description   This property contains the elasticity of the spring. The higher the elasticity is, the stronger the spring.

Example   The following code sets the elasticity of the spring to 0.5:

```
spring.elasticity = 0.5
```

hkSpring.damping

Syntax   hkSpring.damping   **Access**   Get/Set

Description   This property contains the damping value for the spring. Higher damping values cause the spring to come to a rest quickly. If specified too high, however, this can lead to numerically unstable solutions.

Example   This code sets the damping of the spring to 0.5:

```
spring.damping = 0.5
```

hkSpring.onCompression

Syntax   hkSpring.onCompression   **Access**   Get/Set

Description   If this property is set to true, the spring applies a restoring force when compressed (for example, the distance between `pointA` and `pointB` is less than the rest of the length). If the property is false, it does not apply a compressed force.

hkSpring.onExtension

Syntax   hkSpring.onExtension   **Access**   Get/Set

Description   If this property is set to true, the spring applies a restoring force when extended (for example, the distance between `pointA` and `pointB` is greater than the rest length). If the property is false, it does not.

Spring Lingo Function Reference

You can access the functions in the following sections through a Havok spring, which you can obtain from a Havok cast-member using the function:

```
havok.spring(SpringName)
```

or

```
havok.spring[i]
```

The `hkSpring` of each function description indicates your means of access to them. It does not mean that the actual word `hkSpring` is part of the syntax. In the example code, the variable spring is an instance of an `hkSpring`:

```
spring = member(havokCastMemberNumber).spring
➥("Spring01")
```

hkSpring.setRigidBodyA()

Syntax   `hkSpring.setRigidBodyA(RBName)`

Description   This function sets the rigid body connected to the first end of the spring (pointA, by convention).

hkSpring.setRigidBodyB()

Syntax   `hkSpring.setRigidBodyB(RBName)`, `hkSpring.setRigidBodyB("none")`

Description   This function sets the rigid body connected to the second end of the spring (pointB, by convention). If you pass #none as a parameter here the spring will be attached to a world point, specified by the spring property pointB.

hkSpring.getRigidBodyA()

Syntax   `hkSpring.getRigidBodyA(RBName)`

Description   This function returns the name of the rigid body connected to the first end of the spring. If it is not connected to a rigid body, it will return #none.

hkSpring.getRigidBodyB()

Syntax   `hkSpring.getRigidBodyB(RBName)`

Description   This function returns the name of the rigid body connected to the second end of the spring. If it is not connected to a rigid body, it will return #none.

Linear Dashpot Lingo Property Reference

You can access the properties in the following sections through a Havok linear dashpot, which you can obtain from a Havok castmember using the following functions:

`havok.linearDashpot(LinearDashpotName)`

or

`havok.linearDashpot[i]`

The `hkLinearDashpot` of each property description indicates your means of access to them. It does not mean that the actual word `hkLinearDashpot` is part of the syntax. In the example code, the variable linearDashpot is an instance of an `hkLinearDashpot` as shown here:

```
linearDashpot =
member(havokCastMemberNumber).linearDashpot
➥("LinearDashpot")
```

hkLinearDashpot.name

Syntax   `hkLinearDashpot.name`   **Access**   Get

Description   This property contains the name of the linear dashpot.

hkLinearDashpot.pointA

Syntax hkLinearDashpot.pointA   **Access** Get/Set

Description This property contains the position on rigid body A to which the linear dashpot is attached. The position is relative to rigid body A.

Example This code attaches the linear dashpot to the center of mass of rigid body A:

```
newPos = vector(0, 0, 0)
linearDashpot.pointA = newPos
```

hkLinearDashpot.pointB

Syntax hkLinearDashpot.pointB   **Access** Get/Set

Description If the linear dashpot is attached to another rigid body, this property contains the position on rigid body B to which the linear dashpot is attached. The position is relative to rigid body B. If the linear dashpot is attached to a point in world space, this property contains a position relative to the origin of the scene to which the dashpot is attached.

Example The following Lingo code attaches the linear dashpot to the center of mass of rigid body B:

```
newPos = vector(0, 0, 0)
linearDashpot.pointB = newPos
```

hkLinearDashpot.strength

Syntax hkLinearDashpot.strength   **Access** Get/Set

Description This property contains the strength of the linear dashpot and controls how quickly the stable state for the dashpot is achieved. High strength values yield very stiff dashpots, which can lead to unstable results. A good initial range is 0.5–1.

Example This Lingo code sets the strength of the linear dashpot to 10:

```
linearDashpot.strength = 10
```

hkLinearDashpot.damping

Syntax hkLinearDashpot.damping   **Access** Get/Set

Description This property specifies the damping factor for the linear dashpot. The damping factor controls how quickly the dashpot comes to rest. Very high damping factors can yield unstable results. A good initial value is 0.1.

Example The following code sets the damping of the linear dashpot to 0.5:

```
linearDashpot.damping = 0.5
```

Linear Dashpot Lingo Function Reference

You can access the functions in the following sections through a Havok linear dashpot, which you can obtain from a Havok cast member using the following functions:

```
havok.linearDashpot(LinearDashpotName)
```

or

```
havok.linearDashpot[i]
```

The hkLinearDashpot of each function description indicates your means of access to them. It does not mean that the actual word hkLinearDashpot is part of the syntax. In the example code, the variable linearDashpot is an instance of an hkLinearDashpot:

```
linearDashpot =
member(havokCastMemberNumber).linearDashpot
➥("LinearDashpot")
```

hkLinearDashpot.setRigidBodyA()

Syntax hkLinearDashpot.setRigidBodyA(RBName)

Description This function sets the rigid body connected to the first end of the linear dashpot (pointA, by convention).

hkLinearDashpot.setRigidBodyB()

Syntax hkLinearDashpot.setRigidBodyB(RBName), hkLinearDashpot.setRigidBodyB(#none)

Description This function sets the rigid body connected to one end of the linear dashpot. If you pass #none as a parameter, the linear dashpot will be attached to a world point, which is specified in the linearDashpot property pointB.

hkLinearDashpot.getRigidBodyA()

Syntax hkLinearDashpot.getRigidBodyB(RBName)

Description This function returns the name of the rigid body connected to the first end of the linear dashpot. If it is not connected to a rigid body, it will return #none.

hkLinearDashpot.getRigidBodyB()

Syntax hkLinearDashpot.getRigidBodyB(RBName)

Description This function returns the name of the rigid body connected to the second end of the linear dashpot. If it is not connected to a rigid body, it will return #none.

Angular Dashpot Lingo Property Reference

You can access the properties in the following sections through a Havok angular dashpot, which you can obtain from a Havok castmember using the following function:

havok.angularDashpot(AngDashpotName)

or

havok.angularDashpot[i]

The hkAngularDashpot of each property description indicates your means to access the properties. It does not mean that the actual word hkAngularDashpot is part of the syntax. In the example code, the variable angDashpot is an instance of an hkAngularDashpot:

```
angDashpot =
member(havokCastMemberNumber).AngularDashpot
➥("AngDashpot")
```

hkAngularDashpot.name

Syntax hkAngularDashpot.name   **Access** Get

Description This property contains the name of the linear dashpot.

hkAngularDashpot.rotation

Syntax   hkAngularDashpot.rotation   **Access**   Get/Set

Description   This property contains the angle of rotation that the angular dashpot attempts to maintain between another rigid body or world space.

Example   This Lingo code sets the rotation to be zero:

```
newAngle = [vector(1, 1, 1), 0]
angDashpot.rotation = newAngle
```

hkAngularDashpot.strength

Syntax   hkAngularDashpot.strength   **Access**   Get/Set

Description   This property contains the strength of the angular dashpot and controls how quickly the stable state for the dashpot is achieved. High strength values yield very stiff dashpots, which can lead to unstable results. A good initial range is 0.5–1.

Example   This Lingo code sets the strength of the angular dashpot to 10:

```
angDashpot.strength = 10
```

hkAngularDashpot.damping

Syntax   hkAngularDashpot.damping   **Access**   Get/Set

Description   This property specifies the damping factor for the angular dashpot. The damping factor controls how quickly the dashpot comes to rest. Very high damping factors can yield unstable results. A good initial value is 0.1.

Example   The following Lingo sets the damping of the angular dashpot to be 0.5:

```
angDashpot.damping = 0.5
```

Angular Dashpot Lingo Function Reference

You can access the properties discussed in this section through a Havok angular dashpot, which you can obtain from a Havok castmember using the following functions:

```
havok.angularDashpot(AngDashpotName)
```

or

```
havok.angularDashpot[i]
```

The hkAngularDashpot of each property description that follows indicates your means of access to them. It does not mean that the actual word hkAngularDashpot is part of the syntax. In the example code, the variable angDashpot is an instance of an hkAngularDashpot:

```
angularDashpot =
member(havokCastMemberNumber).AngularDashpot
➥("AngularDashpot")
```

hkAngularDashpot.setRigidBodyA()

Syntax   hkAngularDashpot.setRigidBodyA(RBName)

Description   This function sets the rigid body connected to one end of the angular dashpot.

hkAngularDashpot.setRigidBodyB()

Syntax   hkAngularDashpot.setRigidBodyB(RBName or #none)

Description   This function sets the rigid body connected to one end of the angular dashpot. If you pass #none as a parameter, the angular dashpot will be attached to a world point, which is specified in the angularDashpot property rotation.

hkAngularDashpot.getRigidBodyA()

Syntax   hkAngularDashpot.getRigidBodyA(RBName)

Description   This function returns the name of the rigid body connected to the first end of the angular dashpot. If it is not connected to any rigid body, it will return #none.

hkAngularDashpot.getRigidBodyB()

Syntax   hkAngularDashpot.getRigidBodyB(RBName)

Description   This function returns the name of the rigid body connected to the second end of the angular dashpot. If it is not connected to any rigid body, it will return #none.

CHAPTER 6

In This Chapter

Picking a Part of the City, 144

Modeling the Buildings, 147

Editing Photos to Create Textures, 150

Texture Mapping, 152

Exporting the Virtual City Tour Movie, 153

Working with the .W3D File in Director, 153

    Navigation Using Lingo, 155

    Lingo Camera Angles, 156

    Buttons and Sliders, 158

    Sliders and Rotation, 159

    The Hot Spots, 161

Building a Virtual City Tour

In this chapter, I demonstrate how to link camera navigation to on-screen sprites, such as hand-drawn buttons and sliders. With this knowledge, you will be able to draw custom interfaces around your Shockwave 3D movies, and you can use the interfaces to control the navigation in your movie.

This chapter uses a Shockwave 3D movie that was constructed for a company called Virtual City Tours. I walk you through the construction process and discuss how to photograph the city, 3D model it, and then construct the elements in Director **[6.1]**. I owe a special thanks to Ian Fuller, the President and Founder of Virtual City Tours, for not only thinking of the Virtual City idea, but for also allowing it to be discussed here. Visit the Virtual City Tours' web site at **http://www.virtualcity-tours.com** to see their development progress.

The prerequisite for this city is photo-realism. Photo-realism is tough to achieve because of the limitations in the shipping version of Shockwave 3D, such as the fact that you can't use shadows and that lighting is limited. Thus, in order to attempt to satisfy the realism requirement, you have to make up for these limitations with realistic-looking textures. There are literally hundreds of buildings in this project, making it a large and even more complex project.

The creation process includes taking several photos for modeling references and texturing references, building the actual 3D scene (in this case, I used 3ds max), exporting the scene to the .W3D format, constructing the (UI) user interface, and finally programming the model with Lingo. If you are only interested in learning the Lingo code, you can skip to the end of the chapter.

The first thing you have to do is decide how much of the city you want to build as photo-realistic. Believe it or not, this is an important decision, as I found out when I attempted this project for the first time. Hopefully, my experiences will help aid you with decisions like this and with the details of this process.

Picking a Part of the City

When Shockwave 3D was still in the beta stages, I wasn't sure whether or not an entire city, or even a large part of a city, could be built. As you might expect, creating a 3D model of San Francisco is a daunting task. I decided to build a selection of blocks of the city, or more specifically, Union Square.

As you can see, Union Square **[6.2]** has a lot of buildings, and most of them are tightly packed together. Taking photos of

[6.1]

Chapter 6 Building a Virtual City Tour | 145

[6.2] Union Square looking east.

[6.3] Several photo angles are necessary to start the complicated modeling process.

[6.4] Reconnaissance work.

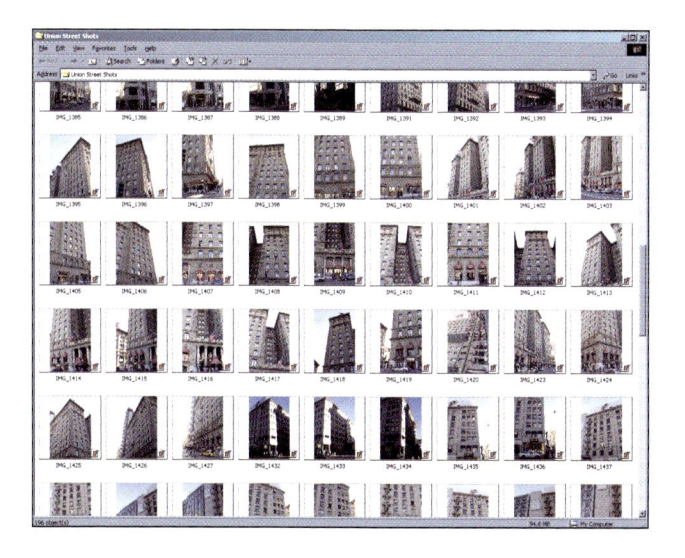

[6.5] Hundreds of photos were used to create the city scene.

these buildings is a tricky thing, not to mention building a 3D model of something so spectacular and complex. To make this task photo-realistic, you have to shoot photos of the buildings and use them as the textures in the 3D model.

Every building in the square requires multiple photographs shot at several different angles [6.3]. In the case of this project, I hired a professional photographer whose name is Andy Berry. Andy is a great photographer. In addition to having him shoot the buildings, I had him shoot several pictures of the surrounding areas of the buildings to use as textures and references for the models [6.4].

Andy delivered to me thousands of photos to go through and to use as references [6.5], but with the delivery of these photos, a problem presented itself.

[6.6] Shooting textures that are at perpendicular angles is tough with 10-story buildings.

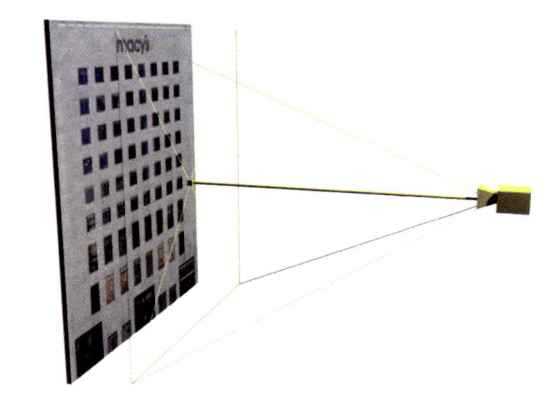

[6.7] Don't try this at home.

The easiest and fastest way to texture buildings is to photograph the front of the buildings, and then cubically (or with a box) map the texture completely around the 3D box. The problem with my photos was that the buildings were so high and close to one another that photographing the buildings at the correct angles was almost impossible. Photos that are going to be used as textures have to be shot perpendicular to the face of buildings **[6.6]**; otherwise, the building textures result in a smudged appearance, which is the opposite effect desired when you are trying to achieve a photo-realistic quality.

At one point, I thought I might use the textures from clip-art buildings or other buildings in the surrounding area. While the photographer worked on the angle problem, I started the geometry construction for some of the buildings. With too much time on my hands, I decided to blow up one of the buildings just to make myself feel better about the photography problem. It worked **[6.7]**.

Eventually, a solution for photographing the buildings arrived. We used a special lens (telephoto), and then shot the buildings from inside other buildings, and from a distance. To get the right angle on the east buildings, we went into the west buildings and took the photographs from about two hundred yards away from the east buildings and five stories above the ground. This allowed us to get a more exact angle. The problem then became the obstructions. Because we shot the buildings from a distance, there were trees, telephone poles or wires, and other obstructions in the view of the pictures. These had to be digitally removed later in the process.

After you have gathered photos of the buildings and the areas surrounding the buildings, you can finish the model. When taking photographs of the surrounding areas, take several shots to ensure that you get the more realistic pictures of the entire scene as we did for this project **[6.8–6.10]**.

Modeling the Buildings

To construct buildings quickly, you only need the top-down view and height for each building. You could rent a helicopter and photograph the scene from above it. For my scene, I was able to find a view on the Internet, because Union Square is a popular place.

Next, you need to lay out your scene. After you have a rough layout of where the buildings, streets, and curbs go, you can start drawing the models.

Start the construction by drawing the buildings from the top view. Outline shapes for where each building should be placed in relation to the other buildings **[6.11]**.

The first building you extrude should be as close to the actual height in relation to the city block as possible. The first building is going to serve as the one that other buildings are drawn in relation to in terms of height; thus, be as accurate as possible so that subsequent buildings in the scene look realistic.

[6.8–6.10] If there had been a kitchen sink next to one of these buildings, we would have photographed it. Remember to take pictures of as many details as you can, including street signs.

[6.11] The top-down view of the Union Square model you are creating.

[6.12] Create the buildings by using the height of the original building.

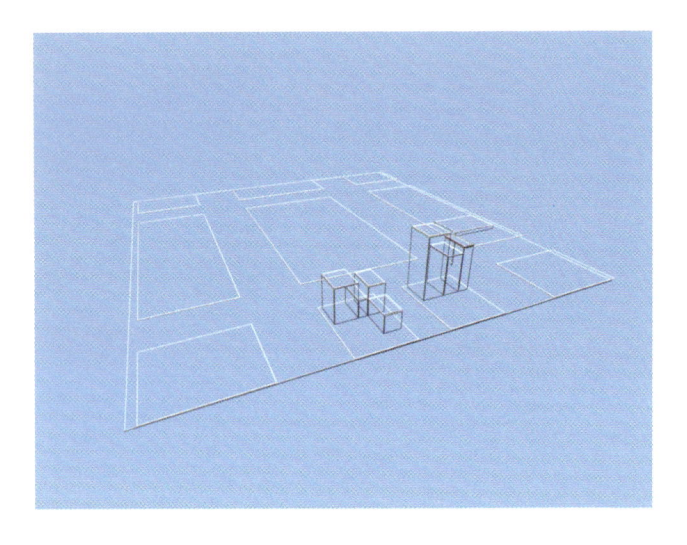

The construction of the buildings progresses quickly after the first one is in place. Create the second building right next to the first one, and keep the height relationship similar to one another [6.12].

I went around my Union Square sketch creating each building this way [6.13]. The more buildings you create, the easier it gets.

After the buildings have been extruded, you should look them over and adjust the heights so that the buildings don't appear to be too small or too large compared to the real street they are on and compared to the other objects you will need to add to the scene later [6.14].

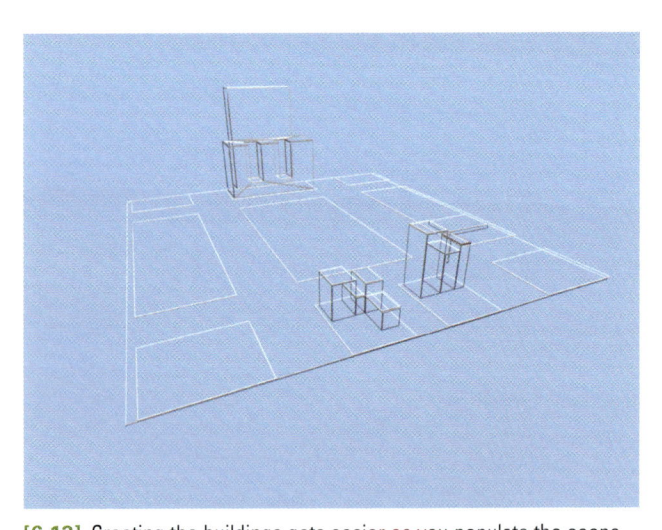

[6.13] Creating the buildings gets easier as you populate the scene.

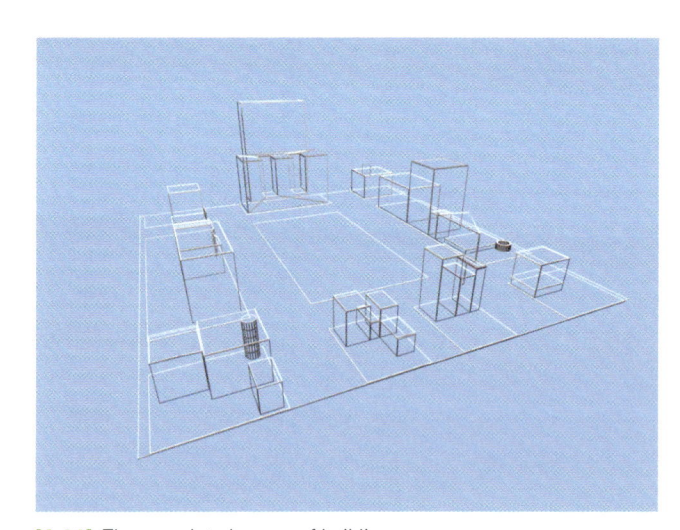

[6.14] The completed scene of buildings.

With the majority of the buildings completed, you can start working on smaller, more detailed objects, such as garbage cans, street lights, signs, benches, and other objects you photographed [6.15–6.18]. If you want, you can also use 3D clip art from CDs or you can search for 3D models online.

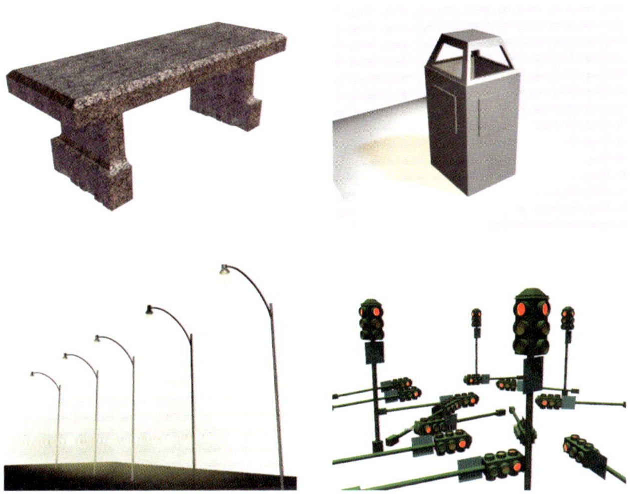

After you create the models, check each one with 3ds max's Poly Count tool (or use another application). If necessary, reduce the geometry by deleting some of the models' parts or by using the Optimize modifier on the model [6.19–6.20].

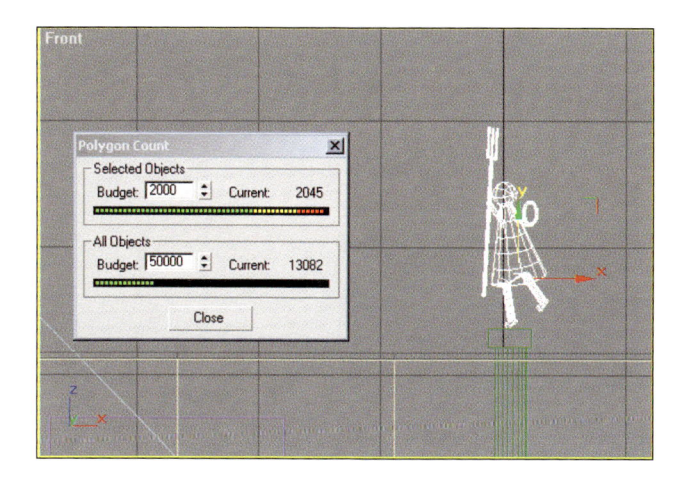

[6.19] The model with a poly count of 2,045 before the Optimize modifier has been applied.

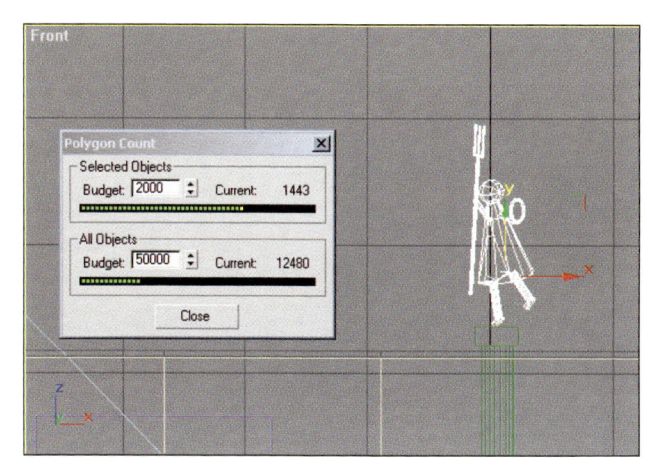

[6.15–6.18] You need to create several models to make the city look realistic.

[6.20] The poly count is reduced by 602 after applying the modifier.

The Optimize modifier is also part of the Modify tab, and you can remove polygons from any 3D object with it. I don't recommend using the modifier if you are rendering or animating. Remember that size doesn't matter in these cases. Using the Optimize modifier speeds the redraw process, as there are fewer polygons to redraw after you have used it.

The Poly Count tool is in the Tools tab in 3ds max. This tool opens a dialog window that shows you both the polygon count of a selected object and the polygon count of the objects in the scene. You can also set a budget value for your scene and the objects in it. After you set a value, an incremental bar displaying various colors slides across the dialog window indicating how close you are to exceeding the preset budget value. This tool was created for the game industry, but it's perfect for creating low-bandwidth content, such as Shockwave 3D files.

After the models are constructed, you can texture-map the photographs, but before you do this, the photos need to be cropped and edited.

Editing Photos to Create Textures

After you have scanned the photographs onto the computer (unless you digitally shot them), they need edits or retouch-ups before they can be called textures. Texture clean-up work is a time-consuming and tedious process that, in this case, takes longer than building the models. Depending on the number of buildings you construct, you could edit hundreds of images with each needing color correction, cropping, rotation, and sizing.

The photographs I used were digitally shot with a Canon D30 to prevent the need for scanning, and to save time. Each image was opened and edited using Photoshop 6. First, I corrected the color by punching up the brightness and contrast. To do this, I used the Auto Brightness and Contrast option. You can see the difference [6.21].

Next, depending on the photographs, the perspective may need to be adjusted to compensate for angles that aren't perfectly perpendicular to the face of the building [6.22].

You can adjust images using the Transform Distortion tool. You can also push and pull on the handles of the images to bring the top of each building closer in perspective and push the bottoms out further. The time spent on editing your images is worth it. Minor edits to the textures can be the determining factor in whether or not a scene looks real.

After the Photoshop work is complete, the images appear to be transformed into realistic-looking textures [6.23–6.24].

After you have edited the photographs, the textures are ready for texture mapping in 3ds max.

[6.21] Color correction was applied by adjusting the brightness and contrast of the photograph.

[6.22] The angle of this building was photographed at a 90-degree angle; however, as you can see, the angle wasn't perfect.

[6.23] Before the images are edited.

[6.24] After the images are edited.

Texture Mapping

The final step in making things "look pretty" is the application of the textures to the buildings. In 3ds max, this is an easy process. The textures of my photographs were saved in Photoshop as JPEGs with a maximum quality setting of 12 in the baseline format. The images were also scaled to the size of 512×512. This is going to be the maximum size that will output to Shockwave 3D.

In the Material Editor, name each of the textures. As stated previously, make sure that the materials and textures have different names. I have encountered problems where textures have been switched in Shockwave 3D, but looked fine in 3ds max. Giving everything a unique name in the Material Editor fixes the problem. In the case of this project, I used simple names, such as building01, building02, and so on.

[6.25] Start applying textures to your buildings.

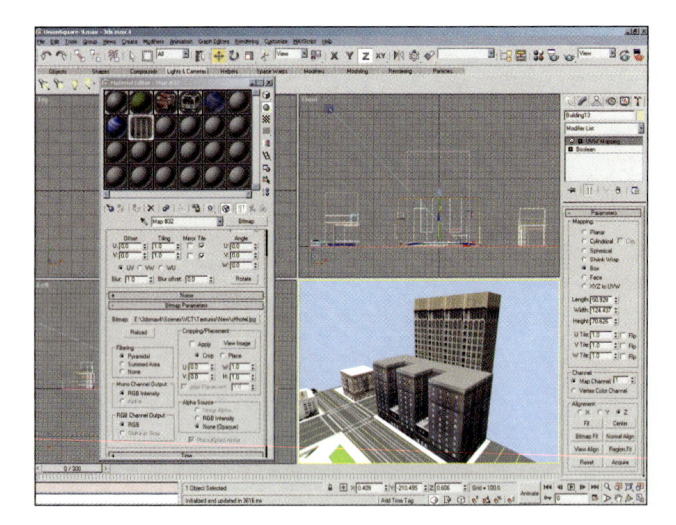

Next, the textures are applied to each building [6.25]. This is an easy process; however, it can be tricky remembering what texture is associated with what building. If you mix them up, you run the risk of your scene not being photo-realistic. When I completed the project, I had to use color prints of Union Square as references while I was applying the textures. You might consider using prints as well. Another option is to name the textures similarly to the buildings to which they are applied to ensure you don't lose track of your files.

After each texture is applied to the correct building, you need to apply the UVW Mapping modifier, which is located in the Modifier tab. Set the mapping type to box or cubic. Some of the textures will also need to be squeezed around the buildings. Use the Z alignment fit button to do this.

Everything looks beautiful, except there is now one problem with box mapping the textures that are on the roof of the buildings. If you construct a city scene the way I did, you will run into the same problem. This is the trade-off for using a faster method of creating so many buildings and texture maps. For the purposes of this exercise, go with this easy solution. Cap the roofs of the building with simple pieces of geometry. These cover the textures and allow for different colors on the roofs of the buildings. Note that the colors do add more polygons to the finished Shockwave movie.

Now, let's add a realistic sky to make this scene even more interesting. To do this, you have to create a giant sphere that surrounds the entire city. Make sure that the sphere encompasses all of your lights and the camera. Generally, for a sky, I would use only half of a hemisphere; however, the ground plane in this prototype is not extended anywhere near the horizon line. If you use half of a hemisphere, half of the sky will look black to the users as they approach the city. Thus, use the full sphere.

The sphere is texture-mapped with a cloud texture that comes with 3ds max. The sphere's "normals" need to be flipped inside out. The normals represent the tangent direction that the texture mapping, spectacular highlighting, reflections, and so on are facing relative to the camera position. In this case, the city is inside the sphere, so we want the texture to map inside it rather than outside it. In 3ds max, you simply select the sphere, go to the Modifier list, and then add the Normal modifier. Click Flip normals. The sky is born, and you can now export the Union Square virtual city tour beta to Director.

Exporting the Virtual City Tour Movie

You should be a pro at exporting your scenes to the .W3D format. Here are the steps for our Union Square movie:

1. In 3ds max, perform a quick rendering (test) of your scene by pressing F10 to make sure everything looks good before exporting.

2. Line up your camera to the view at which you want your Shockwave 3D movie to start. For our purposes, you'll want to show the view from the street level or from a car level.

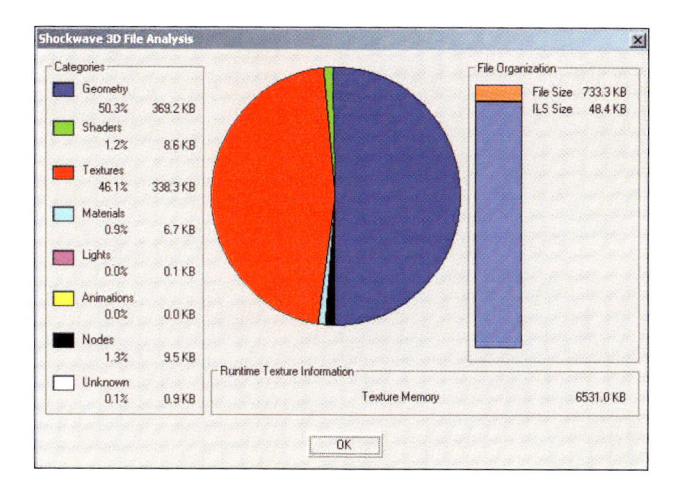

[6.26] If everything exports, you are ready to move on to Director.

3. Make sure that the camera viewport is the one selected (do this by clicking it).

4. Choose File, Export, Shockwave 3D. A dialog appears [6.26].

Working with the .W3D File in Director

In this section, we will link graphical elements (or sprites) to the Shockwave 3D camera. This gives your users the capability to click graphical elements that you create in Photoshop, which allows navigation through the Shockwave 3D city.

First, you'll create the graphical elements. These can be created with Illustrator, Photoshop, or 3D art elements. Import them into Director, and add them to the stage. You can import the elements from the File menu or by right-mouse clicking in the Cast window.

[6.27] Create an interface that your users will interact with to control your Shockwave 3D movie.

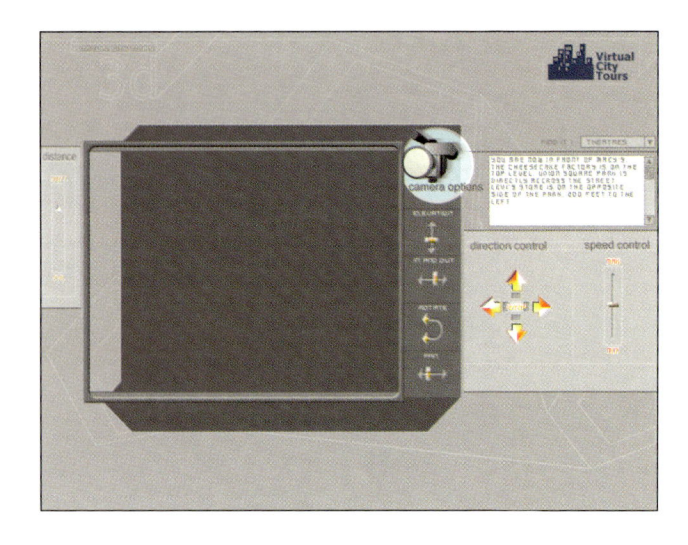

[6.28] The cpuhogticks can be used to make your Shockwave movie perform better.

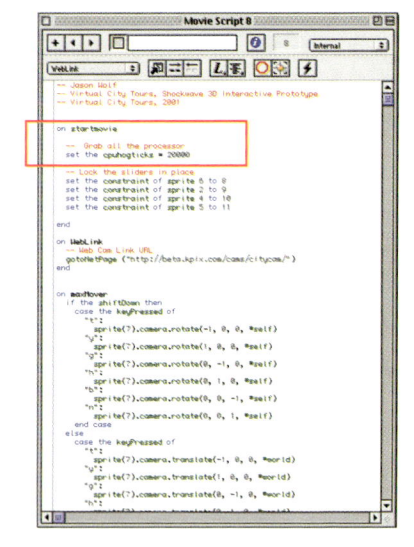

The image [6.27] created in Photoshop will have the Shockwave 3D castmember added on top of it on the stage. Then, the arrows and sliders will be linked to the Shockwave 3D camera.

Before working with the scripts for the graphics on the stage, you have to set up the scripts that will be used within the movie script. Open the Movie Script window by selecting (Command-Shift-U) on the Macintosh and (Ctrl-Shift-U) on the PC.

In the Start Movie handler, I always add the cpuhogticks command [6.28] to grab more of the processor ticks (or time) for the Shockwave 3D movie. The command is responsible for determining when Director gives back control to the CPU so it can check for background events, such as network transactions. Unfortunately, this command only works on the Macintosh.

Tip
One tick equals a sixtieth of a second (1/60). Thus, 60 ticks are equal to one second.

The command's default value is twenty ticks. The higher the value, the more time Director gets from the CPU, up to a point of course [6.28]. I have heard that any value above 1,000 is the same as 1,000. Because CPU cycles are hard to measure, I always use very high values.

The Lingo script to do this is as follows:

```
On startmovie
set the cpuhogticks = 20000
end
```

Navigation Using Lingo

Next, you'll add navigation Lingo code to the movie script that allows the keyboard to control and move the camera in the Shockwave 3D castmember. In this example, the Shockwave 3D castmember was put into sprite channel 7 in the Score window.

Open the movie script and type the following Lingo code:

```
on KeyBoardMover
  if the shiftDown then
      case the keyPressed of
    "t":
        sprite(7).camera.rotate(-1, 0, 0, #self)
    "y":
        sprite(7).camera.rotate(1, 0, 0, #self)
    "g":
        sprite(7).camera.rotate(0, -1, 0, #self)
    "h":
        sprite(7).camera.rotate(0, 1, 0, #self)
    "b":
        sprite(7).camera.rotate(0, 0, -1, #self)
    "n":
        sprite(7).camera.rotate(0, 0, 1, #self)
      end case
  else
    case the keyPressed of
    "t":
        sprite(7).camera.translate(-1, 0, 0, #world)
    "y":
        sprite(7).camera.translate(1, 0, 0, #world)
    "g":
        sprite(7).camera.translate(0, -1, 0, #world)
    "h":
        sprite(7).camera.translate(0, 1, 0, #world)
    "b":
        sprite(7).camera.translate(0, 0, -1, #world)
    "n":
        sprite(7).camera.translate(0, 0, 1, #world)
    end case
  end if
end
```

Lowercase keys equate to the following:

> t = up
> y = down
> g = left
> h = right
> b = Z-axis (in)
> n = Z-axis (out)

When the t, y, g, h, b, or n key is pressed, the camera will move up, down, left, right, in, and out respectively. If, however, the Shift key is held down when the keys are pressed, the camera will rotate around the 3-axis.

Because this handler is part of the movie script, it has to be explicitly called to run. This means that it's not going to function when you click the Play button. To activate it, you have to call KeyBoardMover with another Lingo command.

In this particular movie, there are specific frames in the score that make the keyboard navigation active. For example, in frame 10, there is a Lingo frame script that looks like the following:

```
On exitframe me
    KeyBoardMover
    Go to the frame
End
```

When the playback head hits this script, the movie pauses on frame 10 (or whatever frame this script is on), and the keyboard navigation starts to function.

If you want the keyboard navigation to function for the entire duration of the movie, you can rename the `KeyBoardMover` handler. Name it `enterframe`. This allows the keyboard navigation to function as long as your movie is in playback mode. This also works for Shockwave web movies and projectors.

Lingo Camera Angles

This section explains how to change the angle of your Shockwave 3D camera. We will be "getting" and "setting" the camera transforms for position and rotation.

[6.29] The Shockwave 3D movie with the interface around it.

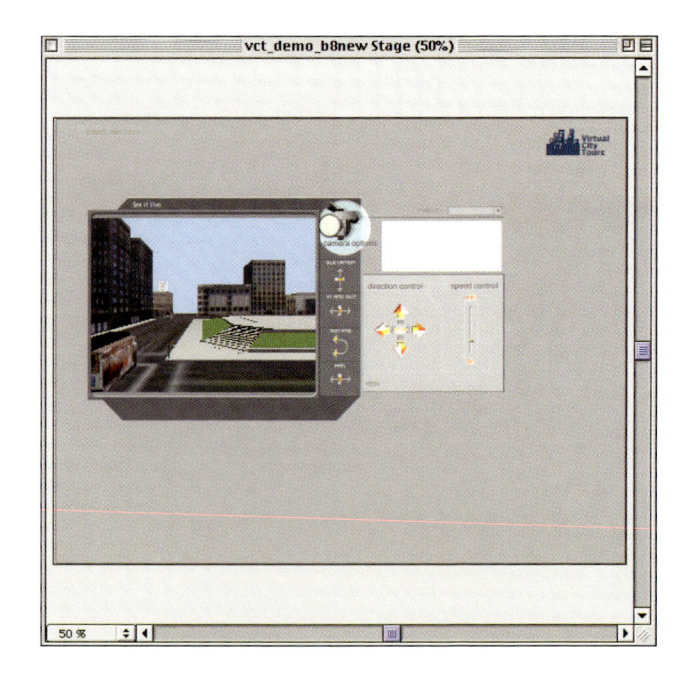

Changing the camera angle allows you to zoom in and out, move up and down, and spin around objects in the Shockwave scene. For the city tour, camera transforms were used to move the user's view to predefined places around the city, giving the users a virtual tour. Accompanying this movement through the city is an audio file that describes what the viewers are seeing.

To do this, you first need to find out where the camera is located in the 3D scene. To get the location vector, use the following Lingo:

```
put sprite(1).camera(1).transform.position
```

`Sprite 1` should be the sprite channel that contains your Shockwave 3D castmember. When you add `put` to the code, Director dumps the result of your position query into the message window. Command-M opens the window. You will see a 3D vector transform that looks like this:

```
-- vector( 120.0000, 0.0000, 10.0000 )
```

This is the current location of your camera in the 3D space. Now, to reposition the camera to a new location, input the location that you want to go to into the command, as shown in the following:

```
sprite(1).camera(1).transform.position = vector(x, x, x)
```

Replace the vector (x, x, x) with the 3D location that you want the camera to move to. Remember, the 3D scene [6.29] is based on the Cartesian coordinate system where X, Y, and Z are planes. Any point in space can be represented with a three-digit number.

In addition to moving the camera to different locations, you can create new cameras for specific locations, and then you can use the Score window to jump between the cameras.

The Score window shows that in sprite channel 7 there is a Shockwave 3D castmember (the highlighted sprite). Notice that in the score script channel there are a series of score scripts [6.30]. Each one of these scripts changes the camera angle by going to a new camera.

Let's look at how this works. First, a new camera is created using the Lingo statement:

```
member("Shockwave3dMember").newCamera("camera02")
```

If you want to use more than one camera, repeat the statement as often as necessary, as shown here:

```
member("Shockwave3dMember").newCamera("camera03")
member("Shockwave3dMember").newCamera("camera04")
member("Shockwave3dMember").newCamera("camera05")
member("Shockwave3dMember").newCamera("camera06")
```

This code creates six cameras in the castmember, which is named Shockwave3dMember. Note that by default there is already a camera named camera01.

Next, the newly created cameras have to be positioned. The Lingo for this follows:

```
set member("Shockwave3dMember").camera("camera02").
transform.position = vector( 258.0, 275.0, 151.0)

set member("Shockwave3dMember").camera("camera02").
transform.rotation = vector( 65.0, 0.0, 133.0)
```

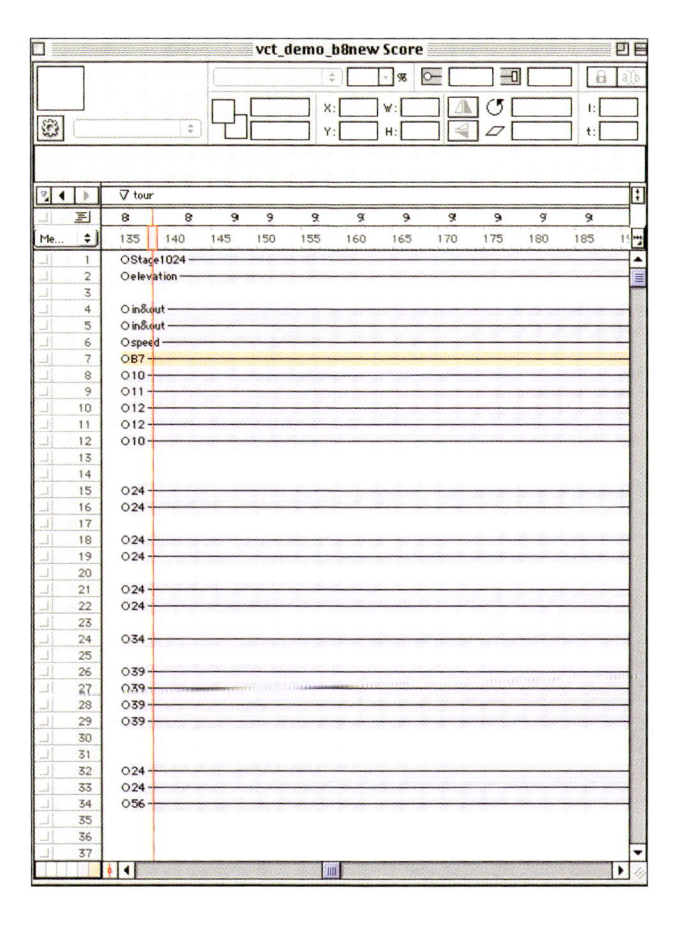

[6.30] You can use different frame scripts on the same Shockwave sprite in the score.

After the cameras are positioned, you can jump from camera angle to camera angle using the following Lingo code:

```
sprite(7).camera = member("Shockwave3dMember ").camera("Camera02")

sprite(7).camera = member("Shockwave3dMember ").camera("Camera03")
```

[6.31] Create bitmapped artwork to represent a button that will control your Shockwave 3D movie.

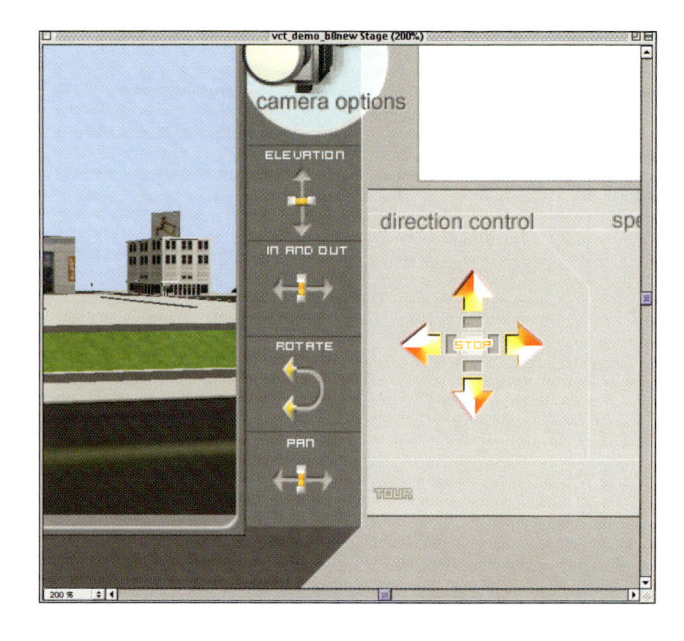

[6.32] Right-click on the PC and Control-click on the Macintosh to bring up the pop-up menu.

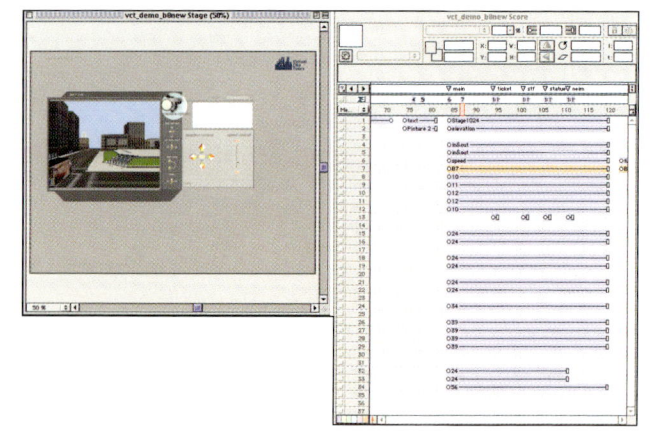

Buttons and Sliders

The previous examples involved forcing the camera to reposition itself using a Lingo statement. Now, you'll attach those same Lingo statements to on-screen buttons and sliders. The buttons and sliders will be hardwired to control your cameras.

The navigation UI elements are used for controlling the camera [6.31]. Following is a list of functions that each UI element has associated to it:

> **Elevation**   This function is used for moving the camera up or down.

> **In and Out**   This function is used for moving forward or backward.

> **Rotate**   The Rotate function is used for spinning the camera around its axis.

> **Panfor**   This function is used to move left or right.

There is also a set of direction arrows that jump the camera forward and backward or left and right a preset distance. The arrows are used to fine-tune the placement of the camera, because the sliders are similar to stopping a remote control car, where you can over- or undershoot your desired stopping point.

First, you attach a script to each direction arrow. If you control-click the sprite, you will receive a pull-down menu that lets you choose Script. After you choose a script, you attach it to the sprite [6.32]. Do this for each sprite and attach the preceding scripts.

For the Up button, which is the navigational equivalent of walking forward in the Shockwave 3D scene, attach the following "walking forward" Lingo script:

```
on mouseUp me
          sprite(7).camera.translate(-10, 0, 0, #world)
end
```

Make sure that you associate sprite(7) [6.33] to the actual Shockwave 3D sprite. If your Shockwave 3D castmember is in channel 2, then use sprite(2). Your sprite number is the channel number that you put your castmember into in the score window.

Now repeat this exact same operation with the other navigation arrows, making sure to attach the correct direction to the matching UI element. Here are the Lingo scripts:

For moving right, attach the following:

```
on mouseUp me
sprite(7).camera.translate(0, 10, 0, #world)
end
```

For moving left, attach the following:

```
on mouseUp me
sprite(7).camera.translate(0, -10, 0, #world)
end
```

For moving backward, attach the following:

```
on mouseUp me
sprite(7).camera.translate(10, 0, 0, #world)
end
```

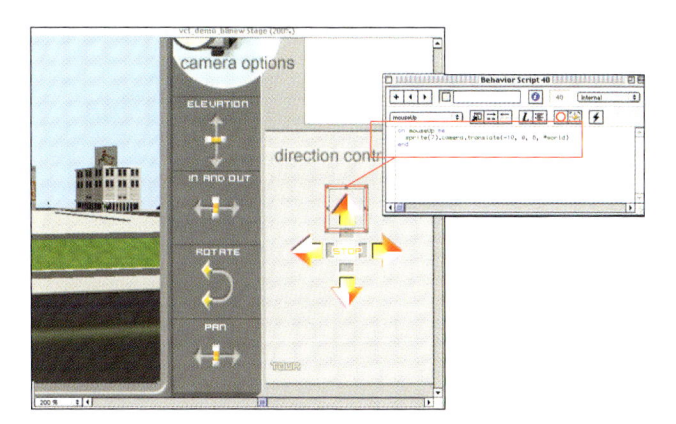

[6.33] The attached script.

Sliders and Rotation

The slider [6.34] is a bit trickier. When you click the part of the slider that slides, you don't want the code to execute just based on the clicking action. If the code executes for each click, it defeats the purpose of a slider. The slider has to have a few other functions associated with it. The slider has to slide along an invisible line. When the slider is higher than its neutral center position, the camera should move up; when the slider is lower than the neutral position [6.35], the camera should move down; and finally, when you let go of the slider (or if you un-click it), the camera should snap back to the middle position (or its starting point). You get all of these results from this one slider function. This should make you respect the software developers more, especially if you think about the little UI functions that most designers take for granted.

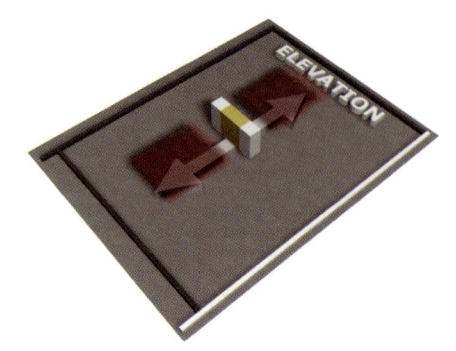

[6.34] The slider's neutral state.

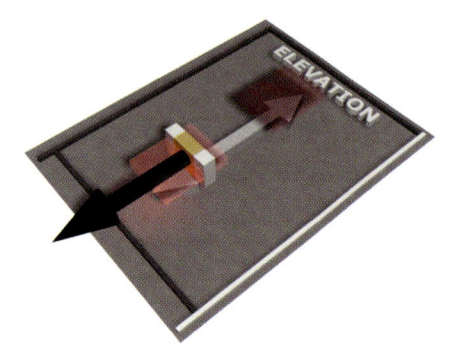

[6.35] The slider enters the invisible spot, which activates the down state.

[6.36] Make the Slider button moveable from the score.

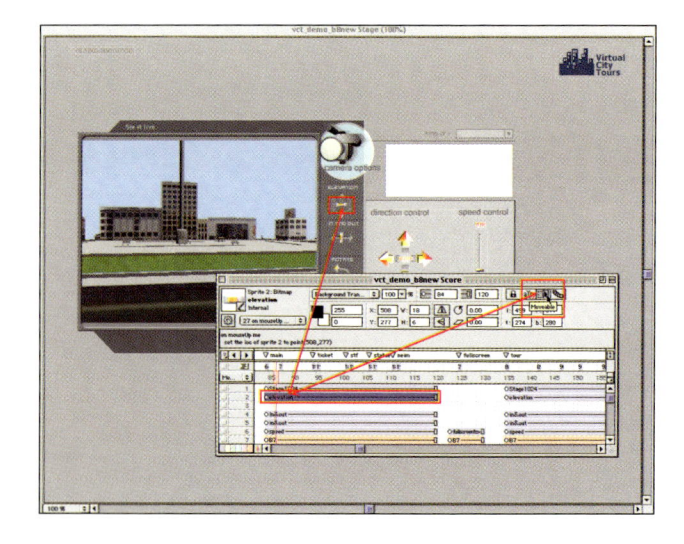

This slider is made up of four parts—invisible lines that represent how far the slider can slide up and down, the slider button, and two invisible hot spots that activate the necessary Lingo code if the slider is inside one of them.

Draw a line from the Tool window (Command-7 on the Macintosh or Ctrl-7 on the PC). This line should be drawn as straight as possible and only as long as you want the slider to slide. Next, open the Movie Script window (Command-Shift-U and Ctrl-Shift-U), and in the start movie handler, add the Constraint command to attach the slider to the line. The script should look like this:

```
On startmovie
set the constraint of sprite 2 to 9
end
```

Make sure that you associate your line to the slider. In the previous Lingo example, sprite 2 is the sliding part and sprite 9 is the line that the slider slides along. In the Score window, select the slider (sprite 2) and click the Moveable button. [6.36].

Now, recall that when you let go of the slider, it should snap back to its point of origin. To make this work, attach the following script to the slider [6.37]:

```
On MouseUp me
set the loc of sprite 2 to point ( 508, 277 )
updatestage
end
```

The trick is the "loc of the sprite" (or point) that you enter will have to be found on your own. In the previous example, the point (508, 277) is in reference to an X, Y location for the Virtual City Tours movie. When you draw your own slider, you will likely put in a different position. Thus, to find out where the slider's point of location is, do the following:

1. Put your slider on the stage in its "final resting place." The final place is where you want the slider to return to when you un-click it.

2. Now, open the Message window (Command-M), and type the following command:

   Put the loc of sprite (X)

The X is the sprite channel of your slider—for example, put the loc of sprite(2).

This command returns the point location that you should use to reset the slider to its custom location. Now that you have the correct value, attach the script.

The Hot Spots

For the slider, both the hot spots are invisible boxes that are created with the Tool window. These are created the same way that the invisible line was created.

Draw a box that is positioned below the slider's resting point. Attach the following script to that invisible box [6.38]:

```
on mouseWithin me
      if sprite 2 intersects sprite 16 then
            sprite(7).camera.translate(0, 0, -1, #world)
      end if
end
```

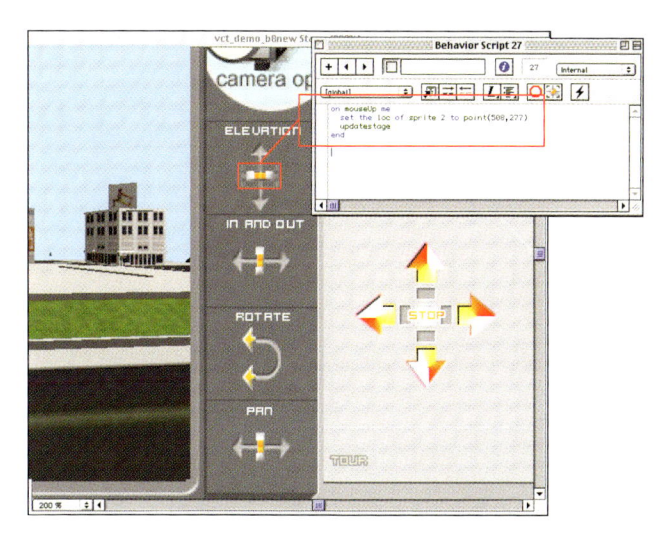

[6.37] Adding the Lingo to the slider.

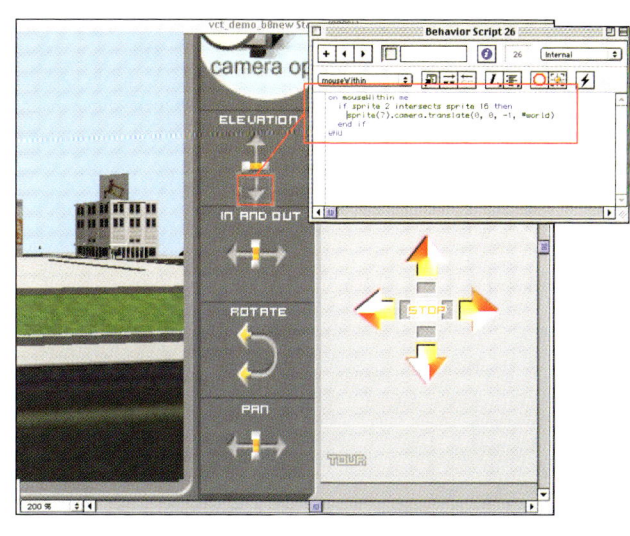

[6.38] Attach the sliders "down state" Lingo command.

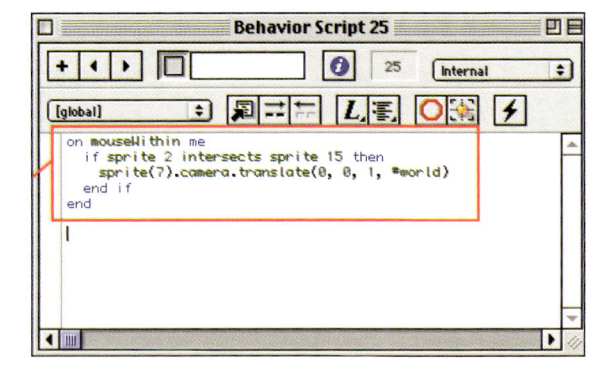

[6.39] Next, attach the sliders "up state" Lingo command.

```
on mouseWithin me
  if sprite 2 intersects sprite 15 then
    sprite(7).camera.translate(0, 0, 1, #world)
  end if
end
```

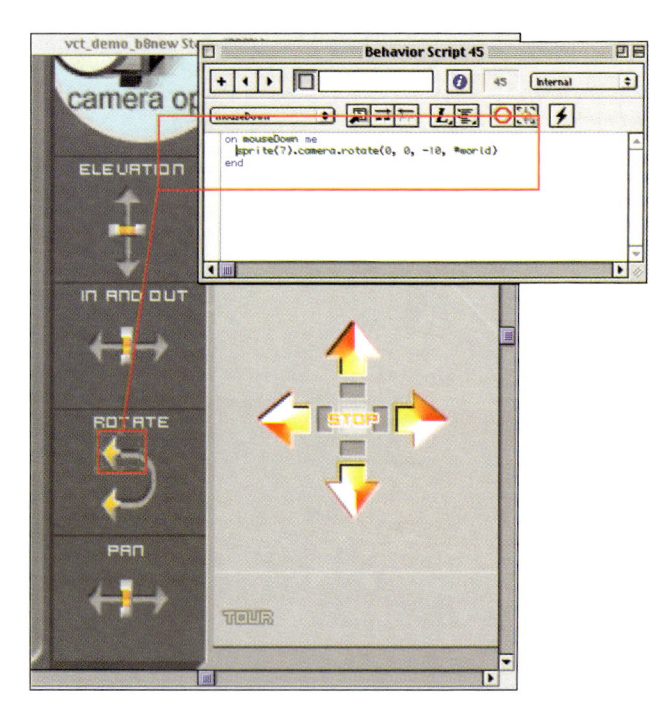

[6.40] Add invisible buttons to your user interface that will control your Shockwave 3D movie.

In the first line, sprite(2) is referring to the sprite channel that the slider is within the score, and sprite (15) is the channel that the invisible box is located in. In the second line, sprite(7) is the channel that the Shockwave 3D castmember is in.

Now, repeat the same process for the invisible box located above the slider by adding the following script **[6.39]**:

```
on mouseWithin me
  if sprite 2 intersects sprite 15 then
    sprite(7).camera.translate(0, 0, 1, #world)
  end if
end
```

The previous script is the same as the "bottom slider" script, except that sprite(16) is the other invisible box, and the camera translate is moving the camera in a different direction.

There are two other sliders that control the in and out motion and the panning motion. Both of these sliders work in exactly the same way that the elevation slider does, Thus, the only other scripts to discuss are the rotation scripts.

The rotation buttons are covered with invisible buttons **[6.40]**. Drawing a box around your buttons and setting the width of that box to no line creates these invisible buttons. Open the Tool Palette from the Window menu and draw a box around your buttons. Then, while the box you just drew is still selected, click the No Line button at the bottom of the Tool Palette window. There is no need to view the boxes, because we already have pretty graphics.

After you create your invisible buttons, add the following Lingo scripts to them [6.41]:

```
on mouseDown me
sprite(7).camera.rotate(0, 0, -10, #world)
end
```

Again, the `sprite(7)` command is referring to the channel that the Shockwave 3D member is located in. When these buttons are clicked, the camera rotates around its axis either positive 10 or minus 10 units.

The example scripts in this chapter use numerical values that were specifically chosen to accommodate the speed needed for the Virtual City Tours demonstration. After you create your own movie and start using these scripts, you will be able to adjust your camera's motion and speed so that it's not too fast or too slow. The speed depends on the size of the 3D world that you create, how fast your target machine can redraw, and the numerical values that you choose to use. Larger values make the camera move faster at the expense of smooth motion. Keep in mind that every movie has its sweet spot, or balance if you will. You can find it!

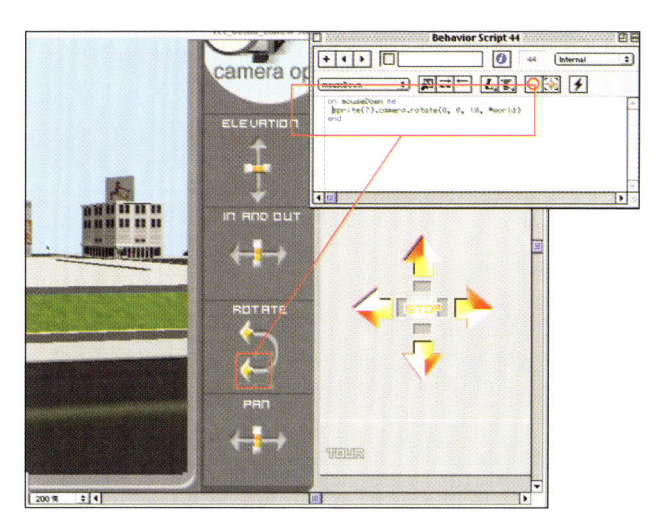

[6.41] Attach the scripts to these invisible buttons.

CHAPTER 7

In This Chapter

Shockwave 3D Software and Application Developers, 167

3D Model Makers and Suppliers, 174

Inspiration Sites, 176

Xtras and Plug-Ins, 180

Shockwave 3D Content Developers, 183

Places to Go, People to See!

Congratulations! You made it to the end of the modeling lessons. You should now know how to create 3D models. Shockwave 3D is such a new technology; thus, there really is no end to its madness! Shockwave is an amazing technology that can create unbelievable objects. It already has an incredibly strong following and commitment from some big name companies, such as Intel, Alias|Wavefront, and Macromedia. This is good news, because when companies invest in technology, the technology usually stays around for a long time.

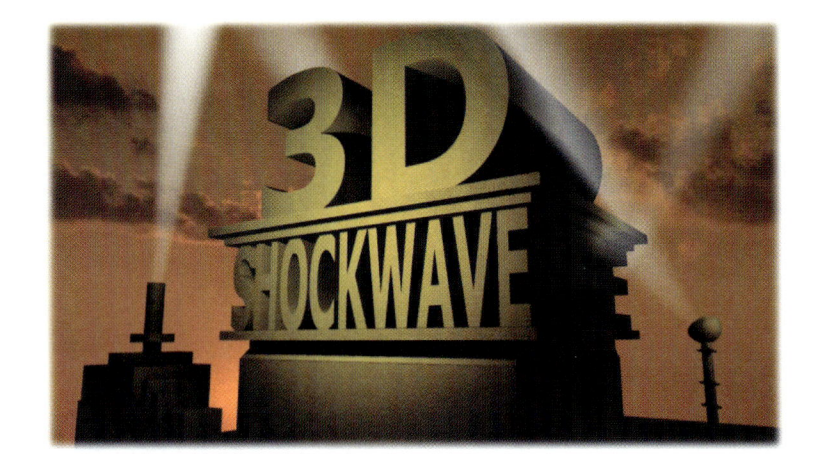

Take Shockwave, for example. The plain, old version of Shockwave allowed the playback of Director movies via a browser. This technology, thanks to some skillful marketing, flourished. Shockwave was the first web-based animation plug-in, and the code base foundation for the Flash vector plug-in that was widely distributed.

If you are like me, you want to know where you can learn more about Shockwave 3D. When I get my hands on a new piece of software or technology, I cannot put it down until I know everything about it, even if I have to take it apart and put it back together again. (Note that I've apologized numerous times to my mother for taking apart appliances throughout my childhood.) I thought it would be beneficial to give you a list of the companies (and web sites) that are using Shockwave 3D. In this chapter, I present you with the links that were available at the time of writing this book. Some links may now be outdated. Knowing this, I tried to select the companies and developers that I thought would be around for a while, or I selected the ones I thought had cool content.

This chapter contains a visual listing of web sites that offer you valuable information about Shockwave 3D. The list includes software providers, Shockwave 3D developers, and inspiration sites that will motivate you to learn more and potentially help you find work in the Shockwave 3D field. The URLs for these sites are located on the CD-ROM that accompanies this book, so you don't have to type them in to your browser.

Shockwave 3D Software and Application Developers

Alias|Wavefront

http://www.aliaswavefront.com

Alias|Wavefront developers created Maya® and the Maya Real-Time Author™ application. Check out the customer examples and gallery section for some inspiration.

Alias|Wavefront might have entered the Shockwave 3D game late, but it was worth the wait.

Ashlar-Vellum

http://www.ashlar-vellum.com/

Ashlar-Vellum creates software for designers and engineers. Their site offers some of the most powerful CAD modeling solutions in the industry.

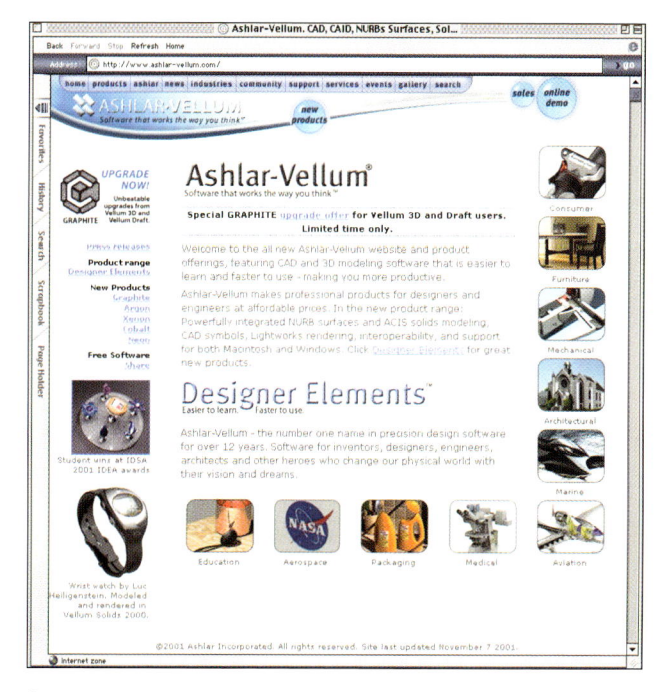

On Ashlar-Vellum's home page, you can sign up for a 3D tip-of-the-day to be emailed to you.

Caligari

http://www.caligari.com/

Caligari created and sells trueSpace 5.1. They offer an excellent collection of textures in the Libraries section.

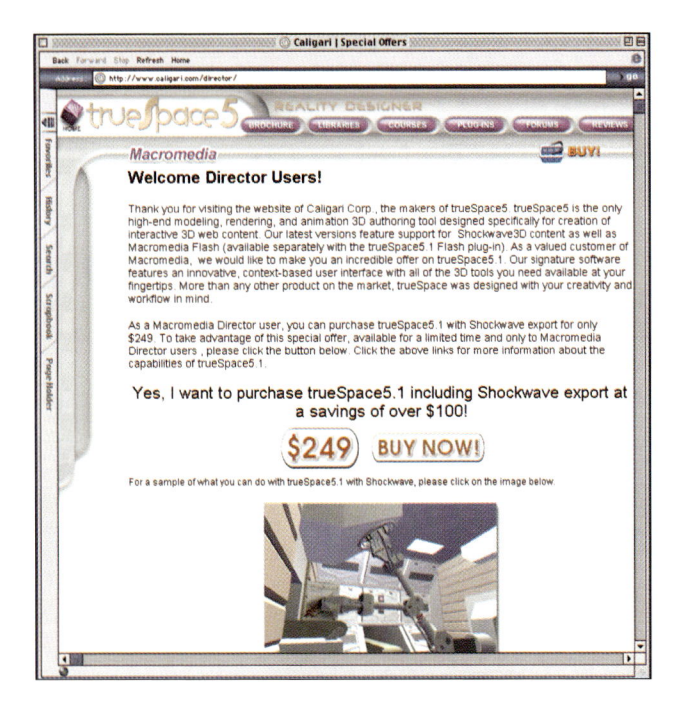

You can get trueSpace with the Shockwave Exporter built in from Caligari.

Curious Labs

http://www.curiouslabs.com/

Curious Labs created Poser. Poser is a must-have application if you are planning on creating 3D humans or figures in your Shockwave 3D movies. Check out the gallery section.

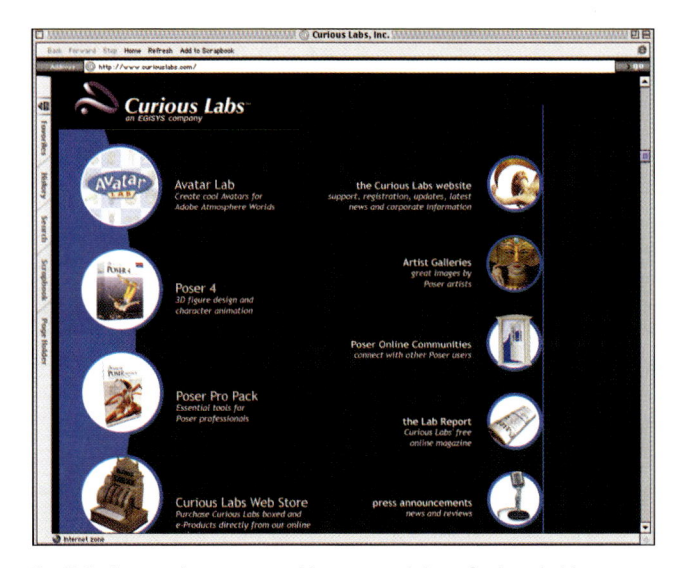

You'll find several textures and human models at Curious Lab's web site.

D Vision Works

http://www.d-vw.com/

D Vision Works created D Sculptor, an image-based modeling program that allows the user to make 3D models of real-world objects using photos from a camera.

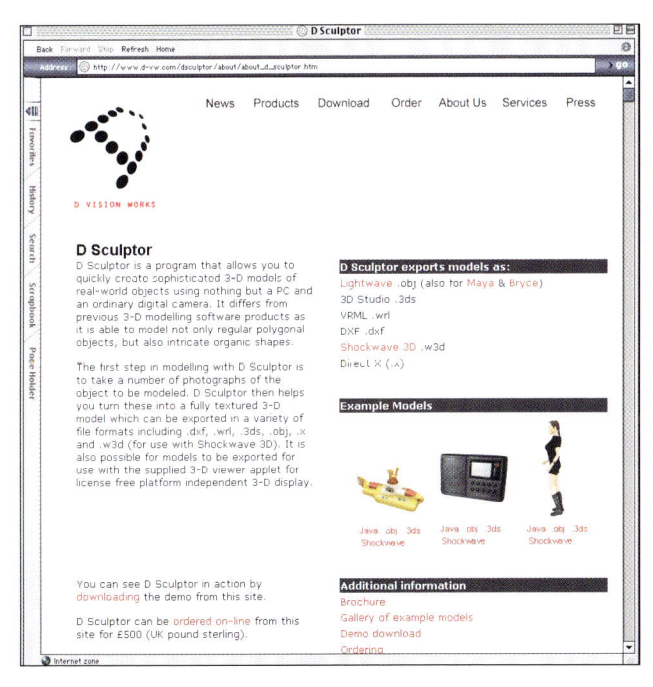

Check out D Sculptor if you need to create 3D models from photos.

Softimage/Avid

http://www.softimage.com/

Softimage builds software that creates 3D content. If you are new to Shockwave 3D and 3D design in general, and you are looking for a way to take your content to the Web, Softimage has several tools for Flash exporting, Shockwave exporting, and runtime engines that build complex characters and interact demonstrations.

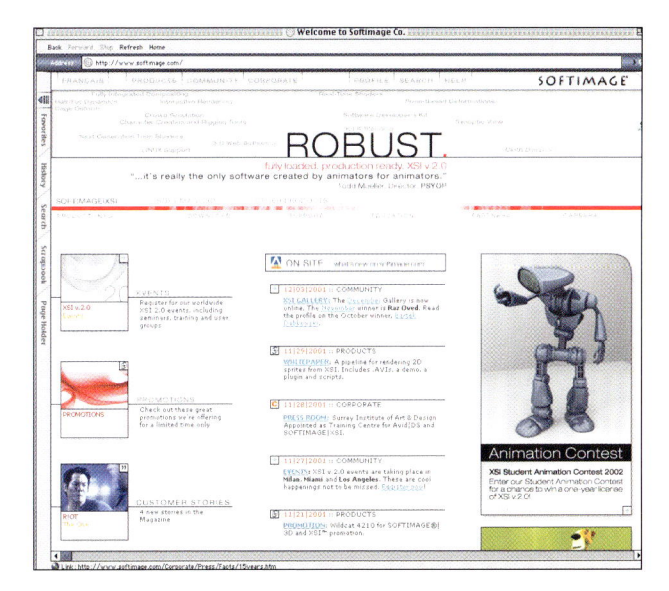

Are you good at 3D? Enter Softimage's regular contests to find out.

Tabuleiro

http://www.shapeshifter3D.com/

ShapeShifter3D is new and it's hot! ShapeShifter is a modeling tool designed specifically for Shockwave 3D. It's inexpensive and worth an experiment. ShapeShifter3D is designed to make low-count polygon models, and it has full support for textures and skeletons. It can also import objects from other 3D programs and convert them into Shockwave 3D objects.

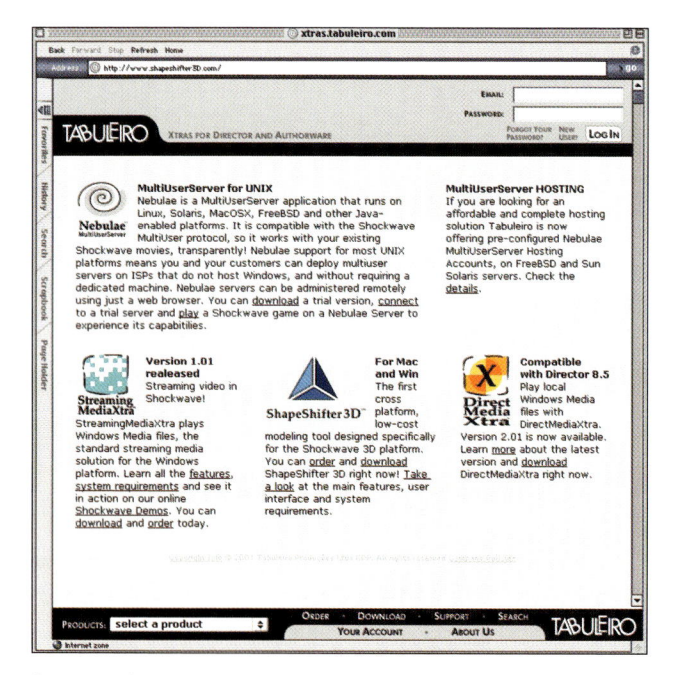

Check out ShapeShifter3D and design low-count polygon models.

Discreet

http://www.discreet.com/

The makers of 3ds max and Reactor bring you one of the best solutions for Shockwave 3D content creation on the market.

Discreet jump-started the Shockwave 3D revolution by adding the Shockwave 3D Exporter to 3ds max.

EON Reality

http://www.eonreality.com

EON Reality makes EonXtra, a plug-in for Director that enables you to embed and run interactive EON applications.

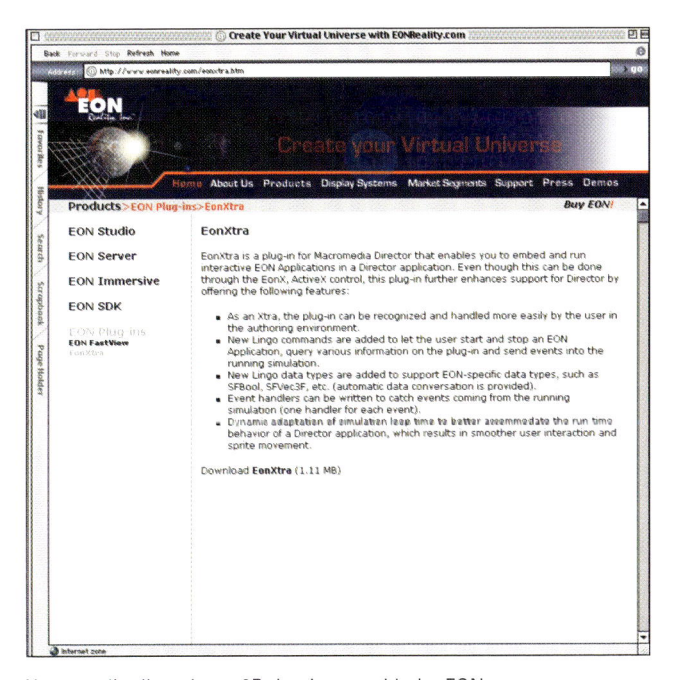

You can distribute large 3D databases with the EON server.

MAXON Computer

http://www.maxoncomputer.com/

Cinema 4D is a very powerful 3D application that you should consider if you want to learn 3D. MAXON Computer makes Cinema 4D, the "jack-of-all-trades" application for 3D everything, including Shockwave 3D exports.

Cinema 4D is a very powerful 3D application that you should consider if you are thinking of learning 3D.

NewTek

http://www.newtek.com/

NewTek created LightWave. If you know anything about 3D, you have heard of LightWave. If you haven't heard of LightWave, then you should check out this site, especially the gallery section, as it contains some of the most compelling and inspirational 3D work I've ever seen.

The makers of LightWave and the famous Video Toaster are entering into the Shockwave 3D game industry.

REALVIZ

http://www.realviz.com/

REALVIZ make some RealCool software. ImageModeler is one of the REALVIZ applications that enable you to photograph an object, scene, or building from a few different angles. Then, the application literally creates a 3D model for you. It can even steal the textures from photos. The application also saves into the Shockwave 3D format.

ImageModeler is worth checking out, as you can create 3D models from photos and save them as Shockwave 3D files.

TGS

http://www.tgs.com/

TGS creates AMAPI 3D, which is a 3D solution for modeling and rendering. AMAPI 3D can publish to the Shockwave 3D format via a translator.

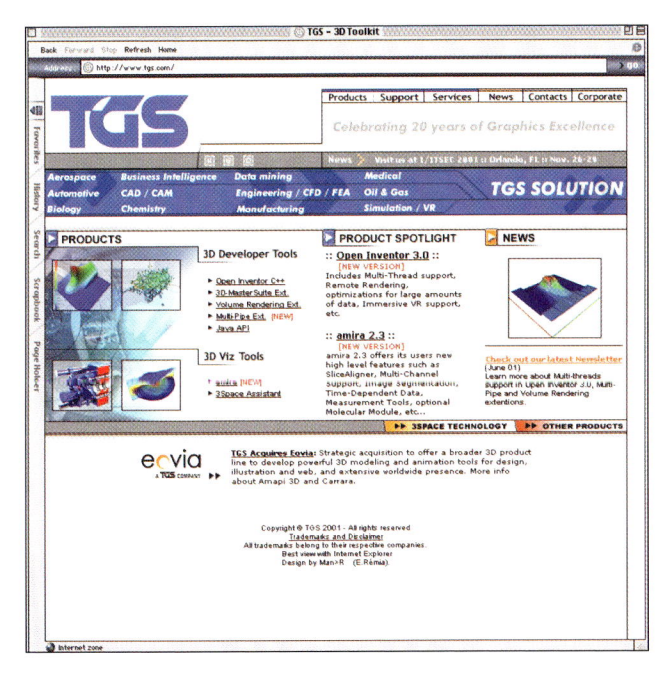

Engineers, scientists, and researchers use TGS to solve visualization issues. You can partner with them to create 3D solutions for almost any industry.

Macromedia

http://www.macromedia.com

Need I say more? Okay, I recommend this site for inspiration and information. I regularly browse the site for ideas, technical notes (which I once wrote), and product updates.

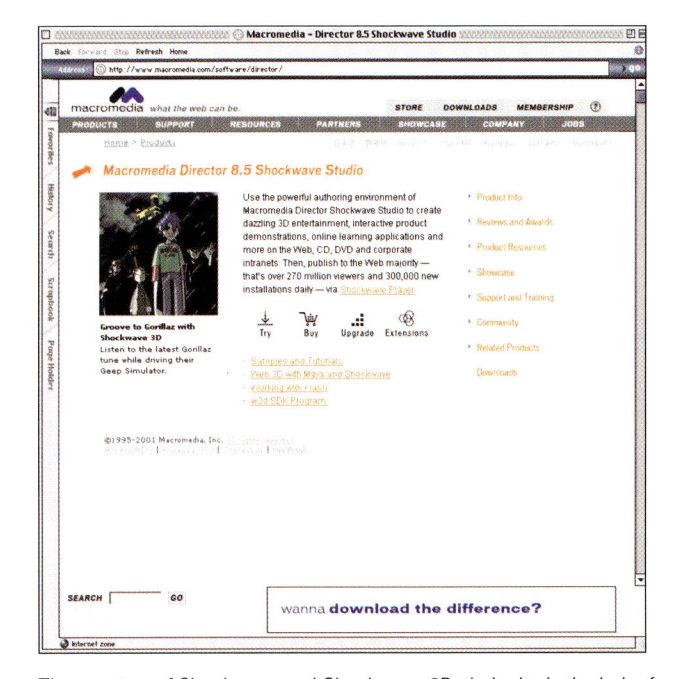

The creators of Shockwave and Shockwave 3D; their site is the hub of things to come regarding Shockwave!

3D Model Makers and Suppliers

Arius3D

http://www.arius3d.com/

When you think high resolution, think of these guys. They have technology that allows super accurate color matching for 3D content. Check out the example on the home page. Don't forget to drag the box around.

Kaon Interactive

http://www.kaon.com/

Kaon Interactive has a great supply of interactive demonstration material that will allow you to see whether their solution is something you are looking for. In addition to Shockwave 3D content, they have a no-plug-in solution for 3D delivery, which is great if you don't want your users to download plug-ins.

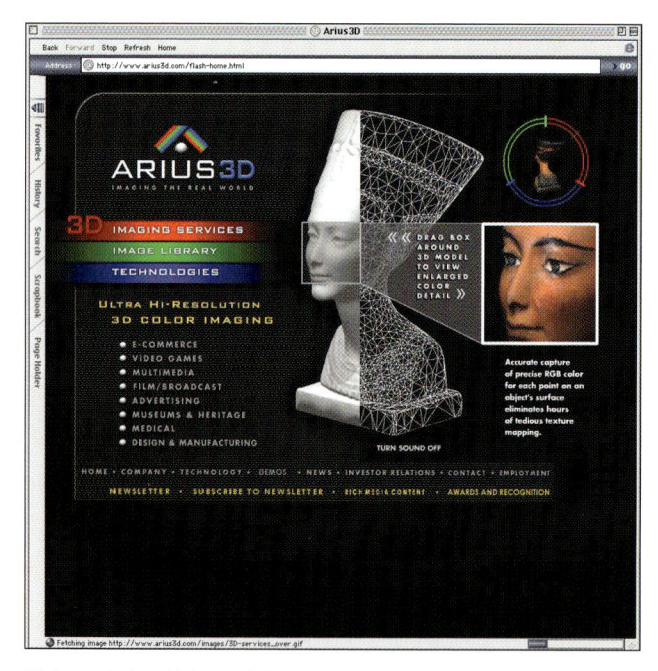

Makers of ultra-high resolution image delivery technology for the web.

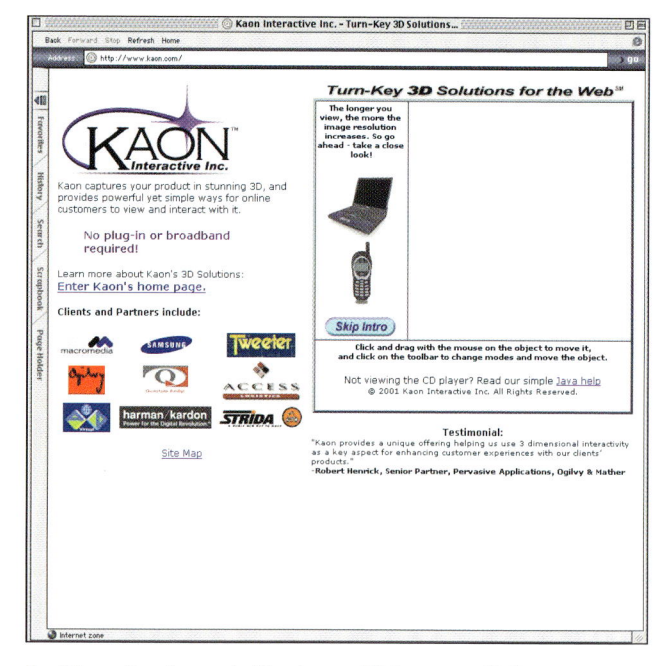

Don't have time to create Shockwave 3D for yourself? Kaon Interactive can produce content for you.

Turbo Squid

http://www.turbosquid.com

Go to the community section on this site and join the Shockwave 3D community! While you are there, join the 3ds max or Maya community, too. You will find games, models, motion capture scripts, and applications for power users.

If you only have time to visit one site, choose this one. There is a wealth of information and fun resources.

Zygote

http://www.zygote.com/

If you can dream it, these guys can make it. Or, they already have made it, and you can download it from the site. This site offers services and models galore.

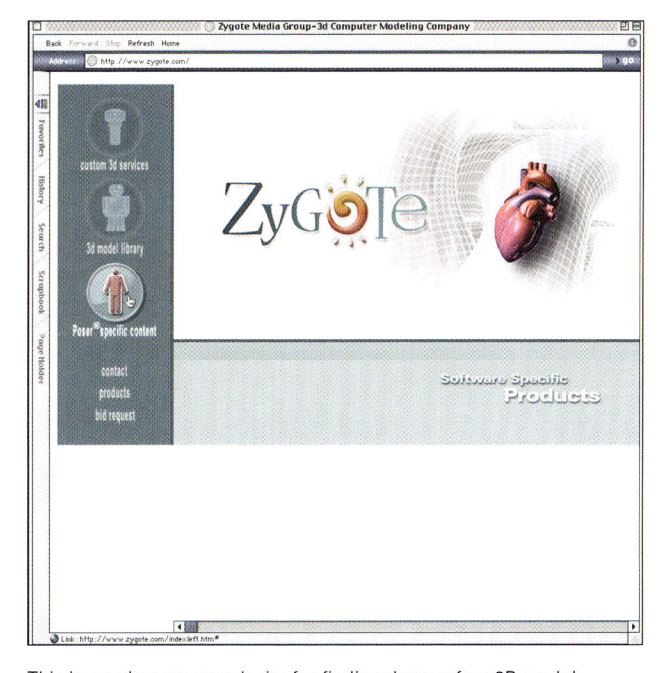

This is another great web site for finding that perfect 3D model.

Viewpoint

http://www.viewpoint.com

Viewpoint has more models than any other site I have seen to date. If they don't have something you are looking for, they will scan it with room-sized laser scanners. They also offer a 3D web playback plug-in technology.

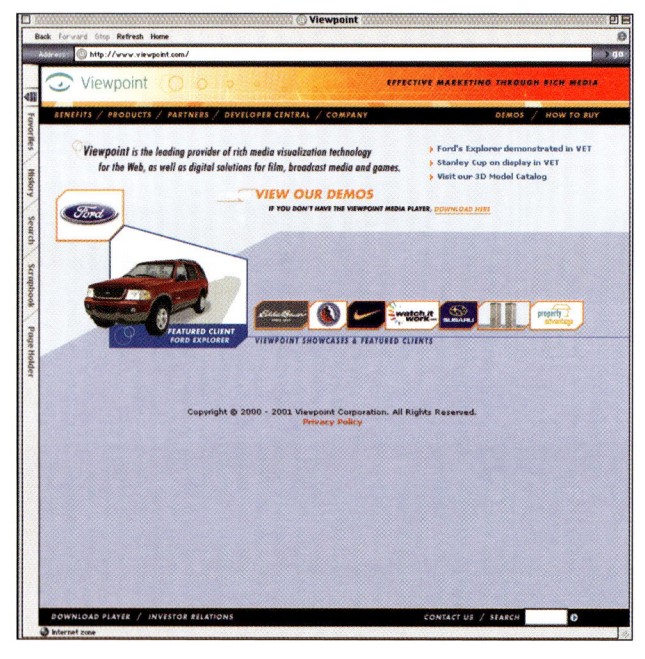

Viewpoint has neatly categorized collections of models. These are not free, but you can preview the look and the poly count of every model before buying online.

Inspiration Sites

3DRender

http://www.3drender.com/

This is my new favorite site. The book (that the site is centered around) is essential for anyone interested in 3D. The site is well designed and has a community where you might even find me.

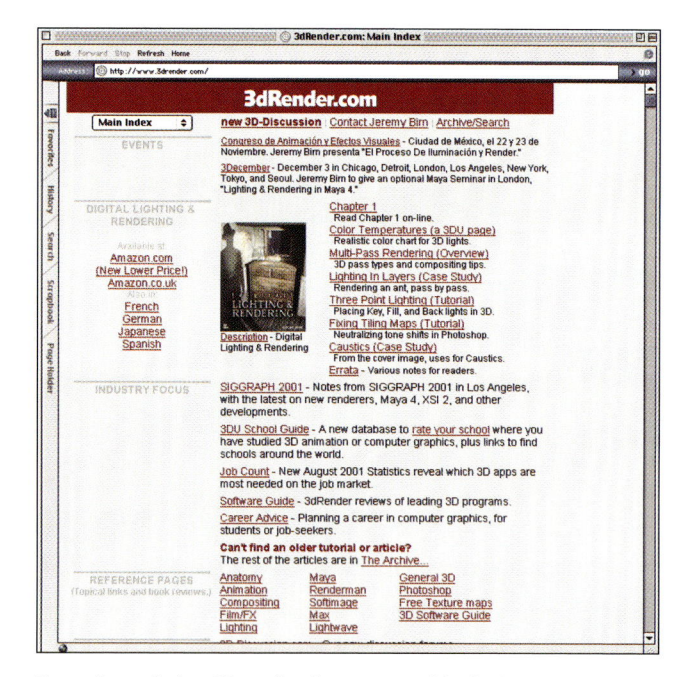

Regardless of what 3D application you use, this site is worth a visit, as you will learn a wealth of information about lighting and rendering.

3Dluvr

http://www.3dluvr.com

This is another great site for inspiration during those 3D modeling slump times. Check out the ArtZone while you are browsing this site.

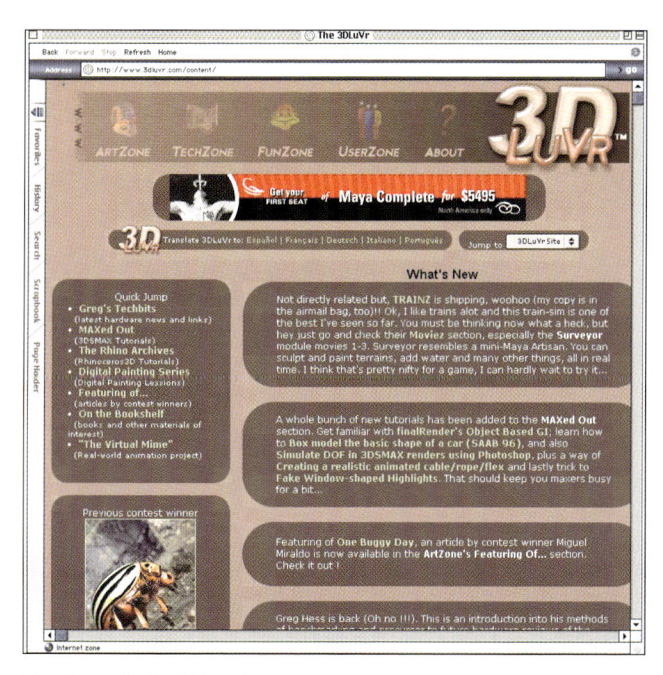

Check out the TechZone for answers to technical questions.

Max3D Lover

http://max3d.3dluvr.com

If you love 3ds max, you will love this site, as the name implies.

Find the latest news about 3ds max.

Animation World

http://mag.awn.com/

This site has everything animation, including articles, reviews, and stories. I consider it my new, second-favorite web site!

You'll find jobs, how-to articles, tips, stories, and tons of other information at this site.

Digimation

http://www.Digimation.com/

The special effects that come out of 3ds max are typically as a result of Digimation. Digimation makes an almost unlimited collection of plug-ins for just about everything you can imagine.

If there is a plug-in for 3ds max, you will be able to find it at this site.

VFX Pro

http://www.vfxpro.com/

This site is the front door of the Visual Effects community. People at ILM, Pixar, Dreamworks, and PDI are browsers of this site, and you should be as well. There is a huge listing of jobs if you are considering employment in the industry. The offerings are worth the required registration.

This site is the king of visual effects!

Trinity

http://www.trinity3d.com/

The Trinity folks specialize in animation and special effects, and their site is a great place to check out the latest technologies in render solutions and hardware devices.

Trinity3D can give you the software tools or do your Shockwave 3D creation for you.

Design in Motion

http://www.designinmotion.com/

This is the CNN of motion graphic designers. This site has an enormous amount of resources related to the world of 3D.

If you work with After Effects, you will love this site of endless resources!

Xtras and Plug-Ins

face2face

http://www.f2f-inc.com/

face2face offers a very unique solution to talking characters that you might want to create. You talk and videotape yourself, and then you analyze the talking motion using software. The resulting data is translated into your 3D models.

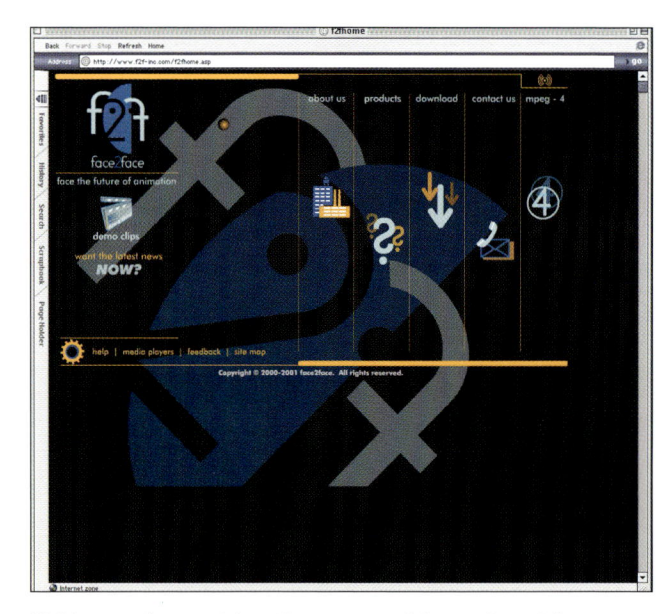

Digitize your face, and face2face can turn it into a 3D model.

famous3D

http://www.famous3d.com/

This company specializes in facial animation and visual characters for the web. Think low poly counts, and you'll get them here.

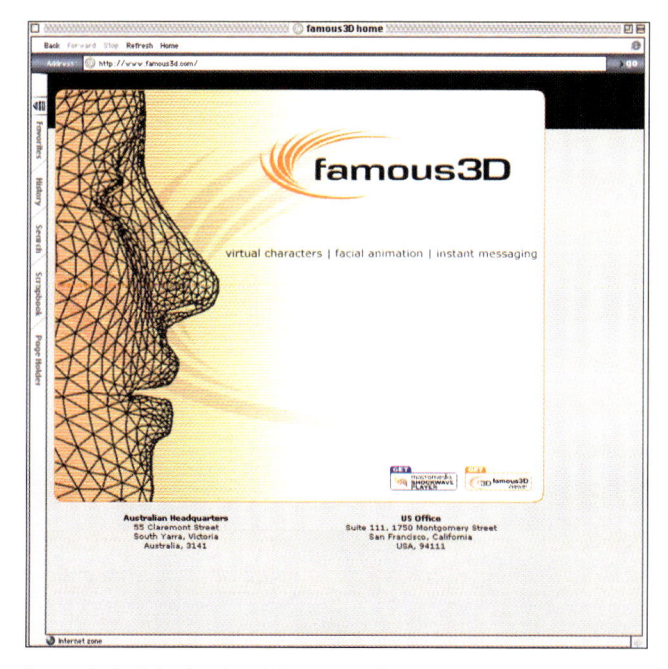

Low poly-facial animation delivered via Shockwave 3D is the specialty at this site.

Havok

http://www.havok.com

Havok is the creator of the real-time physics simulator for 3ds max and Director. They have free plug-ins for 3ds max 3 and 4 that enable physics to be incorporated into your models. This physics interaction can translate to Shockwave 3D through Havok.

The creators of real-time physics libraries for Shockwave 3D.

MGI

http://www.mgisoft.com/

MGI is the creator of Photovista 3D and other cool web tools. These tools let you easily create detailed, photo-realistic, 3D objects that site visitors can use and then export to Shockwave 3D.

The creators of Photovista provide a fast photo-modeling tool for Shockwave 3D content creation.

NxView

http://www.nxview.com/

NxView 5 is a 3D application that allows you to create compelling web content. Make sure to check out the animated truck on the home page of the NxView site.

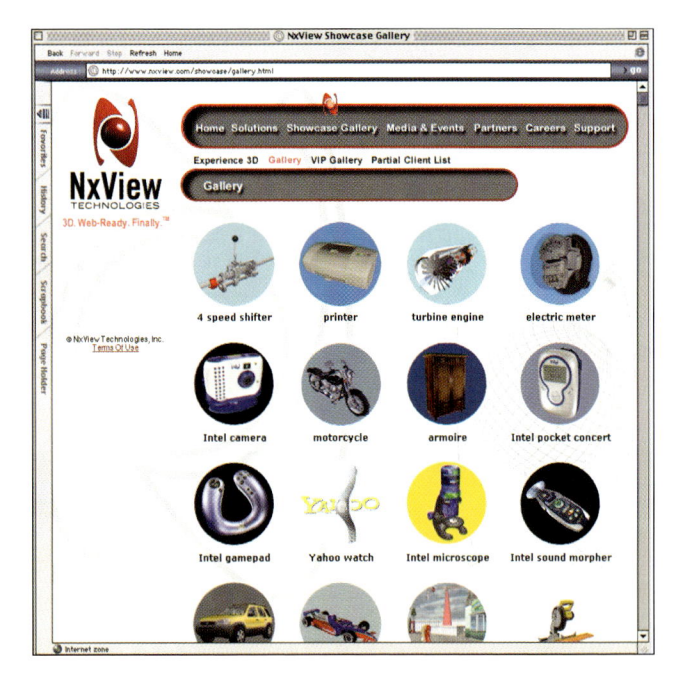

Visit the Gallery section to get a sample of the quality of work these guys can produce.

Shockwave 3D Content Developers

3dvillage

http://www.3dvillage.com/

These guys develop 3D media for other companies. They offer e-Learning, real estate and economic development, eCommerce, and promotional media content creation.

This company will create Shockwave 3D content for you. This site has several resources to help you decide what is right for you.

Dream Theater

http://www.dreamtheater.com/

Dream Theater is a fully integrated company that specializes in conceptualization, design, content writing, and programming.

Dream Theater is a one-stop solution for your digital needs.

ForgeFX

http://www.forgefx.com/

This is a "you must visit it" site. ForgeFX develops killer Shockwave 3D games, and it offers sample code for valuable learning experiences.

Check out this site for a beautiful display of what is possible on the web.

Gigawatt Studios

http://www.gwatt.com/

This is another "must see it" site that is beautifully designed in Flash. The site has several Shockwave 3D games (play the Lunchables game).

Shockwave 3D content creators and their sample games.

Kalisto

http://www.kalisto.com/

Kalisto is a multi-platform game development company. Visit the web games section.

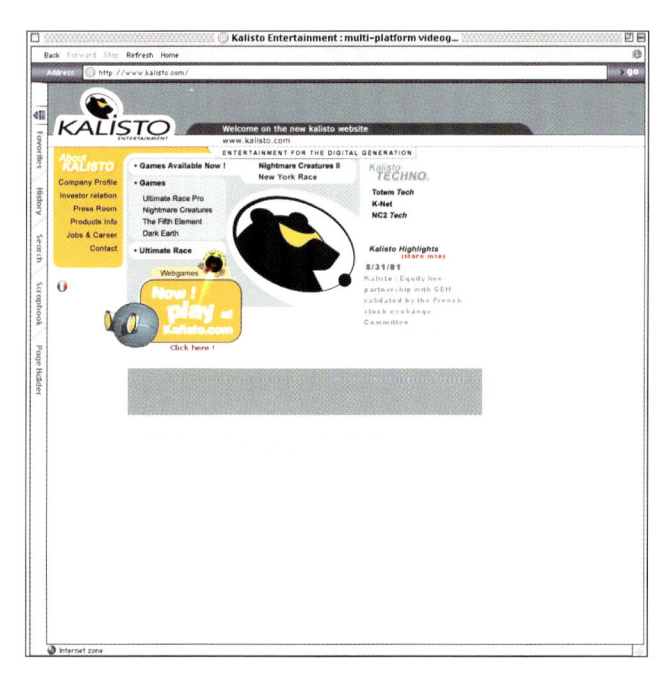

Learn as you play some great games, and don't forget to play The Fifth Element game.

MindComet

http://www.mindcomet.com

This site is one of the most compelling broadband sites I have seen. It is big, fast, and just plain fun. Visit MindComet for some true inspiration.

For those of you who have a fast connection, check out this site.

My Virtual Model

http://www.myvirtualmodel.com

This site is truly unique. Here, you can create a virtual model of yourself or someone that you know, and then use that model to shop for clothing. Attempt to create a model of yourself.

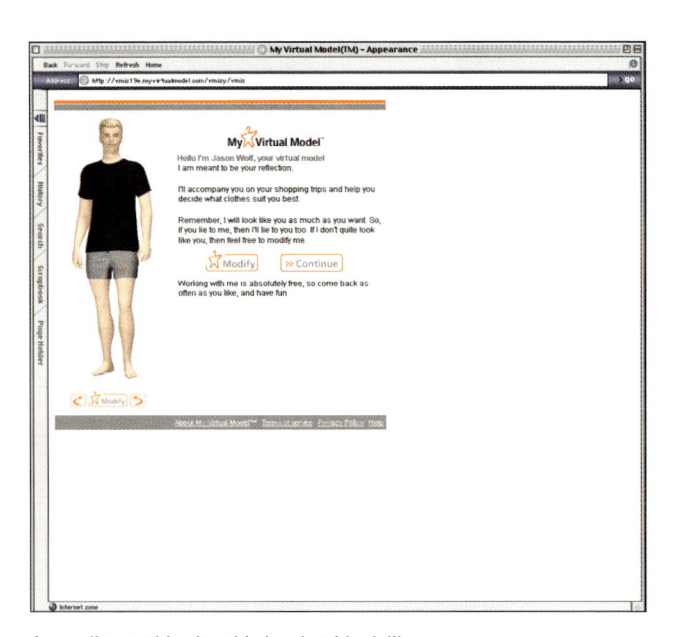

According to this site, this is what I look like.

OradNet

http://www.oradnet.com/

This company makes a technology called TOPlay. With it, you can deliver full-motion 3D graphics, interactive sports entertainment, database information, and online sporting events. It's similar to a real-time Shockwave 3D game based on real-world data.

A blending of live action content and 3D modeling and animation is this company's web site.

Right Hemisphere

http://www.us.righthemisphere.com/

One word describes this site—DeepPaint. Or, is that two words? Check out the DeepPaint application if you are a 3ds max or Maya user. You won't regret it.

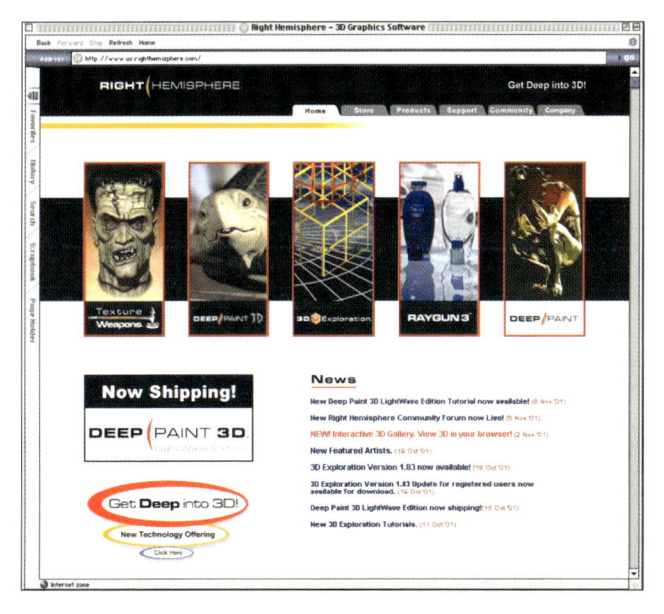

I recommend you check out DeepPaint at this site.

SquidSoup

http://www.squidsoup.com/

These guys built their own set of 3D algorithms for Director a couple of years ago. Some of the work they did (altzero 1) won awards and brought them acknowledgment by Macromedia. They currently produce content for companies such as Intel, Universal Music Group, Levi's, Audi, PlayStation, and The Arts Council of England.

You will love the inventive Shockwave 3D games this company has developed.

TRIK:MEDIA

http://www.trikmedia.com/

These guys are the creators of the "one more" multiplayer Shockwave 3D game. Visit the site and enter the Flash version for inspiration.

Elegant design and inspiration can be found at this company's web site.

CHAPTER 8

■ **In This Chapter**

What Is the RTA?, 191
   What Comes with RTA?, 192
RTA Features, 192
Why RTA?, 194
Concluding Remarks, 196

Sneak Peek at the Maya® RTA™

We've discussed other 3D authoring tools, such as 3ds max. This chapter discusses an exciting and powerful tool that can be used with Shockwave to deliver 3D content to the Internet. This tool is the Maya® Real-Time Author™ setup tool.

Maya provides a 3D perspective of objects in animation [8.1], as well as an Interaction Editor, which shows a view of the animation action including objects and a touch sensor that triggers it [8.1]. A panel (located on the right side of the screen in 8.1) shows the attribute editor of the animation action, where the objects that are part of it and the frame duration are selected.

Maya is a premiere 3D tool. If you've seen a movie with special effects, then you've seen the capabilities of Maya and you probably didn't even realize it. Movies such as *Final Fantasy*, *The Matrix*, and *The Phantom Menace* are products of Maya's 3D capabilities. Why doesn't everyone use it, you ask? Some people don't use it because the full-blown, unlimited version costs $16,000. Maya does have financing plans, if you decide to take the plunge and skip out on buying that new car!

There is an advantage to investing in Maya. It is an application that might help you obtain work in the industry, if you know how to use it. Alias|Wavefront (the creators of Maya) also offers a product called Maya Builder® for around $3,000.

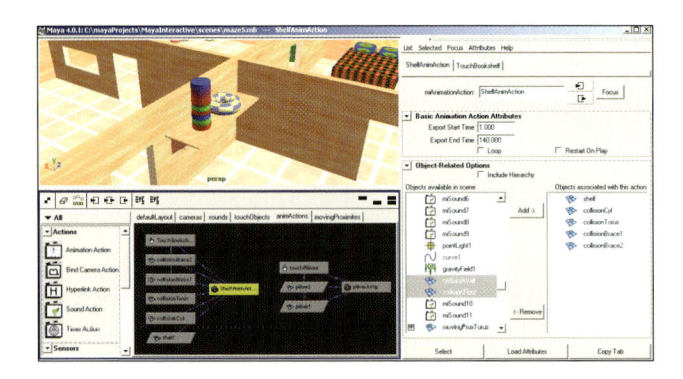

Maya Builder provides Maya's workflow features with a polygon-based toolset that works perfectly for Shockwave 3D authoring.

Maya users are comprised of the best 3D people in the industry today. This elite group can create animation and special effects for high-profile video games, feature films, and television shows. Why would Maya users want to output to Shockwave 3D when it's a medium that isn't traditionally used in their world? Generally, users of Maya animate for feature film; why would they want to move their content to the Internet where quality and size decrease? They do because of the power of Maya RTA.

Just as I was considering the idea of using Maya, Alias|Wavefront, the creators of Maya, released Maya RTA or real-time authoring. One of the amazing features of RTA is the manner in which it allows the Maya 3D artist to create final Shockwave content—complete with behaviors and interactions—all within Maya and without writing custom Lingo code. For the Director developer, a key advantage is that the behaviors and interactions created in RTA are generated as 3D Lingo that can be modified and extended. This combination of attributes leads to some serious productivity advantages in complex Shockwave projects that incorporate 3D content.

Maya's RTA is a solution for animators who are creating interactive 3D content that is integrated into the Maya workflow system. RTA takes your created content and automatically delivers it to the Internet through Shockwave 3D. This includes the Lingo code.

[8.1] Save time by building your user interactions inside Maya.

At the time of writing this book, the Maya RTA application and the new Shockwave 3D exporter were unavailable. However, the features and benefits of how these two technologies work together are worth the review. It is my intention to provide you with a solid understanding of how these technologies work together so that you can decide whether you want to invest in Maya RTA or another tool.

What Is the RTA?

RTA is a Maya plug-in. It introduces a new Interaction Editor into the Maya user interface [8.2].

This new Interaction Editor allows for the creation of and connection to a new set of Maya scene elements called sensors, actions, and viewers. The new Editor is similar to HyperShade (in Maya), where shader networks are created, which allow you to point to various shaders. With the Interaction Editor, you construct networks that control a scene's behaviors and user interactions with the scene's 3D content. Those interactions, behaviors, and scene geometry are exported to Director 8.5 through a new Shockwave 3D exporter.

3D content creation applications are designed for delivering linear animation. That is, the final output is a QuickTime movie, a video, or film; however, for games and the interactive market, the output is different. The output consists of the scene geometry and animations. In both cases, the 3D artist doesn't maintain control over how the 3D content is viewed. This is because the content is edited with other film or video footage. However, with the RTA plug-in, the Maya artist controls the experience that the user has, even if the creator doesn't know Lingo.

Using the RTA plug-in, the artist can create different kinds of interactions and assign different behaviors to objects within the scene. Some interaction examples include the following:

> The user is in the 3D scene and clicks on a model (or object). When he does this, the mouse action causes an animation sequence to start playing a sound file. When the audio file stops playing, a web browser takes the user to a specific web page.

> The user is in the 3D scene and presses a key on the keyboard, which results in a walking or flying action through the scene. The actions automatically avoid objects below and above the user's perspective.

> The user approaches a 3D object within a specific distance, and a sound starts playing. When the sound is completed, an animation sequence starts playing. The user can click a button to shift the camera view to get a better perspective of the animation that is playing.

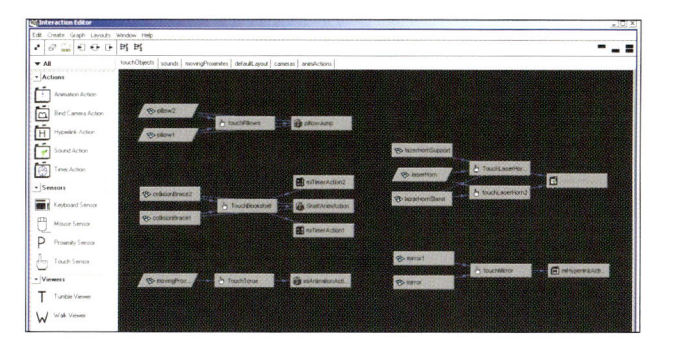

[8.2] The Interaction Editor has a simple drag-and-drop user interface.

These interactions are similar to the behaviors that are built into Director, except that they are built into the 3D application Maya. This allows you to create almost everything in one application. This is a great feature and prevents some of the back-and-forth activity that is required when building a Shockwave 3D movie.

What Comes with RTA?

Three components comprise the RTA product. Two are plug-ins that install into Maya. The third is a script file that installs into Director. Using this script file means you don't have to use Lingo programming. As noted previously, the Maya RTA plug-in also includes the Interaction Editor, which enables the creation of behaviors and interaction networks within Maya.

A new 1.2 version of the Maya Shockwave 3D exporter converts a Maya scene into the .W3D format required for input into Director. The exporter provides a pre-viewer that runs in Maya and allows for testing and refinement of Maya content destined for Shockwave 3D. Interactions and behaviors, as well as scene appearance and animation, can be tested in the Shockwave pre-viewer, saving you from more back-and-forth time.

[8.3] The path from Maya to Shockwave 3D is shown in this figure.

The .W3D file is a closed file that is proprietary and non-extensible; thus, the people at Alias|Wavefront had to come up with a way to get the interactive portion of the content out of Maya and into Director. This was done by writing an ASCII file that contains the Lingo syntax, which allows for interactive scenes. This new file type ends with the .ls suffix, and it must be imported along with your Shockwave .W3D file into Director in order for the Maya scene to function properly [8.3].

Note

New Shockwave 3D Exporter The new 1.2 Maya Shockwave 3D exporter is going to release simultaneously with RTA. It will operate with Maya whether or not RTA is installed. There is no charge for this plug-in. However, as noted previously, there is a charge for Maya.

RTA Features

The Maya-Shockwave duo provides three features to allow for content creation—sensors, actions, and viewers. The sensors are the triggers for the actions in the scene. The actions are events that occur while playing back the content in Shockwave 3D format. The viewers provide behaviors for the cameras that the user controls when in Shockwave 3D.

You can use multiple connections and one sensor that triggers an event to create multiple actions. For example, when a user gets close to an object, he or she can trigger a sound that causes an animated sequence to start playing. Longer interaction networks can also be created allowing an initial action to trigger more subsequent actions, and so on.

These connections can be set up in Maya without having to go into Director or without having to use Lingo script.

The sensors are the first scene elements that detect types of events or user input. The five types of sensors are as follows:

> **Touch** A touch sensor detects a user touching an object in the 3D scene. The user selects the object from a list of geometry meshes in the scene. Touching is defined in a variety of ways and includes clicking with the mouse, or simply rolling the cursor over or off of a specified object(s).

> **Keyboard** This sensor detects the user pressing or releasing a specified keyboard key or key combination (Shift, Alt, Ctrl, and so on).

> **Mouse** The mouse sensor detects the user pressing or releasing a specified mouse button.

> **Proximity** This sensor detects the current camera moving into or out of a volume type selected by the user and placed within the 3D scene. Proximity sensor volume types are cube, cylinder, and sphere. They can be transformed (translated, rotated, scaled), parented, and animated as necessary.

> **Actions as sensors** The completion of most RTA actions can be used to trigger subsequent or additional actions. In other words, when one action ends, another one can begin if the action that completed is also acting as a sensor.

The next scene elements are the actions. Actions are the events that are triggered by RTA sensors. The six types of actions are as follows:

> **Bind Camera** This action switches the 3D display to the view of a specified camera. The camera can have a pre-choreographed animation, or it may be the camera associated with an RTA viewer that allows the end user to control its position and orientation.

> **Timer** This action starts a clock for a user-specified amount of time. The completion of the timer action is generally used to trigger subsequent actions, such as the start of an animation or sound.

> **Animation** The animation action causes the motion of a specified set of objects to play over a specified range of frames. The completion of the animation can be detected and used to trigger subsequent actions. Animation actions can be looped continually.

> **Sound** The sound action plays a specified audio file. Sound can be ambient or spatial. A Maya manipulator that depicts the point of origin and extent in three dimensions controls spatial sound. The spatial positioning of maximum sound volume and minimum sound volume is also controlled. The completion of the sound action can be used to trigger subsequent actions. Sound can be looped as well.

> **Hyperlink** This action launches a specified web page when triggered.

> **Lingo Script**   This is an RTA stub action that is provided for use by Director Lingo programmers. (A *stub action* is a blank action that allows a Lingo programmer the ability to custom-write an action to suit his or her needs.) It allows the Maya artist to put sensors in a Maya scene that are set to trigger Lingo scripts that will be provided by the Director programmer.

The last scene elements are the viewers. Viewers are types of cameras and controls that can be placed into a scene and exported to Director and the Shockwave Player. RTA viewers offer specific control characteristics that are appropriate to the type of 3D content or environment being viewed. Viewers include the following:

> **Walk**   The RTA Walk viewer provides first-person, game-type camera controls that allow a user to walk through a 3D environment. Control attributes provided to the Maya artist are speed, step height, and collision distance.

> **Speed**   This viewer represents the speed with which the camera moves through a 3D scene.

> **Step height**   This viewer represents the height limit of an object in the scene over which the camera moves. Above that height, the object will be blocked. Step height also determines what is defined as a cliff or precipice off of which the camera will not walk.

> **Collision distance**   This is the distance at which the camera bumps into obstructions. Or, this can be defined as the distance allowed between two objects before a collision occurs.

> **Tumble**   The RTA Tumble viewer provides Maya-type camera controls for viewing and interacting with a 3D object. The Tumble viewer defines an up vector as it rotates around the object of focus. It does not lean over like the camera controls provided in Director. It also provides discrete camera pan and zoom, instead of the drifting pan and zoom of the default Director cameras.

> **Moded vs. non-moded viewers**   The option to make RTA viewer cameras moded or non-moded is provided to accommodate a range of content complexity issues.

The moded version is designed for more complex scenes and experienced 3D users. In these cases, the user explicitly determines that the camera will become active by selecting a specified control key to enter camera control mode.

The non-moded option puts the camera immediately into control mode. As soon as the user clicks in the 3D scene, camera control is initiated. This moded viewer is intended for less complex 3D scenes and less experienced 3D users.

Why RTA?

There are many advantages to the RTA solution for both the Maya artist and the Lingo programmer. Although Director offers a comprehensive set of Lingo commands for controlling 3D content in a .W3D file, it does not have a sophisticated 3D user interface to allow elements in a Shockwave 3D scene to be controlled interactively. In addition, you can't customize the content after you've imported the content into Director.

Maya RTA, on the other hand, does provide an interface and allows you to customize your content.

In Shockwave, virtually all of the 3D scene control comes from Lingo scripting. The result is that the authoring of complex 3D scene interactions from within Director requires a deep knowledge of both Lingo and of 3D programming concepts. The number of Director programmers who have this combination of skills is small, a limitation that constrains the potential expansion of compelling Shockwave 3D content. The RTA removes that limitation constraint by simplifying the creation and control of 3D interactions for Director users in a number of ways.

First, there are 3D spatial control tools [8.4] in Maya. With no 3D user interface for controlling 3D content that is imported into a .W3D file, performing the most basic 3D tasks in Director (such as positioning and orienting a 3D sound, or locating and sizing a proximity sensor) requires the use of Lingo scripts. Maya RTA improves this by allowing the creation of a variety of 3D interactions for Shockwave from within the user interface. Maya's 3D spatial control tools, such as manipulators and interactive cameras with instant focus utilities, can be applied to visually position, orient, and scale interactive 3D scene elements, such as proximity sensors and 3D sound sources.

The output that RTA creates for Director is a raw Lingo file. The RTA Lingo scripts are open and accessible to the Lingo programmer. This makes reverse engineering possible, because the scripts can be used as is, or they can be extended. They provide an excellent basis for learning how professional 3D programmers approach 3D problems.

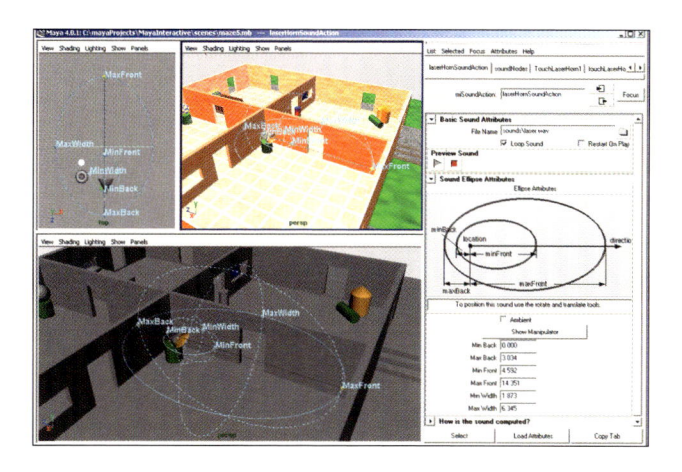

[8.4] The Maya RTA 3D sound control user interface.

Finally, since the RTA toolset and workflow is fully integrated with both Maya and with the Maya Shockwave 3D exporter, there are productivity advantages that include the following:

> **The Scene Checker**   With this feature, a Maya scene can be reviewed for improper use of RTA sensors and actions.

> **Export Express**   After you first export to a Shockwave file, the pre-viewer is calculated and cached; subsequent modifications to RTA interactions or viewers are lightweight exports that are immediately available for testing and tuning.

> **Scene Manifest**   The Maya Scene Manifest file contains detailed information regarding the exported Maya data file. This includes information on the RTA sensors, actions, and viewers. You can use this to check your scenes for redundant actions, or you can check it for errors.

With the arrival of Maya RTA, the rate at which high-quality, interactive 3D content is produced will increase dramatically. Lingo programmers can focus on building more compelling flow-control and effective media integration. When 3D Lingo programming is required, the RTA code base can be used as a starting point of reference. The end result will improve quality, completion times, and even costs. In my opinion, Maya is the best tool for Shockwave 3D content creation, but it's also the most expensive. You should weigh the advantages against the cost and realize that you get what you pay for.

Concluding Remarks

I hope you enjoyed reading this book. The lessons that you learned should springboard your skills ahead of mainstream developers.

I also hope that you enjoyed the opportunity to explore what Shockwave 3D can do for your projects. I have certainly enjoyed explaining just how powerful Shockwave 3D is and how it can be applied in real-world situations. Now, it's up to you to take what you've learned to create your own corner of the 3D web!

Good luck with your development endeavors!

Jason Wolf

Appendix A

What's on the CD-ROM

The accompanying CD-ROM is packed with all sorts of additional files and samples to help you learn more about Shockwave 3D. The following sections contain detailed descriptions of the CD's contents.

For more information about the use of this CD, please use the Read Me file that is included in some of the directories on the CD.

Technical Support Issues
If you have any difficulties with this CD, you can access our web site at **http://www.newriders.com**.

System Requirements

This CD-ROM was configured for use on systems running Windows NT Workstation, Windows 95, Windows 98, Windows 2000, and Macintosh. Your machine will need to meet the following system requirements in order for this CD to operate properly:

> - 4X Speed CD-ROM drive for one of the operating systems listed previously

> - Digital video playback software, such as QuickTime or Windows Media Player

> - Macromedia Director Shockwave Studio 8.5 and 3ds max 4 to open some of the demo files

> - Internet Explorer 5 (or later) or Netscape 6

Loading the CD Files

To load the files from the CD, insert the disc into your CD-ROM drive. The files are located in their own directories. You should copy the directories to your local hard drive if you want to save any changes to the files you are working on. Otherwise, you can simply double-click the files on the CD.

CD Folders

This CD contains the files you'll need to complete the exercises in Shockwave 3D. These files can be found in the root directory's folders. In addition, there are other examples for you to explore.

Here is a complete list of the CD contents:

> **Chapter_2.** This folder contains the "textextrude.dir" Director file referenced in Chapter 2, "Oh Behave!."

> **Chapter_3.** This folder contains the steps used to create the house fly-through example found in Chapter 3, "Architecture Fly-Through." It includes the 3ds max files, the Director source files, and the exported .W3D file.

> **Chapter_4.** This folder contains the examples used to create the car demo in Chapter 4, "Wreaking Havok." This folder includes the 3ds max source file, the Director source file (including the .W3D and .HKE exports from 3ds max), a completed web version of the demo, and the new Havok behaviors.

> **Exporters.** This folder contains the Shockwave 3D exporters that allow 3ds max (version 3 or 4), Maya, and Softimage to save files into the .W3D format. In addition, you will find the Havok exporters for 3ds max (3 and 4), which allow you to export out .HKE files.

> **Chapter_7_URLs.** This folder is referenced in Chapter 7, "Places to Go, People to See!." It contains an HTML link file that holds tons of links to content developers, software manufacturers, and Shockwave 3D inspiration sites.

> **Shockwave3DPlayer.** This folder contains the Shockwave 3D player for your web browser. If you haven't already installed Shockwave 3D for the Macintosh or Windows, you can do so from this folder. Simply double-click the installer file.

> **WebSiteSamples.** This folder contains sample .DCR and .DIR files from the **Havok.com** web site. To play them, drag the .DCR file(s) to your browser or open the .DIR files from within Director 8.5.

> **Chain_animation.** This folder contains a sample QuickTime movie and a 3ds max file showing the linking of a chain together for use with the Havok physics plug-in.

Read This Before Opening the Software

By opening the CD package, you agree to be bound by the following agreement:

You may not copy or redistribute the entire CD-ROM as a whole. Copying and redistribution of individual software programs on the CD-ROM is governed by terms set by individual copyright holders.

The installer, code, images, actions, and brushes from the author(s) are copyrighted by the publisher and the authors.

This software is sold as-is, without warranty of any kind, either expressed or implied, including but not limited to the implied warranties of merchantability and fitness for a particular purpose. Neither the publisher nor its dealers or distributors assumes any liability for any alleged or actual damages arising from the use of these programs. (Some states do not allow for the exclusion of implied warranties, so the exclusion may not apply to you.)

Index

Symbols

3D applications
    need for, 11
    Shockwave 3D plug-in, 11-13
3D model maker web sites, 174-176
3D objects, importing, 7
3ds max, recommendation for, 11
3D text, creating, 41-43
3Dluvr web site, 177
3DMax Lover web site, 177
3DRender web site, 176
3dvillage web site, 183

A

absolute frame rates, 119
actions (behaviors)
    Automatic Model Rotation, 32
    Click Model Go to Marker, 26-27
    Create Box, 20
    Create Particle System, 21-23
    Create Sphere, 23-24
    defined, 19
    Dolly Camera, 28-29
    Drag Camera, 24
    Drag Model, 25
    Drag Model to Rotate, 25
    Fly Through, 26
    Generic Do, 29
    Level of Detail, 32-33
    Model Rollover Cursor, 34
    Orbit Camera, 27
    Pan Camera Horizontal, 30
    Pan Camera Vertical, 30
    Play Animation, 27-28
    Reset Camera, 31
    Rotate Camera, 31
    Show Axis, 34-35
    Sub Division Surface, 35
    Toggle Redraw, 31-32
    Toon, 36-37
actions (Maya RTA), 192-194
    as sensors, 193
actual file sizes versus size on hard drive, 15
Additional Options sub-window (Export Options window), 62
Alias|Wavefront web site, 167
AMAPI 3D web site, 173
angles (camera), linking sprites to camera, 156-157
angular dashpots (Havok)
    defined, 125
    functions, 140-141
    properties, 139-140
animation, Play Animation behavior, 27-28
animation action (Maya RTA), 193
Animation Options sub-window (Export Options window), 61
animation quality setting versus sampling interval setting, 62
animation speed, building models, 46-47

Animation World web site, 178
AntiGravity behavior (Havok control behavior), 104
application developer web sites, 167-173
Apply Constant Force behavior (Havok control behavior), 105
Apply Constant Impulse behavior (Havok control behavior), 106
applying textures to buildings for Virtual City Tours project, 152-153
Arius3D web site, 174
Ashlar-Vellum web site, 167
attaching behaviors to sprites, 41
attenuation, 54
Automatic Model Rotation behavior, 32
availability of Shockwave 3D plug-in, 11-13
axes, Show Axis behavior, 34-35

B

behaviors
    actions
        Automatic Model Rotation, 32
        Click Model Go to Marker, 26-27
        Create Box, 20
        Create Particle System, 21-23
        Create Sphere, 23-24
        Dolly Camera, 28-29
        Drag Camera, 24
        Drag Model, 25
        Drag Model to Rotate, 25
        Fly Through, 26
        Generic Do, 29
        Level of Detail, 32-33
        Model Rollover Cursor, 34
        Orbit Camera, 27
        Pan Camera Horizontal, 30
        Pan Camera Vertical, 30
        Play Animation, 27-28
        Reset Camera, 31
        Rotate Camera, 31
        Show Axis, 34-35
        Sub Division Surface, 35
        Toggle Redraw, 31-32
        Toon, 36-37
    attaching to sprites, 41
    for car simulation, installing, 97
    changing settings, 41
    compared to Lingo, 19-20
    defined, 7, 18-19
    Havok (physics engine), 97
        control behaviors, 102-106
        mouse interactions ("playing God"), 110-111
        setup behaviors, 99-102
    overview, 10
    triggers
        Keyboard Input, 40
        Mouse Enter, 38
        Mouse Leave, 38
        Mouse Left, 37-38
        Mouse Right, 39
        Mouse Within, 40
bind camera action (Maya RTA), 193
Boolean subtractions, 48-51
boxes, Create Box behavior, 20
browser testing movies, 75-76
building models (fly-through house project), 46-49, 52
buildings (Virtual City Tours project)
    applying textures, 152-153
    creating textures, 150-151
    modeling, 147-150
    photographing, 144-147

C

Caligari web site, 168
cameras
    creating, 157
    Dolly Camera behavior, 28-29

Drag Camera behavior, 24
fly-through house project, 57
FOV (field of view) setting, 57
linking sprites to, 153-154
   direction arrow scripts, 158-159
   hot spot scripts, 161-162
   keyboard navigation, 155-156
   rotation button scripts, 162-163
   setting up camera angles, 156-157
   slider scripts, 159-161
Orbit Camera behavior, 27
Pan Camera Horizontal behavior, 30
Pan Camera Vertical behavior, 30
ray casting, 69-72
Reset Camera behavior, 31
Rotate Camera behavior, 31

car simulation
   convex objects versus concave objects in Havok, 91
   creating cross-platform file, 111-112
   creating scene for, 81-85
   exporting, 94
      pie chart in warning window, 96
      as Shockwave file, 94-95
      warning window, 96
   exporting movie, 111
   friction of objects, setting in Havok, 91
   importing into Director, 107-110
   increasing performance speed in Havok, 92
   installing behaviors for, 97
   lighting, 86-87
   mass of objects, setting in Havok, 89-90
   mouse interactions ("playing God"), 110-111
   rigid body collection in Havok, 88-89
   storyboarding, 80-81
   testing, 93-94
   texture mapping, 85-86
   units of measurement in Havok, 87-88
Cartesian coordinate system, Z-axis, 6-7
cartoons, Toon behavior, 36-37

castmembers. *See also* sprites
   Havok
      functions, 117-126
      properties, 114-117
   preloading, 67-68
   redrawing problems, 66-67
   scaling, 8-9
   visibility, reducing lag time in score, 66
chamfered box for car simulation, 82
Cinema 4D web site, 171
cities. *See* Virtual City Tours project
Click Model Go to Marker behavior, 26-27
collision distance viewer (Maya RTA), 194
collision tolerance (Havok simulations), 118-119
collision-tolerance force field in Havok, 83
collisions (Havok)
   havok.registerInterest( ) function, 121-123
   positioning rigid bodies, 127
colors, Toon behavior, 36-37
commands (Lingo)
   cpuhogticks, 154
   Frame Ready, 9
   Open Movie, 14
compressing movies, 13
compressing projector, 78
Compression Settings sub-window (Export Options window), 61
concave objects in Havok, 91
content developer web sites, 183-188
control behaviors, Havok (physics engine), 102-106
convex hulls and rigid bodies (Havok), 121
convex objects in Havok, 91
coordinates, Z-axis, 6-7
costs
   Maya, 190
   Maya Builder, 190
cpuhogticks command (Lingo), 154

Create Box behavior, 20
Create Particle System behavior, 21-23
Create Sphere behavior, 23-24
creating
    3D text, 41-43
    cameras, 157
    cross-platform file (car simulation), 111-112
    invisible buttons, 162
    projectors, 78
    rigid bodies (Havok), 121
    scene for car simulation, 81-85
    textures for Virtual City Tours, 150-151
cross-platform file, creating (car simulation), 111-112
Curious Labs web site, 168
cursors, Model Rollover Cursor behavior, 34

D

D Vision Works web site, 169
DCR format, exporting movies for the web, 15
delivery options. *See* exporting movies
Design in Motion web site, 180
Digimation web site, 178
direction arrow scripts, linking sprites to camera, 158-159
Director Dev web site, 7
Discreet web site, 170
display proxy in Havok, 92
dithering graphics, 77
Dolly Camera behavior, 28-29
DOUG web site, 7
downloading movies, progressive streaming, 8-10
Drag Camera behavior, 24
Drag Model behavior, 25
Drag Model to Rotate behavior, 25
Dream Theater web site, 183

Drive Model behavior (Havok control behavior), 104-105
DXR format, exporting movies as, 14
dynamic friction, 91

E

editing photos to create textures, 150-151
embedding Xtras in movies, 76-77
EON Reality web site, 171
Export Express (Maya RTA), 195
Export Options window, 58
    Additional Options sub-window, 62
    Animation Options sub-window, 61
    Compression Settings sub-window, 61
    Preview Options sub-window, 59
    Shockwave 3D Resources to Export sub-window, 60
    Texture Size Limits sub-window, 62
exporting
    car simulation
        from Havok, 94
        pie chart in warning window, 96
        as Shockwave file, 94-95
        warning window, 96
    Maya scenes to .W3D file format, 192
    models to Shockwave (fly-through house project), 57-64
    movies, 13
        car simulation, 111
        as DCR format for the web, 15
        as DXR format stand-alone applications, 14
        as stand-alone applications, 13-14
        to .W3D format, 153

F

face2face web site, 180
famous3D web site, 181
file formats. *See* .W3D file format

file size
    actual versus on hard drive, 15
    reducing, 65
        by compressing projector, 78
        by graphic dithering, 77
Fly Through behavior, 26
fly-through house project, 45-46
    building model for, 46-49, 52
    camera setup, 57
    creating projector, 78
    embedding Xtras, 76-77
    exporting to Shockwave, 57-64
    file size, reducing, 65
    graphic dithering, 77
    lighting, 53-54
    Lingo scripts for, 67-73
    naming model, 52-53
    publishing the movie, 78
    redrawing problems, 66-67
    saving and compacting the movie, 78
    score setup, 65-66
        reducing lag time, 66
    storyboarding, 46
    testing, 73
        browser testing, 75-76
        projector testing, 74-75
    texture mapping, 55-56
ForgeFX web site, 184
FOV (field of view) setting, 57
frame rates, absolute, 119
Frame Ready command (Lingo), 9
frames, score setup, 65-66
framing windows (fly-through house project), 51
friction (Havok)
    of objects, 91
    of rigid bodies, 128

functions (Havok)
    angular dashpots, 140-141
    castmembers, 117-126
    linear dashpots, 138-139
    rigid bodies, 132-135
    springs, 136-137

G

Generic Do behavior, 29
Gigawatt Studios web site, 184
graphic dithering, 77
graphical elements. *See* sprites
gravity in Havok, 87-88
    Set Gravity behavior, 102

H

Havok (physics engine), 11, 79-80
    angular dashpots
        functions, 140-141
        properties, 139-140
    behaviors, 97
        control behaviors, 102-106
        setup behaviors, 99-102
    car simulation
        convex objects versus concave objects, 91
        creating cross-platform file, 111-112
        creating scene for, 81-85
        exporting, 94
        exporting as Shockwave file, 94-95
        exporting movie, 111
        friction of objects, setting, 91
        importing into Director, 107-110
        increasing performance speed, 92
        installing behaviors for, 97
        lighting, 86-87

mass of objects, setting, 89-90
mouse interactions ("playing God"), 110-111
pie chart in warning window, 96
rigid body collection, 88-89
storyboarding, 80-81
testing, 93-94
texture mapping, 85-86
units of measurement, 87-88
warning window when exporting, 96
castmembers
   functions, 117-126
   properties, 114-117
linear dashpots
   functions, 138-139
   properties, 137-138
overlapping objects, 84
relationship with Reactor, 80
rigid bodies
   functions, 132-135
   properties, 126-131
springs
   functions, 136-137
   properties, 135-136
web site, 181
Havok Physics (HKE) behavior (Havok setup behavior), 100
Havok Physics (No HKE) behavior (Havok setup behavior), 101-102
havok.angularDashpot property, 116
havok.angularDashpot( ) function, 125
havok.collisionList property, 116
havok.deactivationParameters property, 116-117
havok.deleteAngularDashpot( ) function, 126
havok.deleteLinearDashpot( ) function, 125
havok.deleteRigidBody( ) function, 120
havok.deleteSpring( ) function, 124
havok.disableAllCollisions( ) function, 123
havok.disableCollision( ) function, 123

havok.dragParameters property, 117
havok.enableAllCollisions( ) function, 123
havok.enableCollision( ) function, 123
havok.gravity property, 115
havok.initialize( ) function, 117-119
havok.initialized property, 114
havok.linearDashpot property, 116
havok.linearDashpot( ) function, 124-125
havok.makeAngularDashpot( ) function, 125-126
havok.makeFixedRigidBody( ) function, 121
havok.makeLinearDashpot( ) function, 125
havok.makeMovableRigidBody( ) function, 120-121
havok.makeSpring( ) function, 124
havok.registerInterest( ) function, 121-123
havok.registerStepCallback( ) function, 123-124
havok.removeInterest( ) function, 123
havok.removeStepCallback( ) function, 124
havok.reset( ) function, 119
havok.rigidBody property, 115
havok.rigidBody( ) function, 120
havok.scale property, 114-115
havok.shutdown( ) function, 119
havok.simTime property, 115
havok.spring property, 116
havok.spring( ) function, 124
havok.step( ) function, 119
havok.subSteps property, 115
havok.timeStep property, 115
havok.tolerance property, 114
hkAngularDashpot.damping property, 140
hkAngularDashpot.getRigidBodyA( ) function, 141
hkAngularDashpot.getRigidBodyB( ) function, 141
hkAngularDashpot.name property, 139

hkAngularDashpot.rotation property, 140
hkAngularDashpot.setRigidBodyA( ) function, 140
hkAngularDashpot.setRigidBodyB( ) function, 141
hkAngularDashpot.strength property, 140

.HKE file format
    exporting, 94
    importing car simulation, 107-110

hkLinearDashpot.damping property, 138
hkLinearDashpot.getRigidBodyA( ) function, 139
hkLinearDashpot.getRigidBodyB( ) function, 139
hkLinearDashpot.name property, 137
hkLinearDashpot.pointA property, 138
hkLinearDashpot.pointB property, 138
hkLinearDashpot.setRigidBodyA( ) function, 139
hkLinearDashpot.setRigidBodyB( ) function, 139
hkLinearDashpot.strength property, 138
hkRigidBody.active property, 128-129
hkRigidBody.angularMomentum property, 130
hkRigidBody.angularVelocity property, 129-130
hkRigidBody.applyAngularImpulse( ) function, 133
hkRigidBody.applyForce( ) function, 132
hkRigidBody.applyForceAtPoint( ) function, 132
hkRigidBody.applyImpulse( ) function, 132
hkRigidBody.applyImpulseAtPoint( ) function, 133
hkRigidBody.applyTorque( ) function, 133
hkRigidBody.attemptMoveTo( ) function, 133-134
hkRigidBody.centerOfMass property, 130
hkRigidBody.corrector.enabled property, 131
hkRigidBody.corrector.level property, 131
hkRigidBody.corrector.maxDistance property, 131
hkRigidBody.corrector.maxTries property, 131
hkRigidBody.corrector.multiplier property, 131
hkRigidBody.corrector.threshold property, 131
hkRigidBody.correctorMoveTo( ) function, 135

hkRigidBody.force property, 130
hkRigidBody.friction property, 128
hkRigidBody.interpolatingMoveTo( ) function, 134
hkRigidBody.linearMomentum property, 130
hkRigidBody.linearVelocity property, 129
hkRigidBody.mass property, 127
hkRigidBody.name property, 126
hkRigidBody.pinned property, 129
hkRigidBody.position property, 126-127
hkRigidBody.restitution property, 128
hkRigidBody.rotation property, 127
hkRigidBody.torque property, 130
hkSpring.damping property, 136
hkSpring.elasticity property, 136
hkSpring.getRigidBodyA( ) function, 137
hkSpring.getRigidBodyB( ) function, 137
hkSpring.name property, 135
hkSpring.onCompression property, 136
hkSpring.onExtension property, 136
hkSpring.pointA property, 135
hkSpring.pointB property, 135-136
hkSpring.restLength property, 136
hkSpring.setRigidBodyA( ) function, 137
hkSpring.setRigidBodyB( ) function, 137
hot spot scripts, linking sprites to camera, 161-162
house project. *See* fly-through house project
hyperlink action (Maya RTA), 193

I-J

Image Modeler web site, 172
importing
    3D objects, 7
    car simulation into Director, 107-110

inspiration, web sites for, 176-180
installing behaviors for car simulation, 97
Interaction Editor (Maya RTA), 191-192
invisible buttons, creating, 162

K

Kalisto web site, 185
Kaon Interactive web site, 174
Keyboard Input trigger, 40
keyboard navigation, linking sprites to camera, 155-156
keyboard sensors (Maya RTA), 193

L

lag time in score, reducing, 66
Level of Detail behavior, 32-33
Library palette, 18
lighting
    attenuation, 54
    car simulation, 86-87
    fly-through house project, 53-54
LightWave web site, 172
linear dashpots (Havok)
    defined, 125
    functions, 138-139
    properties, 137-138
Lingo
    behaviors. *See* behaviors
    commands
        cpuhogticks, 154
        Frame Ready, 9
        Open Movie, 14
    compared to behaviors, 19-20
    defined, 7
    for fly-through house project, 67-73

Generic Do behavior, 29
Havok angular dashpots
    functions, 140-141
    properties, 139-140
Havok castmembers
    functions, 117-126
    properties, 114-117
Havok linear dashpots
    functions, 138-139
    properties, 137-138
Havok rigid bodies
    functions, 132-135
    properties, 126-131
Havok springs
    functions, 136-137
    properties, 135-136
web resources for information, 7
Lingo script action (Maya RTA), 194
linking sprites to camera, 153-154
    direction arrow scripts, 158-159
    hot spot scripts, 161-162
    keyboard navigation, 155-156
    rotation button scripts, 162-163
    setting up camera angles, 156-157
    slider scripts, 159-161
LOD setting (Shockwave), 47

M

Macromedia web site, 173
Make Angular Dashpot behavior (Havok setup behavior), 101
Make Fixed Rigid Body behavior (Havok setup behavior), 98
Make Linear Dashpot behavior (Havok setup behavior), 98-99
Make Movable Rigid Body behavior (Havok setup behavior), 99
Make Spring behavior (Havok setup behavior), 99-100
markers, Click Model Go to Marker behavior, 26-27
mass of objects, setting in Havok, 89-90
MAXON Computer web site, 171

Maya, 189-190
    cost of, 190
    web site, 167
Maya Builder, 190
Maya RTA (real-time authoring), 190-191
    actions, 192-194
    advantages of, 194, 196
    components of, 192
    Interaction Editor, 191-192
    sensors, 192-193
    viewers, 192, 194
measurement units. *See* units of measurement
MGI web site, 182
MindComet web site, 185
moded viewers (Maya RTA), 194
Model Rollover Cursor behavior, 34
modeling buildings for Virtual City Tours project, 147-150
models
    3D model maker web sites, 174-176
    Automatic Model Rotation behavior, 32
    Click Model Go to Marker behavior, 26-27
    Drag Model behavior, 25
    Drag Model to Rotate behavior, 25
    fly-through house project
        building, 46-49, 52
        camera setup, 57
        exporting to Shockwave, 57-64
        lighting, 53-54
        naming, 52-53
        storyboarding, 46
        texture mapping, 55-56
    Model Rollover Cursor behavior, 34
Mouse Enter trigger, 38
mouse interactions ("playing God"), car simulation, 110-111
Mouse Leave trigger, 38
Mouse Left trigger, 37-38
Mouse Right trigger, 39

mouse sensors (Maya RTA), 193
Mouse Within trigger, 40
Move Model behavior (Havok control behavior), 103-104
movies
    compressing, 13
    creating projector, 78
    downloading (progressive streaming), 8-10
    embedding Xtras, 76-77
    exporting, 13
        car simulation, 111
        as DCR format for the web, 15
        as DXR format stand-alone applications, 14
        as stand-alone applications, 13-14
        to .W3D format, 153
    graphic dithering, 77
    navigation in, 72
    pausing, 68-69
    publishing, 78
    saving and compacting, 78
    scaling, 8-9
    testing, 73
        browser testing, 75 76
        projector testing, 74-75
My Virtual Model web site, 186

N

naming models (fly-through house project), 52-53
navigation
    linking sprites to camera, 153-154
        direction arrow scripts, 158-159
        hot spot scripts, 161-162
        keyboard navigation, 155-156
        rotation button scripts, 162-163
        setting up camera angles, 156-157
        slider scripts, 159-161
    in movies, 72
NewTek web site, 172
non-moded viewers (Maya RTA), 194
NxView web site, 182

O-P

objects, overlapping and Havok (physics engine), 84
Open Movie command (Lingo), 14
OradNet web site, 186
Orbit Camera behavior, 27
overlapping objects and Havok (physics engine), 84

Pan Camera Horizontal behavior, 30
Pan Camera Vertical behavior, 30
particle systems, Create Particle System behavior, 21-23
pausing movies, 68-69
performance speed in Havok, increasing, 92
photo-realism for Virtual City Tours, 144
photographing buildings for Virtual City Tours project, 144-147
photos, editing to create textures, 150-151
physical properties of objects, setting in Havok, 89-90
physics engine. *See* Havok (physics engine)
pie chart in warning window, exporting car simulation, 96
Pie Chart window, 63
Play Animation behavior, 27-28
Play While Downloading Movie option (progressive streaming), 9
plug-ins
    Shockwave 3D plug-in, availability of, 11-13
    .W3D file exporter, 57-58
        troubleshooting, 64
    web sites for, 180-182
point of location for sliders, determining, 161
Polygon Addition tool (Shockwave), 47
Polygon Counter tool (3ds max), 47
Polygon Reduction tool (Shockwave), 47
polygons in models, reducing, 149-150
Poser web site, 168
positioning rigid bodies (Havok), 127
preloading castmembers, 67-68

Preview Options sub-window (Export Options window), 59
progressive streaming, 8-10
projector testing movies, 74-75
projectors
    creating, 78
    embedding Xtras in, 76-77
    exporting movies as, 13-14
properties (Havok)
    angular dashpots, 139-140
    castmembers, 114-117
    linear dashpots, 137-138
    rigid bodies, 126-131
    springs, 135-136
Property Inspector, changing behavior settings, 41
proximity sensors (Maya RTA), 193
publishing movies, 78
Push Model behavior (Havok control behavior), 102-103

Q-R

QA (Quality Assurance), 73

ray casting, 69-72
Reactor, relationsip with Havok (physics engine), 80
real-time authoring. *See* Maya RTA
real-time physics engine. *See* Havok
REALVIZ web site, 172
redrawing problems for castmembers, 66-67
reducing
    file size, 65
        by compressing projector, 78
        by graphic dithering, 77
    lag time in score, 66
    polygons in models, 149-150
Reset Camera behavior, 31
resolution, scaling movies, 8-9

Right Hemisphere web site, 187
rigid bodies (Havok)
    and convex hulls, 121
    creating, 121
    functions, 132-135
    positioning, 127
    properties, 126-131
rigid body collection in Havok, 88-89
Rocket Model behavior (Havok control behavior), 103
rollovers, Model Rollover Cursor behavior, 34
Rotate Camera behavior, 31
rotating
    cameras, Rotate Camera behavior, 31
    models
        Automatic Model Rotation behavior, 32
        Drag Model to Rotate behavior, 25
rotation button scripts, linking sprites to camera, 162-163
RTA. *See* Maya RTA

S

sampling interval setting versus animation quality setting, 62
saving and compacting movies, 78
scale of Havok simulations, 118
scaling movies, 8-9
Scene Checker (Maya RTA), 195
scene for car simulation, creating, 81-85
Scene Manifest (Maya RTA), 195
score
    reducing lag time, 66
    setup, 65-66
scripts (Lingo). *See* Lingo
sensors (Maya RTA), 192-193
Set Gravity behavior (Havok control behavior), 102
setup behaviors, Havok (physics engine), 99-102

ShapeShifter 3D web site, 170
Shockwave 3D plug-in, availability of, 11-13
Shockwave 3D Resources to Export sub-window (Export Options window), 60
Show Axis behavior, 34-35
shutdown( ) function versus havok.shutdown( ) function, 119
simulations. *See* car simulation
sky, adding to scenes, 152
slider scripts, linking sprites to camera, 159-161
    adding hot spots to slider, 161-162
sliders, determining point of location, 161
Softimage/Avid web site, 169
software developer web sites, 167-173
sound action (Maya RTA), 193
speed
    of animation, building models, 46-47
    of simulations in Havok, increasing, 92
speed viewer (Maya RTA), 194
spheres, Create Sphere behavior, 23-24
springs (Havok)
    defined, 124
    functions, 136-137
    properties, 135-136
sprites. *See also* castmembers
    attaching behaviors to, 41
    linking to camera, 153-154
        direction arrow scripts, 158-159
        hot spot scripts, 161-162
        keyboard navigation, 155-156
        rotation button scripts, 162-163
        setting up camera angles, 156-157
        slider scripts, 159-161
SquidSoup web site, 187
stand-alone applications, exporting movies as, 13-14
    in DXR format, 14
static friction, 91

step height viewer (Maya RTA), 194
storyboarding
    car simulation, 80-81
    models (fly-through house project), 46
streaming, progressive, 8-10
stub actions, defined, 194
Sub Division Surface behavior, 35

T

Tabuleiro web site, 170
testing
    car simulation in Havok, 93-94
    movies, 73
        browser testing, 75-76
        projector testing, 74-75
text, creating 3D text, 41-43
texture mapping
    car simulation, 85-86
    fly-through house project, 55-56
Texture Size Limits sub-window (Export Options window), 62
textures
    applying to buildings for Virtual City Tours project, 152-153
    editing photos to create, 150-151
    photographing buildings for, 144-147
TGS web site, 173
ticks, defined, 154
timer action (Maya RTA), 193
Toggle Redraw behavior, 31-32
Toon behavior, 36-37
touch sensors (Maya RTA), 193
Track Camera Model behavior (Havok control behavior), 106
triggers (behaviors)
    defined, 19
    Keyboard Input, 40
    Mouse Enter, 38

Mouse Leave, 38
Mouse Left, 37-38
Mouse Right, 39
Mouse Within, 40
TRIK:MEDIA web site, 188
Trinity web site, 179
troubleshooting exporting models to Shockwave, 64
trueSpace web site, 168
tumble viewer (Maya RTA), 194
Turbo Squid web site, 175

U-V

units of measurement in Havok, 87-88
VFX Pro web site, 179
viewers (Maya RTA), 192, 194
ViewPoint web site, 176
Virtual City Tours
    applying textures to buildings, 152-153
    creating textures for buildings, 150-151
    exporting movie to .W3D format, 153
    modeling the buildings, 147-150
    photo-realism, 144
    photographing the buildings, 144-147
    web site, 144
visibility of castmembers, reducing lag time in score, 66

W

.W3D file exporter
    need for, 11
    troubleshooting, 64
.W3D file format, 7
    exporting
        Maya scenes to, 192
        models, 57-58
        movies to, 153
    importing car simulation, 107-110

walk viewer (Maya RTA), 194
warning window, exporting car simulation, 96
Web 3D. *See* .W3D file format
web applications, exporting movies as DCR format, 15
web sites
    3D model makers, 174-176
    3Dluvr, 177
    3DMax Lover, 177
    3DRender, 176
    3dvillage, 183
    Alias|Wavefront, 167
    AMAPI 3D, 173
    Animation World, 178
    Arius3D, 174
    Ashlar-Vellum, 167
    Caligari, 168
    Cinema 4D, 171
    content developers, 183-188
    Curious Labs, 168
    D Vision Works, 169
    Design in Motion, 180
    Digimation, 178
    Discreet, 170
    Dream Theater, 183
    EON Reality, 171
    face2face, 180
    famous3D, 181
    ForgeFX, 184
    Gigawatt Studios, 184
    Havok, 181
    Image Modeler, 172
    for inspiration, 176-180
    Kalisto, 185
    Kaon Interactive, 174
    LightWave, 172
    Lingo information, 7
    Macromedia, 173
    MAXON Computer, 171
    Maya, 167
    MGI, 182
    MindComet, 185
    My Virtual Model, 186
    NewTek, 172
    NxView, 182
    OradNet, 186
    for plug-ins and Xtras, 180-182
    Poser, 168
    REALVIZ, 172
    Right Hemisphere, 187
    ShapeShifter 3D, 170
    Softimage/Avid, 169
    software and application developers, 167-173
    SquidSoup, 187
    Tabuleiro, 170
    TGS, 173
    TRIK:MEDIA, 188
    Trinity, 179
    trueSpace, 168
    Turbo Squid, 175
    VFX Pro, 179
    ViewPoint, 176
    Virtual City Tours, 144
    Zygote, 175
web testing movies, 75-76
windows, framing (fly-through house project), 51

X-Z

Xtras
    embedding in movies, 76-77
    web sites for, 180-182

Z-axis, 6-7
Zygote web site, 175

Solutions from experts you know and trust.

www.informit.com

OPERATING SYSTEMS

WEB DEVELOPMENT

PROGRAMMING

NETWORKING

CERTIFICATION

AND MORE...

**Expert Access.
Free Content.**

New Riders has partnered with **InformIT.com** to bring technical information to your desktop. Drawing on New Riders authors and reviewers to provide additional information on topics you're interested in, **InformIT.com** has free, in-depth information you won't find anywhere else.

- Master the skills you need, when you need them

- Call on resources from some of the best minds in the industry

- Get answers when you need them, using InformIT's comprehensive library or live experts online

- Go above and beyond what you find in New Riders books, extending your knowledge

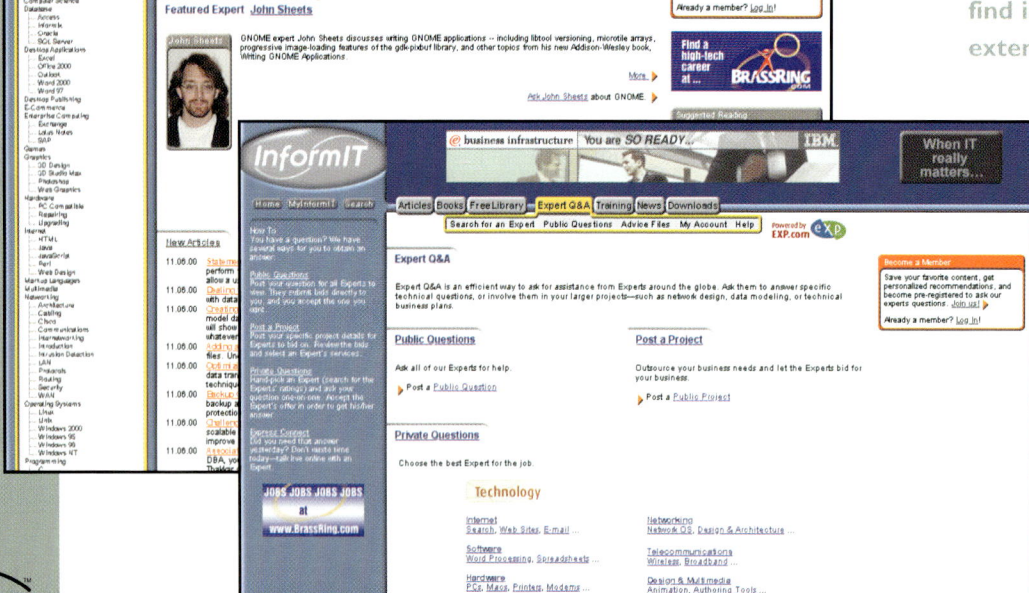

As an **InformIT** partner, **New Riders** has shared the wisdom and knowledge of our authors with you online. Visit **InformIT.com** to see what you're missing.

InformIT

www.informit.com

New Riders

www.newriders.com

HOW TO CONTACT US

VISIT OUR WEB SITE

WWW.NEWRIDERS.COM

On our web site, you'll find information about our other books, authors, tables of contents, and book errata. You will also find information about book registration and how to purchase our books, both domestically and internationally.

EMAIL US

Contact us at: **nrfeedback@newriders.com**

- If you have comments or questions about this book
- To report errors that you have found in this book
- If you have a book proposal to submit or are interested in writing for New Riders
- If you are an expert in a computer topic or technology and are interested in being a technical editor who reviews manuscripts for technical accuracy

Contact us at: **nreducation@newriders.com**

- If you are an instructor from an educational institution who wants to preview New Riders books for classroom use. Email should include your name, title, school, department, address, phone number, office days/hours, text in use, and enrollment, along with your request for desk/examination copies and/or additional information.

Contact us at: **nrmedia@newriders.com**

- If you are a member of the media who is interested in reviewing copies of New Riders books. Send your name, mailing address, and email address, along with the name of the publication or web site you work for.

BULK PURCHASES/CORPORATE SALES

If you are interested in buying 10 or more copies of a title or want to set up an account for your company to purchase directly from the publisher at a substantial discount, contact us at 800-382-3419 or email your contact information to corpsales@pearsontechgroup.com. A sales representative will contact you with more information.

WRITE TO US

New Riders Publishing
201 W. 103rd St.
Indianapolis, IN 46290-1097

CALL/FAX US

Toll-free (800) 571-5840
If outside U.S. (317) 581-3500
Ask for New Riders
FAX: (317) 581-4663

New Riders

WWW.NEWRIDERS.COM

0735711895
Jim Lammers and
Lee Gooding
US$45.00

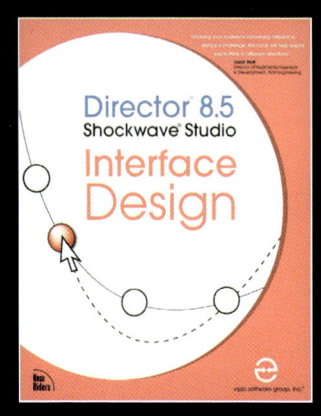

0735712182
Epic Software
US$39.99

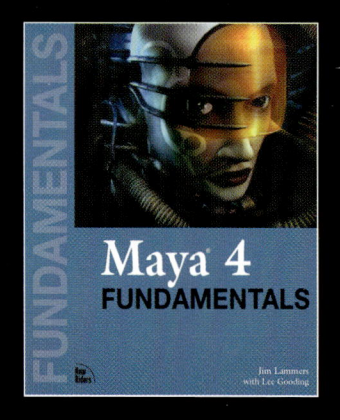

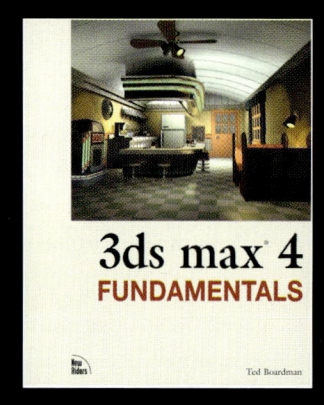

073571066X
Ted Boardman
US$39.99

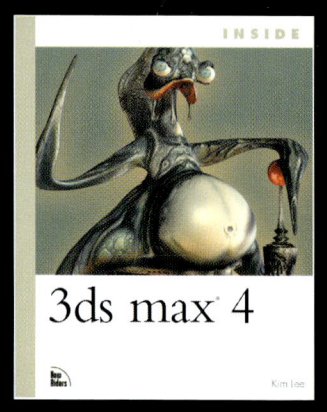

0735710945
Kim Lee
US$49.99

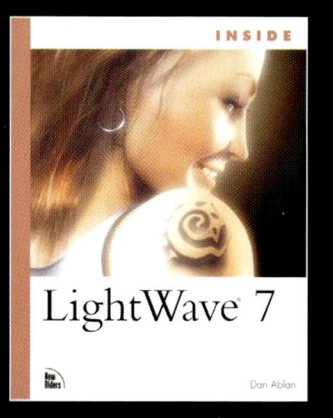

0735711348
Dan Ablan
US$59.99

VOICES
THAT MATTER™

Be creative. Be inspired.
Get the Voices That Matter
from New Riders.

New Riders

WWW.NEWRIDERS.COM